Human Rights Diploma[c]

In this insightful analysis of human rights diplomacy, Rein Müllerson examines the ways in which foreign policy instruments are used to promote human rights abroad, and how human rights issues are used for the sake of other foreign policy aims.

The book explores the relationship between human rights and international stability and the role of non-governmental organizations, the business community and mass media in formulating human rights agendas for governments and inter-governmental organizations. Also addressed are issues such as the universality of human rights in a multi-cultural world and the impact of religious and nationalistic extremism. Rein Müllerson concludes by looking at the role of the UN and other international bodies engaged in the promotion of human rights, and how military force can be an option in settling violations.

The author argues that it tends to be regimes that are hostile to human rights that in turn cause instability in the international community. Throughout the book it is demonstrated that a concern for human rights is legitimate because of the impact human rights have on international relations, and because of the common bonds that link all people.

Rein Müllerson is Professor and Chair of International Law at King's College, London. In 1995 he was elected to the *Institut de Droit International*. He is also the author of *International Law, Rights and Politics* (1994).

Human Rights Diplomacy

Rein Müllerson

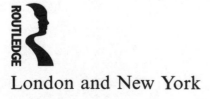

London and New York

First published 1997 by Routledge
11 New Fetter Lane, London EC4P 4EE

Simultaneously published in the USA and Canada
by Routledge
29 West 35th Street, New York, NY 10001

© 1997 Rein Müllerson

Typeset in Times by Routledge
Printed and bound in Great Britain by Mackays of
Chatham PLC, Chatham, Kent

British Library Cataloguing in Publication Data
A catalogue record for this book is available from the British Library

Library of Congress Cataloguing in Publication Data
Mullerson, R. A.
Human rights diplomacy / Rein Müllerson.
Includes bibliographical references and index.
1. Human rights. 2. Diplomacy. 3. International relations.
I. Title.
JC571.M899   1996   92–26289
323–dc20   CIP

ISBN 0–415–15390–5 (hbk)
ISBN 0–415–15391–3 (pbk)

Contents

vi *Contents*

Acknowledgements

The idea and the beginning for this book came from the International Institute for Strategic Studies (IISS) where I was a Research Fellow (non-resident) in 1994–95. The director of the IISS, John Chipman, and the Deputy Director, Rose Gottemoeller, as well as Dr Mats Berdal and many others who participated in numerous discussions on the manuscript, or parts of it, helped me immensely. My special thanks go to Dr Gerry Segal, who read the whole manuscript several times and whose comments were invaluable. Professor James Crawford of Cambridge University provided critical remarks of great help. I am also thankful to those anonymous reviewers who made many interesting comments and drew my attention to issues I had originally neglected.

Cairo Robb's critical eye and mind helped me to improve the content and form of the manuscript. It is, moreover, always a pleasure to work with Routledge staff. Gordon Smith, Caroline Wintersgill, Philip Gooch and James Whiting have helped me in every possible way.

George, Jan and Irina once more heroically withstood all the inconveniences related to my work on the book.

Rein Müllerson
Kings College, London

Introduction

The end of the Cold War and the bipolar international system forces us to reconsider many of the traditional issues of international law and politics. The role of human rights in international relations and in the foreign policy of different governments is one of them.[1]

Although human rights mainly concern relations between the individual and the state, they have become, especially since the Second World War, an important international issue as well. There are hundreds of legally binding human rights instruments which either cover a wide range of human rights, like the two United Nations Covenants on human rights, or deal with specific rights (e.g., labour rights in the International Labour Organization's conventions, or cultural and educational rights in UNESCO instruments). Some documents aim to protect or promote the rights of special categories of persons, such as the Convention on the Right of the Child or instruments on women's rights. Some instruments are universal, while others are of regional character.

As a starting point for our discussion on human rights in international relations and foreign policy I rely basically on those human rights instruments which are accepted by an overwhelming majority of states. These states represent all levels of economic, political and societal development, various cultures and religions of the world.[2] Hundreds of non-governmental human rights organizations (NGOs), many of which are international while others are nationally based, similarly rely on and, at the same time, actively support the implementation of rights and freedoms enshrined in these instruments. These are civil and political, social, economic and cultural rights, which are all equally important, though it may be that sometimes for some societies certain rights or freedoms seem to be more important than others.[3]

In Chapter Two I will discuss in some detail the interplay between civil and political rights on the one hand and social and economic rights on the other. Here, suffice it to say that it is widely accepted that at least some civil and political rights have acquired the character of customary norms of international law, which means that they have become obligatory for all states notwithstanding whether they participate in international human rights treaties or not. At a minimum, such a list of customary human rights includes norms prohibiting genocide; slavery and the slave trade; murder and the practice of disappearances; torture or cruel, inhuman or degrading treatment; prolonged arbitrary detention; and systematic racial discrimination.[4]

This book tries to analyse the reasons for and consequences of such an internationalization of human rights. Therefore, the emphasis is not so much on human rights as such but on human rights diplomacy, its determinants, objectives and future perspectives. Human rights diplomacy can be defined as the use of foreign policy instruments in order to promote human rights, as well as the use of human rights issues for the sake of other foreign policy aims. Human rights diplomacy may be closely related to, but does not exactly overlap with, humanitarian diplomacy. The latter is used by many states and non-governmental bodies in order to ease human suffering, which may be either man-made or caused by natural disasters such as droughts or earthquakes. Though in some cases it may be difficult to distinguish between human rights diplomacy and humanitarian diplomacy, the latter is always an emergency policy while the former is aimed at changing laws and practices, which means that long-term approaches are usually needed.

Though human rights issues have become a permanent component of the diplomacy of practically every state, they seldom rank high among political priorities. Policy-makers think more in terms of political 'hardware' than 'software'. When Joseph Stalin was told that the Pope had great influence in worldly affairs, Uncle Joe's ironical response was completely in line with the tenets of *Realpolitik*: 'how many divisions does the Pope have?' For the 'great leader of all of the working people of the world', only divisions mattered, and in this he was not unique. However, the end of the Cold War and the collapse of the Soviet Union has shown clearly that, though divisions do matter, there are other important factors, other issues which have to be called strategic, besides the balance of power, nuclear deterrence and the number of divisions and tanks. The Cold War itself was ultimately not about the bomb, it was more about ideas, including the idea of human dignity, and the idea of the rights and freedoms of human beings. The outcome of this struggle shows that, ultimately, ideas may be even more important than the number of divisions, missiles or nuclear warheads.

This does not mean to say that divisions or missiles do not matter. They certainly matter, if only because in order to have something in the long run it is often necessary to guarantee the immediate future. What I am trying to suggest, however, is that human rights issues in international relations are often either neglected or mishandled, with disastrous consequences, not only for human rights themselves, but also for the so-called 'hard' or strategic problems of international relations; and that 'soft' issues such as human rights and democracy may have serious implications for international peace and national security.

There seems to be a dialectic contradiction, in the spirit of Hegel or Marx, between human rights and international relations. Writing seriously on human rights in international relations involves steering constantly a path between the Scylla of idealism and the Charybdis of cynicism, between concerns for stability and for justice, between a vision of the unity of mankind and the constraints of parochialism or cultural relativism, between the imperatives of state sovereignty and non-interference in internal affairs, and between concerns for human life and dignity.

These contradictions are not only philosophical, they are firmly rooted in real-world issues, and they can probably never be resolved once and for all. Nevertheless, constant efforts towards their resolution in everyday practice, often through compromises, is the way in which human rights issues in international relations should be dealt with. One should not approach these contradictions on an all-or-nothing basis. In the following chapters I will discuss in detail the interface between the trend towards globalization and homogenization, on the one hand, and the pull of cultural and religious traditions, on the other. It is equally important to take into account the effect of differences in levels of societal development on human rights.

There are also contradictions between emotional and rational approaches to human rights. For someone to become and remain – notwithstanding the all-too-many frustrations – genuinely interested in human rights, passion and compassion are needed. At the same time, without a cool and sober head and the ability to compromise, it is impossible to find realistic ways for feasible progress. There are strains also between the feeling that 'something should be done' and the awareness that what can be done is not always enough and what is necessary may often be simply impossible. However, this strained relationship between passion and compassion, on the one hand, and reason, on the other, is not exclusively negative. While the former enlarges the scope of the possible, the latter may help to channel bursts of indignation into practical measures – unfortunately, not always, and not everywhere. Although it may not be possible to put an end to human rights emergencies everywhere, it does not mean that something, or something more, could not and should not be done somewhere.

What seems to be insufficiently represented in the literature on human rights is a serious and unbiased discourse encompassing the noble normative ideals and legal requirements enshrined in the Universal Declaration on Human Rights, and in hundreds of other legal and political instruments; the righteous indignation expressed over the existing reality, mainly by human rights NGOs, journalists and public opinion in many countries; and the hard-headed pursuit of realistic improvements, which is mainly a task of governments and inter-governmental bodies and which is probably the most difficult and controversial side of this triangle.

In this book an attempt is made to combine these different visions of and approaches to human rights strategies in international relations: legalistic–moralistic and 'realist', universalist and relativist; and to think about ideals without losing touch with reality, which is all too often quite different from ideals and normative prescriptions.

Chapter One tries to answer the question: why are states at all concerned with human rights situations in other countries? Why, for example, did the governments of the Commonwealth countries in Auckland discuss human rights in Nigeria, or why did the US pressurize the warring factions in the conflict in Bosnia-Herzegovina to sign the Dayton Peace Agreement which, in Annexe 6, contains extensive human rights clauses as well as procedures and mechanisms for their implementation?

Recent developments in the former Yugoslavia, Rwanda and Liberia, for example, earlier crises in Cambodia (at that time Democratic Kampuchea under the Pol Pot regime) and in Uganda under Idi Amin, as well as many other events which have had a disruptive effect on international relations, have all had human rights violations as a factor which contributed to the emergence of threats to international stability. Neglect of interests or violation of the rights of ethnic minorities in Eastern and Central Europe as well as in some former Soviet republics have contributed either to breaches of peace (e.g., the war between Armenia and Azerbaijan over Nagorny-Karabakh, and armed conflicts in Ossetia and Abkhazia in Georgia) or to strained relations between neighbouring countries (e.g., Russia's relations with Estonia and Latvia, Hungarian–Romanian and Hungarian–Slovakian relations).

Human rights, however, have become an international issue not only because their violation may negatively affect relations between states. It is argued in this book that there are indeed imperatives of *Realpolitik* as well as humanitarian reasons which necessitate states having human rights diplomacy as a component of their foreign policy. Though the improvement of human rights situations in some countries and regions may be a necessary component in the movement towards more stable international relations, the ultimate aim of the human rights movement in the world is not to be an instrument for peace and stability but to promote and protect human rights and fundamental freedoms. This means that sometimes, in order to achieve improvements in the field of human rights, states may have to be ready to risk a certain deterioration of inter-state relations.

Today, practically no state can afford not to participate in some form of human rights diplomacy. Human rights are discussed and voting often takes place on human rights issues in the UN (e.g., in the Commission on Human Rights, the General Assembly, even in the Security Council) and other international fora. As is shown in the book, different international organizations whose mandate may seem to be unrelated to human rights, such as the European Union or international financial institutions, often become engaged in human rights diplomacy, since certain human rights situations may have significant impact on issues which these organizations are dealing with. In order to respond to these challenges most foreign ministries have special departments which specialize in human rights issues.

Even if a state considers human rights to be principally or exclusively an internal matter, this is its position on the issue and it may often have to defend it. Some states have created their own human rights bodies (usually called commissions, committees or centres) whose primary task is often not to improve their country's human rights situation but to try to justify the existing situation and ward off domestic and international criticism.

Sometimes even states which traditionally emphasize the cultural diversity of the world as an obstacle for the existence of universal human rights, and consider these issues to belong exclusively to the domain of domestic affairs, can take an unexpected view. For instance Bangladesh, Indonesia, Iran, Jordan, Malaysia, Oman, Pakistan, Quatar, Senegal, Sudan and Tunisia, states which are not usually among the active promoters of human rights in the world, submitted a draft resolution at the fiftieth Session of the UN Commission on Human Rights in 1994 which was critical of the Serbian authorities' human rights violations in Kosovo.[5] The draft was adopted without a vote.

Human rights diplomacy, expressed for example in the voting in international fora, in the participation or refusal to participate in various human rights instruments and in attitudes towards human rights monitoring bodies (a policy which practically every state has to have), may be rather passive and reactive, or even negative, aimed simply at beating off attacks by other countries or international bodies relating to the human rights situation in the country. When Cuba responds to the accusations by Washington of human rights violations by virtually sending thousands of its citizens to American shores, or in response to the draft resolution of the UN Commission on Human Rights on Cuba by putting forward a draft resolution on the violation of human rights by the United States, this also is human rights diplomacy – or rather it is human rights counter-diplomacy. In contrast, active human rights diplomacy aims to achieve concrete positive changes in human rights situations in other countries. Only states which feel more or less confident on human rights at home, and which have strong human rights 'constituencies', can afford to have coherent and assertive human rights diplomacy as a part of their foreign policy.

The human rights aspect of foreign policy is exercised not only through the different multilateral fora, but often by means of bilateral diplomacy as well. Human rights issues often affect bilateral trade and security relations; they have become an important topic of many high level negotiations and meetings.

There are a number of countries which pursue rather distinctive human rights diplomacy. Norway, Sweden, Denmark, the Netherlands, Canada and Australia certainly belong to this category. The United Kingdom and Germany have also become more active in their human rights diplomacy. The United States has to be considered as a special case for a number of reasons: its place in the international system as one of the two superpowers, and now the only one remaining; its specific moralistic–legalistic, sometimes messianic, approach to international affairs; its global interests and responsibilities; and because in the Cold War ideological struggle, which was led by the US and the USSR, human rights issues played an important if rather specific role. The foreign policy of practically all Western countries now has an important human rights component. In addition, many other states have also recently started to conduct more active human rights diplomacy, especially on the issue of the protection of ethnic or religious minorities.

In the post-Cold War world, discipline, which was previously imposed by the competing superpowers, has diminished. This has brought about the decrease of the stability of the international system as well. The new situation has certainly created important windows of opportunity for positive developments in different parts of the world. And not all developments in our chaotic world have been negative. Often it seems to be the loss of previous certainties and predictability that leads to the pessimistic after-taste that develops when people reflect upon trends of world development. However, the end of the Cold War has also opened the way for previously suppressed negative tendencies, like extreme nationalism or religious extremism. Old abominations, such as economic and social underdevelopment and politically repressive regimes, have not disappeared either. In today's much looser international system these factors, which have mainly domestic roots, have a tendency to spill over and affect the stability of international relations.

It seems that in the post-Cold War world, human rights have to be seen as part of a wider context – that of the issue of stability. Domestic and international stability and instability are often mutually conditioned, and one of the factors which tends to affect both of them is a country's situation with regard to human rights.

Most contemporary threats (nuclear proliferation, drugs, terrorism, civil wars and human rights violations), unlike the threat of a nuclear conflict between the superpowers during the Cold War, do not put the survival of most states directly in danger. They are not necessarily threats to international security, especially in its traditional – military – sense. However, these 'amorphous challenges', as they are called in the Strategic Survey for 1994–95 prepared by the International Institute on Strategic Studies, have crept up in the present era and they are not easily countered, or conquered, by simple direct actions.[6] However, if not curtailed, these threats endanger domestic as well as international stability.

As is discussed in Chapter Two, stability is not to be equated with preservation of the *status quo* or the absence of changes either domestically or in international relations. Rather, it is 'the power to make changes...without pulling the whole political fabric down on the heads of the reformers';[7] as such it is like the stability of a bicycle which does not fall, only so long as it keeps moving.

An interesting observation – an observation which, however,

remained without any development – was made on the final page of James Baker's recent memoirs *The Politics of Diplomacy*. He wrote:

> In three and a half years... the very nature of the international system as we had known it was transformed. In this transformation, diplomats can – and should – take only modest credit. For the true responsibility for the changes... lies in the ordinary men and women who sought freedom, who struggled against the darkness of totalitarianism, and who rose up to seize liberty for themselves.[8]

The former Secretary of State is right. Often, especially in crucial moments of history, domestic issues, including human rights, matter more for international relations than international relations themselves. However, this truth is rarely recognized by diplomats and students of international relations, and James Baker himself makes this important comment only on the last page of his memoirs, which otherwise are no more than an interesting but rather traditional book by a high level diplomat.

The end of the Cold War, caused mainly by internal changes in the former Soviet Union, has destabilized the existing international system which, in turn, contributed to the destabilization of domestic affairs in various countries. In a society, be it domestic or international, order does not usually come out of disorder automatically, without purposeful efforts by different social forces. The character of a new order will depend on the direction of these efforts. I agree with those who believe that 'the modern international system is increasingly being reproduced on an intentional basis',[9] which means that purposeful efforts are needed to manage human rights situations which adversely affect not only domestic but also international stability.

In Chapter Two, I will consider how manifestations of extreme nationalism or religious extremism affect human rights and international stability. I will also discuss threats to international stability stemming from the liberalization and democratization of authoritarian or totalitarian regimes and the introduction of human rights into societies where there are few preconditions for their acceptance. However, it is argued that such threats should not be seen as a warning against the processes of liberalization and democratization, but rather as a call for an approach to the promotion of human rights which takes into account all the complexities of the problem.

One of the most controversial problems in the field of human rights at the international level is the issue of the universality of human rights in a multicultural world. In Chapter Three I will try to show where cultural peculiarities really matter and where they are used (or abused) to conceal the real political aims of power-holders. It is contended that the implementation of universal human rights standards may be inhibited to a lesser extent by cultural differences than by differences in levels of societal development. In the contemporary world, societies where the concept and practices of human rights have developed over centuries coexist and even interpenetrate with societies where human rights ideas are still in a rather embryonic stage. Human rights ideals and even practices start to penetrate societies where the social preconditions for the development of human rights are either weak or completely lacking. This may, of course, help to speed up the development of some societies, but at the same time, such a situation not only puts limits on the possibility of promotion of human rights, but it may also have a destabilizing effect on societal and international relations. However, it may be even more difficult to prevent the spread of human rights than to put an end to the proliferation of weapons of mass destruction. How and to what extent it is possible to manage these processes is a crucial question which is discussed in Chapters Two and Three of this book.

The beginning of active human rights diplomacy coincided with the start of the Cold War, and was greatly influenced by the latter. Therefore it is now necessary to try to distinguish between patterns which ought to be developed and improved and practices which should not have a place in the post-Cold War world. Chapter Four will show that there are many lessons to be learned from past experience: for example, that support for a 'friendly' dictator may contribute to the emergence of an unfriendly one, or that one cannot force a dictator to respect human rights if the *conditio sine qua non* of his staying in power is the suppression of any opposition to this power. One of the general lessons regarding human rights diplomacy to be drawn from the Cold War, and even from the short post-Cold War period, seems to be that such diplomacy should be principled and differentiated at the same time. Though this may sound like a call to combine the incompatible, it is hoped that further analysis will show that these requirements can be realized in a rather consistent human rights diplomacy, provided that there is determination to deal with, and to understand, the causes and implications of different human rights situations in the world.

One can distinguish, generally speaking, two categories of human rights problems: first, complete denial of human rights or their gross and massive violation which has a systematic or systemic character; and second, if one may call them so, 'ordinary' or individual violations of the specific rights of human beings, which are mainly due to shortcomings in the existing normative or institutional systems of protection of human rights as well as simply to imperfections of human nature.[10] At the international level the second category of violations can be considered, and often a remedy can be found, by different legal mechanisms and procedures (e.g., UN and regional monitoring bodies, individual complaints procedures). As a rule, however, such human rights violations have to be and can be remedied at the domestic level, and international mechanisms and procedures play a secondary, though sometimes important, role in dealing with such violations. On the other hand, to deal with the first category of violations, i.e., gross and systematic violation or complete denial of human rights, one needs long-term strategies. Sometimes involvement of the political bodies of the UN (e.g., the Security Council) may be helpful. Such violations usually do not stem from the shortcomings of legal procedures and mechanisms. They have deeper roots which lie in the social, economic, or political characteristics of society.

In this context, it is possible to distinguish between two categories of state where the denial of human rights or their gross violation have systemic character. There are countries where human rights may be completely absent, but different historical, cultural or religious traditions give legitimacy to governing regimes which are neither democratically elected nor respect human rights. The second category comprises states where repression is the way of dealing with discontent and opposition to the regime. Though some countries combine certain characteristics of both of these patterns, such a distinction could help the world community and individual states to choose adequate ways and means of addressing different situations. These various situations, as well as ways and means of dealing with them, are discussed in the following chapters.

In Chapter Five, in the light of the analysis of the causes and effects of various human rights situations which may negatively affect international stability, I try to outline some strategies for the future in the domain of human rights diplomacy. These include long-term strategies aimed at the promotion of human rights, as well as at changing the underlying factors which cause or facilitate human rights emergencies as well as various responses to concrete human rights situations. Possible ways and means of doing this, and also the relative advantages and disadvantages of bilateral and multilateral human rights diplomacy, are discussed in some detail.

The final chapter, Chapter Six, addresses the controversial issue of humanitarian intervention, and concentrates on some new developments related to the UN field operations on the maintenance of international peace and security which have a humanitarian component.

This book is not an exposé of my personal experience on human rights issues. I have relied heavily on the materials of different international organizations, states' practice, press reports and, of course, on the wisdom of those philosophers, lawyers, historians, IR (international relations) specialists and sociologists from different countries who have written on human rights in their numerous books and articles. However, I believe that, somehow, and in the background, as is practically always the case with authors, my personal experience and background are also present.

Richard Falk, whom I always admire and sometimes criticize, recently wrote (I understand with some regret or reproach) that, in my writings, I, like my teacher Professor Tunkin, almost exclusively rely on non-Marxist, i.e., Western, scholarship.[11] I do not know how true this is and how much it matters. Professor Tunkin himself used to say (usually not very loudly and, I believe, often only to those whom he really trusted), when a young postgraduate in his or her dissertation tried to assert that he or she had said something which was new in the Soviet doctrine of international law, that it did not matter whether this was new in the Soviet doctrine of international law or not. What mattered, from Tunkin's point of view, was whether this was new and significant in the doctrine of international law. This is contrary to the belief, which was propagated first of all by official Soviet doctrine, that the Soviet approach to international law was and should have been something different from bourgeois doctrines.

However, I believe that, though there should be, and certainly there are, different approaches to international legal studies and different schools of international legal thought, there is one science of international law. It may be Western in the sense that it originated in the West and that Western authors have contributed more than anybody else to its development. However, there have been scholars from India, Egypt, Japan, Nigeria, from many Latin American countries as well as from other regions of the world, who have excelled in this field. They may have emphasized their specific problems, brought some new facets to the doctrine of international law, but it has not created separate Latin American or African sciences of international law. I believe that something like that is happening in the domain of human rights.

I am an Estonian, born in the former USSR and educated at Moscow University. This was a country where there were no human rights. Not everything was absolutely bad, of course, and for example the health care system may even have been superior to that of some Western democracies. However, even these social benefits were not rights but rather privileges for conformism and obedience. Dissidents were deprived not only of these benefits but usually of their liberty as well. This practice of the absence of human rights was very well explained in terms of the differences between bourgeois approaches to human rights, which, as it was alleged, were called upon to conceal the absence of real rights, and the genuine socialist approach to human rights. Moreover, the doctrine went on, as the Soviet Union was also surrounded by hostile imperialist powers, it was necessary to be vigilant and therefore it was not possible to ignore those few madmen, like Andrei Sakharov or Sergei Kovaljov, who did not understand the obvious advantages of socialism. It was necessary to isolate them in order to prevent them from 'pouring water on the water-mill of imperialism'.

Does all this sound painfully familiar? Is it not all about cultural, religious or ideological relativism and special circumstances?

After 1985, when Michael Gorbachev came to power, Soviet society woke from a long hibernation and human rights issues became a hot topic for discussion in the mass media, academic circles and, later, also in the Supreme Soviet (a kind of Parliament) and other official fora. I participated in drafting various laws and programmes on, or related to, human rights. It was interesting to observe how those who represented the establishment (the Central Committee of the Communist Party, the KGB, the Army), even though sometimes they agreed in principle with the necessity of reforms (often, I believe, only in words), tried to argue that these concrete proposed reforms were not for us because we were different and our situation was different. They argued against the abolition of the notorious 'propiska' system (internal resident permits), against the abolition of exit visas, and against the abrogation of articles in the Criminal Code under which dissidents were sentenced, and so on and so forth.

Later, working in the Foreign Ministry in my native Estonia, I found that similar arguments were sometimes used when politicians wanted to resort to practices which were contrary to international human rights standards. As Estonia was looking Westwards, and therefore it was impossible, in principle, to say that these standards were not applicable because they were based on an alien concept, they used the argument of special circumstances. These arguments concerned, for example, issues of citizenship and the status of foreigners, which are discussed in some detail in this book.

However, as further developments in Eastern and Central European states have shown, it was possible to get rid of many of the old practices rather quickly. These practices were rooted not so much in the traditions or habits of people as in the power interests of ruling elites. Often even traditions and habits were called to serve the interests of the communist elite. This does not mean, of course, that there are not any traditions or other objective factors (these issues are discussed in Chapters Two and Three) which may negatively affect the acceptance or implementation of international human rights standards. However, more often than not human rights are suppressed because this is the only way the leaders can retain their power.

Therefore I am somewhat sceptical when I read or hear that human rights are not or cannot be universal because of cultural differences between societies. Pressure to limit human rights comes from interested groups, and references to one's 'otherness' (often, I think, believed rather sincerely, because a strong interest seems to become accepted not only as an interest but also as a virtue or necessity) serve to conceal power interests. My own personal experience (rather limited, as every personal experience usually is) shows that what was called the 'Western concept of human rights' – something different from and alien to the 'socialist concept of human rights' – was not Western at all. Many Western countries themselves still have to work hard to comply fully with universal human rights.

And certainly there are double standards in the human rights diplomacy of Western countries. For example, recently the US established diplomatic relations with Vietnam and it continues to trade even with Nigeria, while retaining in place the embargo against Cuba. No principle, only interests, can explain such policies. *The Economist* seems to be quite right when it observes that 'the embargo remains because of the worst of America: the power of a well-organised lobby to dictate policy. Here, the lobby is the Cuban-American National Foundation. The foundation is implacably against any softening of policy towards Cuba.... It is a force to be reckoned with at any time, but especially in an election season. Of the 1.1 million Cuban Americans, some 700,000 live in South Florida'.[12]

In March 1996 the US congress passed a new piece of anti-Cuban legislation. The Cuban Liberty and Democratic Solidarity (Libertad) Act of 1996[13] aims 'to bring democratic institutions to Cuba through the pressure of general economic embargo at a time when the Castro regime has proven to be vulnerable to international economic pressure'.[14] However, this Act is not only evidence of double standards in human rights policy. Its effects also seem to be counter-productive to declared aims, as they may even strengthen the fading popularity of Fidel Castro. As sanctions can also be applied against third-country nationals who trade with Cuba, the EU, Canada, Mexico, Russia and other countries protested against this legislation. Sir Leon Brittan, in his letter to Warren Christopher, stated that 'the European Union (EU) has consistently expressed its opposition, as a matter of law and policy, to extraterritorial applications of US jurisdiction which would also restrict EU trade in goods and services with Cuba' and that these measures 'would risk complicating not only third-country relations with Cuba, *but also any transitional process in Cuba itself*' (emphasis added).[15]

It is necessary to get rid of such double standards as well as to improve human rights practices and laws in the West. It is also necessary to work further on the problem of the universality of human rights in the multicultural and multi-dimensional world. However, it would be foolish to throw out the baby (universal human rights) with the bathwater (double standards and other deficiencies of the human rights policy of many countries).

When some Western scholars use arguments based on cultural relativism[16] and believe that people in the West, the East and the South are so different that human rights ideas and norms which were developed mainly in the West are not applicable in other places, it sounds rather arrogant and imperialistic. It seems to me that sometimes Western intellectuals, being disillusioned (often rightly so) with how Western governments resolve (or refuse, or are unable, to resolve) domestic or international problems, as well as with the injustice of their domestic and international politics, try to find remedies where they cannot be found. Taking for granted democratic freedoms and human rights at home, habitually using the fruits of the market economy, being acutely aware of the injustices carried out by the West against the South not only during the colonial period but also in the Cold War context, they sometimes see the resurgence of Western imperialism not only in the conditionality of economic assistance but even in Western human rights diplomacy.

1 The *raison d'être* of human rights diplomacy

Governments, even in democratic countries, are not, and can hardly be expected to act as, human rights organizations. As Louis Henkin writes, 'state egoism, selfishness, is the hallmark of the international state system. . . . The occasional reference to mankind is rhetoric; it has no significant normative implications'.[1] Governments have to take care of many other interests and, naturally, they have to take care of their own interest in staying in power. Their concern for human rights in other countries is only one, and certainly not the most important, of the imperatives of their foreign policy. Moreover, all too often human rights diplomacy does not fit comfortably with other foreign policy priorities.

Therefore, before turning to issues of efficiency (or inefficiency) and other problems of human rights diplomacy, it is necessary to ask: why should governments, which are, or at least should be, responsible to and before their own people, be at all concerned with human rights in far away places? Why should, for example, the British or French governments think of human rights in East Timor, Bahrain or Chechnya? Why should states create, finance and pay attention to activities of international bodies such as the UN Human Rights Commission, and the so-called 'treaty-bodies' which monitor the implementation of various human rights instruments; keep in Geneva the UN Centre for Human Rights; or have several regional human rights bodies?

Human rights issues have become part and parcel of everyday diplomatic discourse, and therefore these questions may seem too obvious to be asked. However, it seems that answers to and reflections on these questions may help to provide new approaches to concerns of practical diplomacy.

This chapter attempts to answer these questions. Starting from a historical point of view I will show that it was the rights and interests of religious and ethnic minorities, with the threat to international security that their violation often brought, which raised the issue of human rights to the international level.

I shall then go on to argue that undemocratic regimes, hostile to human rights, sometimes tend to choose foreign policy options which may threaten international stability; that most serious post-Cold War human rights violations are committed by weak regimes with insufficient legitimacy, with the attendant risk that such regimes may implode, thereby threatening international stability; that business interests may not always be inimical to human rights; that, on the contrary, under certain circumstances it is in the interests of business to support human rights; and that international concern for human rights is legitimate not only because of these links between human rights and international relations, but also because there are common bonds between different peoples and there is a certain meaning in the word 'humankind' which induces states to take human rights into consideration in their foreign policy.

FROM CHRISTIANS IN THE OTTOMAN EMPIRE TO MUSLIMS IN EUROPE

An interesting point as to the *raison d'être* of human rights diplomacy can be made by comparing the genesis of domestic human rights norms with that of international ones. England's Magna Carta of 1215, the Habeas Corpus Acts and Bill of Rights of 1689; the French Declaration of the Rights of Man and the Citizen of 1789; and the US Declaration of Rights of 1774, are all texts which, with certain qualifications and exclusions dependent on the historical time period, of course, spoke of the rights of human beings generally. In contradistinction to such an approach, which was concerned with the human rights of all individuals, or at least those of all white male Protestant property owners, international concern for human rights started with attention to the rights of only one category of individuals: persons belonging to religious or ethnic minorities.

Reflection on this difference of genesis of domestic and international concern for human rights helps to shed some light on the questions of why states may be interested at all in human rights in other countries, and why human rights and freedoms, which are in principle an issue between the individual and the state, have become an international issue.

International concern with the rights of religious and ethnic minorities was from the very beginning related to the most important issue of international relations – war.[2]

Armed conflicts are usually divided into international wars and civil wars, though this rather clear-cut normative distinction is becoming now more and more blurred. However, from the point of view of the evolution of international concern for human rights (not only from this point of view of course, but that is what interests us here), wars, or armed conflicts as they are now usually called, can be characterized not only as being of an internal or international nature, but as involving or not involving ethnic or religious issues.

The history of humankind has proven that religion and war, like ethnicity and war, are closely related phenomena. Though there have been various reasons for armed conflicts, many of them could be characterized as religious or ethnic crusades. Religious or ethnic factors may not have always been the real or main cause of some so-called religious or inter-ethnic wars, but they have certainly been an important catalyst in many of them. Therefore it is not surprising that, in order to suppress or limit such armed conflicts, their sources, i.e., religious or ethnic issues, must have been addressed. Similarly, those who wanted to exploit these issues for the sake of their secular or material aims and interests had to fan the flames of religious or ethnic animosity in order to achieve their aims.

Though all international wars may ultimately be considered, at least to a certain extent, as inter-ethnic conflicts, there have been some international wars where ethnic factors have played a prominent role in the genesis of the conflict. For example, the medieval crusades were to a great extent religious wars, and the Thirty Years' War (1618–48) also had important religious causes as well as consequences. It was caused mainly by the political rivalry between the Catholic and Protestant princes of Germany, as well as by the interests of other powers in Germany. The Treaty of Westphalia, which ended the war, established an important principle – *cuius regio, eius religio* (literally, 'whose the region, his the religion') – with important religious implications.

In the Second World War the Nazis used ethnic arguments as a pretext to attack their neighbours (for example, the claimed necessity to protect ethnic Germans in other countries). In his Proclamation of 15 March 1939 on the German occupation of Bohemia and Moravia, Hitler referred to 'assaults on the life and liberty of minorities, and the purpose of disarming Czech troops and terrorist bans threatening the lives of minorities'.[3] In their genocidal policy the Nazis singled out for extermination and tried to dehumanize certain ethnic groups (Jews, Gypsies and Slavs).

As for civil wars, some, like the American Civil War (1861–65) or the Russian Civil War (1918–20), may not have had any significant inter-ethnic or inter-religious characteristics, while others did, being caused by religious or ethnic factors, waged for the sake of religion or ethnicity and often resulting in outcomes which had religious or ethnic implications.

While many of the medieval domestic conflicts were based on religious differences, (for example the Wars of Religion in France, which started with the massacre of the Huguenots by the troops of the Duc de Guise, and tore France asunder for many years in the second half of the sixteenth century) most current conflicts (for example, in the former Soviet Union, Yugoslavia and in many places in Africa) have their roots in ethnic rivalries and hatred.

These and other internal conflicts with significant religious or ethnic elements, i.e., conflicts which very often originate from the oppression of religious or ethnic minorities, have always considerably affected international relations.

Therefore, it is not accidental and should not be surprising at all that the first international documents purporting to define and protect the rights of certain categories of human beings were treaties on the protection of religious minorities. For example, the Treaty between the King of Hungary and the Prince of Transylvania of 1606 accorded to the Protestant minority in Transylvania free exercise of its religion.[4] Again, one of the most famous treaties of that time – the Treaty of Westphalia, concluded in 1648 between France and the Holy Roman Empire and their respective allies – granted religious freedom to the Protestants in Germany in terms of equality with Roman Catholics.[5] At approximately the same time, the European powers started to conclude treaties with the Ottoman Empire in order to protect their respective religious minorities. Article 7 of the Austro–Ottoman Treaty of 1615 purported to protect Christians in the Ottoman Empire,[6] where European countries intervened more than once in order to guarantee the rights of its Christian subjects. For example, in 1827 England, France and Russia used armed force in order to assist Greek Christian insurgents;[7] and in 1860–61 French troops occupied parts of Syria to protect Maronite Christians against massacre by the Turks.[8]

After the First World War a system of treaties aimed at the protection of ethnic minorities in some European countries came into being under the aegis of the League of Nations. Here also the *raison d'être* of these efforts was the link between the rights and interests of minorities and the stability of the new international system in Europe after the break-up of the Austro-Hungarian and Ottoman Empires. US

President Woodrow Wilson, in his statement of 31 May 1919 at a plenary meeting of the Peace Conference in Paris, stated that 'nothing... is more likely to disturb the peace of the world than the treatment which might in certain circumstances be meted out to minorities...'[9]

The League of Nations system for the protection of minorities consisted of five treaties with the new states which had emerged or had enlarged their territory in the aftermath of the Second World War (Poland, Serbia, Romania, Greece, Czechoslovakia), four special chapters in the peace treaties with vanquished states (Austria, Bulgaria, Hungary, Turkey), and five unilateral declarations made between 1921 and 1932 by some states which were admitted to the League of Nations (Albania, Lithuania, Latvia, Estonia, Iraq).[10]

Although these first efforts at human rights protection were concerned only with specific categories of individuals in specific countries, and were one-sided and often used as a pretext for intervention in weaker states, they also show that, even at a time when few people spoke of human rights in their own countries, there were good reasons for attempts to try to take care of certain categories of persons in other states. Oppression of a whole population by its ruler of the same religion or, later, of the same ethnicity, could lead, at worst, to a rebellion or mutiny; oppression of groups which professed a different faith or were ethnically different could lead to the break-up of states and could drag other countries into the conflict as well.

There was also a sense of belongingness based on religion or ethnicity between the populations of different countries. And even if there were not any such feelings, they could be artificially created or fanned by religious or nationalistic leaders. These spiritual bonds between religious and ethnic kinsmen who lived in different states could be mobilized for the protection of the interests of those who were religiously or ethnically close to the 'protecting' powers. Therefore, the plight of minorities, especially those who had their religious or ethnic brethren in other countries, could directly affect inter-state relations. For example, the argument over who should protect the rights of the Christian subjects of the Sublime Porte played a role in the genesis of the Crimean War (1853–56) – the war which, in the words of Disraeli, was 'a just but unnecessary war' and which Sir Robert Morier called 'the only perfectly useless modern war that has been waged'.[11]

Chapter Two will deal in some detail with contemporary issues related to the rights of ethnic and religious minorities, and with the influence which their violation may exert on international relations. Here it should be emphasized that it was this relationship between the interests and rights of ethnic or religious minorities and inter-state relations which raised human rights issues to the international level.

Issues of minority rights remain most explosive at the end of the millennium, and international peace and security may often depend on how states resolve issues related to religious or ethnic minorities. How many perfectly useless and unnecessary wars are currently being waged in the name of religion or ethnicity in different parts of the world? Though religious or ethnic motivation, as I shall try to show later, is not always the only or even the principal cause (contrary to what may be claimed by the participants in a conflict) leading to wars and humanitarian disasters, it certainly plays an important role in triggering many human rights violations, some of which may constitute a threat to international stability.

All this shows that problems of ethnic and religious minorities are often as much issues of international security as they are human rights issues. As violation of the rights of minorities may result in refugee flows, wars of secession, irredentist claims and foreign interference, it is natural that other states and the world community as a whole should be concerned with the issue.

Moreover, repressions against religious or ethnic minorities have always involved, and unfortunately continue to involve, some of the most inhumane atrocities which a human being is able to commit against a fellow human being. The genocide by the Turks of the Armenians at the beginning of this century, the Holocaust, massacres of the Hutus by the Tutsis and the Tutsis by the Hutus, and of the Bosnian Muslims by their Serb or Croat neighbours, upstage most human rights violations committed by tyrants against their own ethnic or religious brethren. Even ideological murderers such as Stalin or Pol Pot who, as a rule, did not discriminate as to the ethnic origin or religion of their victims, occasionally singled out certain religious or ethnic groups as special targets (for example, the Jews, Chechens and Crimean Tatars by Stalin, ethnic Vietnamese and Buddhist monks by Pol Pot).

In summary, it is a mixture of idealistic or even emotional motives, practical political considerations, and the possibility for the cynical use of the idea of the rights and interests of minorities as justification for acts having, in reality, very little to do with these ideals, which is at the basis of the emergence of international norms on the protection of minorities. The same mixture of idealism, pragmatism and cynicism can be found in the emergence and development of other international human rights standards.

For many people in many countries the international effort to promote human rights everywhere, and especially in places where they are most egregiously trampled upon, is seen as an end in itself. For them, human rights are for the sake of human rights. Human rights NGOs whose number and influence is constantly growing represent this trend, without which there would not be any human rights movement in the world. There are those who believe that at least some human rights violations may negatively affect inter-state relations by creating refugee flows, dragging neighbouring countries into internal disturbances and generally destabilizing international relations. In addition, many governments have used human rights as it suited them, cynically manipulating public opinion at home and exerting pressure on their political and ideological adversaries, while at the same time ignoring violations by friendly dictators.

These three categories of reasons for the existence of human rights discourse at the international level will remain in the foreseeable future. There is reason to believe, however, that as time goes on there will be less ground for the abusive or manipulative use of human rights issues in international relations, and that governments will be able to see that, at least in the long run, it is in their interest to take human rights seriously in their foreign policy-making.

ARE OPPRESSORS ALSO POTENTIAL AGGRESSORS?

The most important reason for the post-Second World War rapid development of international human rights law was the link, real or perceived, between massive human rights violations and threats to international peace and security. The idea was put most eloquently in 1948 by George Marshall, the former US Secretary of State:

> Governments which systematically disregard the rights of their own people are not likely to respect the rights of other nations and other people and are likely to seek their objectives by coercion and force.[12]

Article 55 of the UN Charter states that, 'with a view to the creation of conditions of stability and well-being which are necessary for peaceful and friendly relations among nations', the United Nations shall promote, *inter alia*, 'universal respect for, and observance of, human rights and fundamental freedoms for all without distinction as to race, sex, language, or religion'. The Universal Declaration of Human Rights of 1948 is equally clear: 'Recognition of the inherent dignity and of the equal and inalienable rights of all members of the human family is the foundation of... peace in the world'.

Nazi Germany is often given as an irrefutable example of how human rights violations at home lead to or are accompanied by an aggressive foreign policy.

This example rings true in the sense that domestic repression in Germany, before and during the Second World War, really did go hand in hand with its aggressive foreign policy, and the former was, if not a necessary precondition of the latter, then at least a factor which facilitated Germany's adventures abroad. Repressions at home cleared the way for aggression against other states. This example also serves to show how nationalism, violation of human rights at home and aggressive foreign policy may feed on each other. There are other examples, such as Iraq, Iran and Libya, which tend to show that domestic repression and adventurous behaviour abroad have certain, if not always direct then at least indirect, causal links. Oppression of domestic opposition and attempts to export religious fundamentalism or terrorism are caused by the same characteristics of some regimes. Often, a regime's hold of power needs to be justified in terms of foreign threats. This, in turn, can be achieved by demonizing other countries, peoples or faith. Though such policies do not always lead to armed conflicts or even terrorism, there is no doubt that they negatively affect relations between states and peoples.

However, even gross and massive human rights violations are rarely, if ever, the single or direct cause of wars or other threats to international stability. As Bruce Russet writes: 'Not all authoritarian states are necessarily aggressive. In fact, at any particular time, the great majority are not'.[13] The human rights situation in a country is usually only one element in the complex web of causes and conditions which may eventually lead to a breach of the peace, act of aggression, intervention, regional conflict, or to the creation of tension and friction with other states.

Yet, if there are territorial problems, unsatisfied imperial ambitions, simmering passions to remedy historical grievances, offences or perceived injustices, then an undemocratic and human rights-hostile regime may, more easily than a democratic state, choose violent means of resolving the problem. Such states are also more prone to engage in foolhardy external policies in an attempt to distract criticism from domestic problems. This was evidenced by the Argentine military under the Galtieri government which decided to invade the Malvinas-Falklands.[14] The bloody regimes of Idi Amin in Uganda and the Khmer Rouge in Cambodia provoked their respective neighbours, Tanzania and Vietnam, contrary to the self-interest of those governments in survival. External adventures which eventually accelerated the demise of the oppressive cliques of Idi Amin and Pol Pot were undertaken to help consolidate their power and distract the attention of the population from domestic problems. A serious human rights situation may sometimes be a condition facilitating the furtherance of other negative tendencies, all of which in combination may create a threat to international stability. For example, the striving of the Serbian leadership to create a Greater Serbia was generated by Serbian nationalism and Serbia's hostile policy towards its minorities, and was facilitated also by the Croatian policy of discrimination against Serbs in Croatia. There were many other factors which influenced the outcome which we now have in the former Yugoslavia, but serious human rights violations, which were ethnically based, began long before the armed struggle broke out.

Nazi Germany did not attack its neighbours just because it was a fascist dictatorship. So was Franco's Spain. The search for the *Lebensraum*, a desire to unite all Germans, and economic interests, were the principal reasons for Germany's aggressive foreign policy. However, the upsurge of extreme nationalism leading to the suppression of any opposition to the regime and to 'ethnic cleansing' at home certainly made the adoption of such an aggressive attitude towards its neighbours much easier. Suppression of domestic opposition to an oppressive regime usually means at the same time the suppression of opposition to aggressive foreign policy.

Iraq, Libya, North Korea, Sudan and Iran, all have human rights-hostile regimes, and they all constitute in one way or another a potential threat to international peace and security. Fred Halliday writes, for example, that 'the concept of "export of revolution" (*suchur-i-inqilab*) was commonly used by Iranian officials. It included the conventional means of exporting political radicalism – arms, financial support, training, international congresses, propaganda and radio programmes'.[15] The imminent causes of such a threat are not the abominable human rights records of such countries, but the acts of aggression they commit against their neighbours, their export of terrorism and religious fundamentalism, or their nuclear ambitions. However, repression at home constitutes a *conditio sine qua non* for the pursuit of these policies. Without internal oppression many, if not all, of these regimes would quickly lose their power.

This relationship between domestic and foreign policy may be called a 'two-sides-of-the-same-coin' link between the human rights situation in a country and international stability. This link, in order to be realized, depends on other circumstances and does not necessarily mean that oppressive regimes put international stability at risk by initiating wars against their neighbours. There are finer links between domestic oppression and international stability.

Repressive regimes have used real or imagined foreign threats in order to consolidate their hold on power and to justify their lack of human rights. It would have been more difficult to fabricate spy trials in the USSR in the 1930s, when not dissidents but convinced communists were accused of being British, Japanese or German spies, had there been friendly, or simply normal, relations between the Soviet Union and its neighbours. Moscow had a domestic interest in the existence of international tension. Several other totalitarian or authoritarian regimes have used alleged external threats in order to consolidate their power, and have thereby contributed to the increase of international tension.

On the other hand, extreme international tension may be, if not a cause, then at least a contributing factor to human rights limitations even in democratic countries; the Cold War and McCarthyism were not isolated phenomena. The witch-hunt in the United States could hardly have been possible without extreme international tension. Similarly, the threat from the North was a factor which contributed to the continuance of the national security state and encroachments on human rights in South Korea. Even after the reformist President Kim Young Sam came to power in 1993, fear of North Korea, with its supposed spies, saboteurs and propagandists, as *The Economist* reports, has prevented South Korea's Agency for National Security Planning from shedding all its old habits: 'Its news releases are still unreliable, and its respect for human rights remains less than full'.[16]

The atrocities committed by the North Korean authorities against their own population, and the isolation of one of the last communist regimes in the world, are both features which have a direct bearing on North Korea's nuclear ambition, which in its turn has a destabilizing effect on regional and world security. The failed ideology and political and economic system, repression against the population at home to keep the system going, the consequent isolation in the world, and an unpredictable and threatening foreign policy, are all links in the same chain.

The militant Islamic revolution in Iran resulted not only in the further limitation of the rights and freedoms of Iranians (I am not of course suggesting that they had unlimited rights under the Shah), but resulted also in the Teheran hostage crisis, support of terrorism in the Middle East, as well as in the *fatwa* against the writer Salman Rushdie.

I believe that these examples demonstrate the existence of links between domestic and international relations generally and internal repressions and destabilizing foreign policy in particular. This thesis, that non-democratic and human rights-hostile states, through their foreign policy which is a reflection of their domestic policies, are prone under certain circumstances to having a destabilizing effect on international relations, has another aspect to it. It asserts that democratic and human rights-friendly states are more peaceful than states which lack these characteristics.

The end of the Cold War has given new impetus to the discussion on whether democratic states are more peaceful than authoritarian ones. Without going into great detail on this exciting and important dispute, and referring the reader to the works of Michael Doyle,[17] Bruce Russet[18] and others who support the thesis of peacefulness of democratic states, as well as to their critics,[19] I would like to make some observations which tend to confirm, with certain qualifications of course, the thesis that democratic states are usually less aggressive than non-democratic ones.

There are examples from earlier times which show that the character of a regime has direct relevance to its readiness to become engaged in armed conflict. Analysing the causes of the Crimean War of 1853–56, David Welch comes to the conclusion that, had the political system in Russia been a bit less authoritarian and more open, the war – which none of the participants really wanted – could have been avoided.[20] In our time, it is difficult to imagine that, had there been a less repressive and more open regime in Iraq in 1990, it could have committed a surprise attack on Kuwait.

This does not mean that democracies never go to war. For example, colonialism and colonial wars are an especially black spot on the history of Western democracies. Similarly, the US record in Latin America or Vietnam is far from exemplary. However, political stability and a political culture which favours the peaceful resolution of conflicts and compromises, together with certain institutional constraints, are the features of democratic states which limit their likelihood to engage in war in the international system.[21]

There are, of course, different views expressed on the issue. *The Economist*, for example, argues that 'if democracies are really the best bulwark against war, many seemingly hard choices between idealism and *Realpolitik* can be simplified abruptly. All good things can be made together'.[22] It is simply too good to be true, believes *The Economist*, and adds that too great a confidence in a simple correlation between democracy and peace may lull the world into a false sense of security.

However, such a danger hardly exists. Although the recent studies of international crises demonstrate that democracies are significantly less likely to allow these crises to escalate into war, even when facing non-democratic opponents,[23] the problem rests that there are not enough democracies in the world to make this simple correlation safeguard peace in all parts of all continents. It will probably take more time and effort from different societies to achieve democracy in most countries than it will to achieve peace in the whole world. In any foreseeable future, both objectives would be simply utopian. Therefore, in the absence of a significant number of mature democracies, there is also no chance of being lulled into any kind of false sense of security.

It is also necessary to make clear that, even when a state has had its first free elections (usually such elections are semi-free), and has even had its period of *glasnost*, this does not mean that such a state immediately becomes democratic or more peaceful. On the contrary, as I will show in Chapter Two, during the initial stages of the liberalization and democratization of authoritarian regimes, such states may constitute an even greater threat to international stability than their authoritarian predecessors. Therefore, when one speaks of a correlation between democracy and peace, one should have in mind only stable, established, developed and mature democracies. There is usually quite a long road between first elections, which do not yet bring about democracy but are only the first step towards it, and the fruits of a developed democracy such as internal peace and prosperity and the contribution to international stability that this may bring.

Analysis of certain events of the mid-1990s shows rather clearly that there is a difference between the approaches of democratic states and non-democratic states involved, for whatever reason, in wars. While, for example, Western governments are constantly concerned with the lives of their troops on peacekeeping missions in hot-spots all over the world, and sometimes tend to worry more about the safety of their personnel than the achievement of peacekeeping or peace-making objectives, the authorities, for instance, of Russia – a country which has taken only its first steps along the road towards liberalization and democratization and whose society contains elements of democracy, authoritarianism and chaos – feel proud of Russian soldiers who lose their lives in Tadjikistan or Chechnya. Pavel Grachev, the former Russian Minister of Defence, in his infamous televised speech, described for example how 'Russian boys are dying in Chechnya with smiles on their faces'.[24] The way the Russian authorities handled the hostage crisis in Chechnya's neighbour, Dagestan, in January 1996, where the village of Pervomayskoye was destroyed, many hostages were killed and many terrorists escaped, shows gross neglect by the authorities for that most sacred of human rights – the right to life.

This, of course, is not only evidence of the strength of democracy but maybe its weakness, too, in the face of such challenges as General Aideed or Doctor Karadjic. Nevertheless, the comparison shows that there is a positive correlation between the values society ascribes to human life and its behaviour in the international arena: not being involved in armed conflicts and helping to avoid them is one of the ways to save the lives of citizens. I believe that this remains true even if we recognize that, for democratic governments, there is often rather a great difference between the value they ascribe to the lives of their own citizens (i.e., their electorate) and that which they ascribe to the lives of the nationals of other countries.

The existence of a positive link between human rights and international security can also be demonstrated when one compares the current Federal Republic of Germany with its Nazi predecessor. Though there are many factors which influence the current foreign policy of Germany (including, for example, its close integration into European structures), it would probably not be an overestimation to conclude that the strongest guarantee against a revival of Germany's aggressiveness, which has twice in this century led Europe and the whole world to catastrophic results, is the democratic nature of Germany and its attitude towards human rights.

The same can be said about Japan. Although democratic ideas were implanted into the Japanese soil from outside after its defeat in the Second World War, they nevertheless took root rather well. The historic development of both Germany and Japan shows clearly that there is a link between democracy and human rights at home and a state's behaviour in the international arena.

Currently, the best hopes for Russia's foreign policy becoming stable, irreversibly civilized and non-threatening for its neighbours lie, to a great extent, in the success of its domestic political, social and economic reforms. Zhirinovsky's promises to establish a dictatorship at home, and his threats to dump nuclear waste in the Baltic countries, are certainly two sides of the same coin. It seems to me that even the dispute between Russia and the West over NATO's enlargement is not completely detached from human rights problems. Russia has not yet established itself as a stable democracy. The December 1995 elections to the state Duma saw the return of the neo-communists. Moreover, paranoid military and extreme nationalists have an important say in Moscow's policy-making. These forces in Russia see themselves threatened by NATO moving eastwards. At the same time, Russia's neighbours have an interest in putting themselves under the NATO umbrella, not only because of their previous experiences with the Russian and Soviet Empires, but also because they see that Russia is still far from becoming a stable democratic country that would not pose any security threat* to its neighbours. And, in a vicious circle, the more bellicosely Russia responds to NATO's enlargement, the stronger will be the interest of Eastern Europeans and the Balts to join NATO. The stronger their desire to get under the NATO umbrella and the greater the likelihood that NATO's enlargement may become a reality, the more influential will become the voices of those in Russia who are against NATO moving eastwards.

THE CHANGE OF PARADIGM: WEAK STATES VIOLATE HUMAN RIGHTS AND THREATEN INTERNATIONAL STABILITY

Even if an undemocratic and oppressive regime does not pursue aggressive foreign policy aims and does not directly threaten in any other way its neighbours, struggle against internal oppression may spill over and create at least regional security problems (for example, in Liberia in the 1990s, in Eastern Pakistan in 1971 and in Rwanda in 1994).

One of the widespread forms of spill-over from gross and massive repression and other forms of human rights violations is the flow of refugees. The UNHCR report for 1993 states: 'As the year [1993] began, the number of people forced to leave their countries for fear of persecution and violence had risen to a total of 18.2 million'.[25] This statistic becomes even more significant from the point of view of human rights when one considers that virtually all of the refugee-producing conflicts taking place in the world during 1993 were *within* states rather than between them. The UNHCR report found that 'the lack of representative political institutions, an independent judiciary, impartial law enforcement or free elections may lead people to conclude that armed resistance is the only way to bring about change'.[26] This confirms the existence of a recurrent pattern: human rights violations lead to internal disturbances which, in their turn, adversely affect international relations.

In the post-Cold War world, most armed conflicts are not inter-state clashes but civil wars or inter-ethnic conflicts[27] which very often have their roots in ethnically or religiously based human rights violations. Georgia's problems with its Ossetian and Abkhazian minorities; the Yugoslav pandemonium; the massacres in Rwanda and Burundi; Sri Lanka's and Indonesia's problems, are all conflicts which have at their basis, if not outright violations of the elementary rights of ethnic minorities, then at least the neglect of their legitimate interests.

During the Cold War, most serious human rights abuses were caused mainly by strong centralized regimes. In the post-Cold War era, human rights are more often violated in countries with weak and unresponsive governments.[28] Such governments, in order to stay in power, to quell rebellions or to prevail in civil wars, often resort to gross human rights abuses. Liberia, Nigeria, Zaire and Tajikistan are current prominent examples of countries under unstable governments (or, in the case of Liberia, no government at all). In these countries, human rights abuses have significant effects, not only on the stability of the country itself but also on the stability of international relations. Even when weak governments would like to protect their people against abuses by insurgents or warlords, which is rarely the case, they are unable to do so.

Internal conflicts involving massive human rights violations create refugee flows, strain relations with neighbouring states, and may eventually drag the latter into such conflicts, especially if they are the 'motherlands' of ethnic or religious brethren who are, or are deemed to be, oppressed. In addition, in some countries corrupt and ineffective regimes are the cause of the absolute poverty and the great social inequality of a majority of the population, which in human rights terms is tantamount to the absence of any economic or social rights. In these circumstances a regime can usually stay in power only by suppressing any dissent or discontent. This can lead to the implosion of such countries, thereby causing even greater human rights emergencies which, again, have a tendency to adversely affect relations between states. Haiti and Liberia went through such a scenario.

It may sound paradoxical, but it is a thin line that separates a strong and a weak state. Many of today's weak states, only yesterday, had strong, authoritarian, repressive regimes in power. For example, the Soviet Union was able to suppress with a strong hand any opposition to Communist party rule for seventy years. However, today, the Russian government is unable to deal with a rising crime rate or secessionist tendencies without serious human rights violations. Chechnya is a prime example.[29] And the problem is that such strong and weak regimes have a tendency to replace each other on a regular basis, thereby throwing the society from oppression into chaos and from chaos into oppression. Strong authoritarian regimes are often under the threat of turning disorderly and violent, while social disorder usually calls for a strong hand. Hobbes's 'Leviathan', a centralized state enabled 'by terror... to form the wills of them all to peace at home and mutual aid against their enemies abroad',[30] and 'Behemoth', a kind of non-state, a chaos, a condition of lawlessness, of rebellion, anarchy and civil war,[31] are both not only equally inimical to human rights. Often they seem to call for each other. Ralf Dahrendorf writes that 'the absence of a credible state, lawlessness, the resulting mix of chaos and rebellion describe not totalitarianism, but the condition which gives rise to it'.[32] Recently *The Economist* noted that 'Bad governments help worse ones into power: it was the corruption and authoritarianism of Cambodia in the 1960s that helped to create the Khmer Rouge.'[33] For the sake, not only of human rights, but also of international stability, it is necessary to try to break, where possible, such vicious circles. Once again it can be seen that domestic conflicts, even if they do not directly lead to international security threats, may have a destabilizing effect on international relations.

It is necessary to caution against the view, stated by Max Singer and Aaron Wildavski,[34] that the world can be neatly divided into zones of peace and zones of turmoil. Fred Halliday contends rightly that 'the greatest mistake would be to maintain the idea that conflicts at the international level can be isolated from that within states'.[35] Internal conflicts within so-called zones of turmoil (basically, those in the Third World) inevitably affect states in so-called zones of peace. As Robert Keohane observes: 'Threats to the rich democracies from the zones of conflict may include terrorism, unwanted migration, the proliferation of nuclear weapons, and economic damage'.[36]

Stanley Hoffmann shows convincingly that:

> we live in a world in which apathy about what happens in 'far away countries of which we know nothing' [the phrase coined by Neville Chamberlain and used on the occasion of Hitler's annexation of Czechoslovakia in 1938] can all too easily lead – through contagion, through the message such moral passivity sends to troublemakers, would-be tyrants, and ethnic cleansers elsewhere – not to the kind of Armageddon we feared during the Cold War but to a creeping escalation of disorder and beastliness that will, sooner or later, reach the shores of the complacent, the rich, and the indifferent.[37]

That is why Western European states are not acting simply out of pure altruism when they try to integrate the former communist countries into European structures. Similarly, when they met at the end of 1995 in Barcelona with representatives of states across the Mediterranean in order to promote economic growth and stability in the Magreb area and the Middle East, they were not thinking only of countries across the Mediterranean. Western Europeans are rightly worried about illegal immigration, the export of drugs, terrorism, religious fundamentalism and instability from their 'near abroad'. Issues of economic cooperation, terrorism, drugs, immigration and also of human rights were discussed in Barcelona, and the EU proposed to double its funds for the Mediterranean region over the next five years.[38] On 28 November 1995, the EU and its twelve Mediterranean neighbours signed a cooperation pact aimed at improving regional stability by lifting trade barriers, pouring cash into struggling economies and strengthening political ties.[39]

The more interconnected and interdependent the world becomes, the greater the interest which states have in affairs which, until quite recently, were considered to be exclusively internal matters. Human rights are often at the centre of such intermestic (international/domestic) affairs.

IS BUSINESS PRO OR ANTI HUMAN RIGHTS?

If public opinion, the mass media and NGOs often push governments towards more active human rights diplomacy, the attitude of business communities to human rights is more controversial. We may recall that in 1972, after Ferdinand Marcos had declared martial law in the Philippines, the American Chamber of Commerce sent him a telegram in which the American business community wished him every success in his 'endeavor to restore peace and order, business confidence, economic growth and the well-being of the Filipino people'.[40] US grain farmers were not supportive of Washington's attempts to link trade with the Soviet Union to the latter's human rights record. Recently, American businesses were against tying Chinese MFN (Most Favoured Nation) status to its human rights record. Similarly, they have been against pushing India too hard on its human rights violations in Kashmir.

Such an attitude is, if not always justifiable, then at least understandable. The purpose of business is to make money, not to promote human rights. It just so happens that while business is making money, consumers usually become better off. Interestingly enough, something similar may happen with the link between business interests and human rights in countries where these interests lie.

Businesses may be against linking trade with human rights, but they are interested in the stability and predictability of their business transactions. This means that they have an interest in the stability of law and order wherever they do business. Safety of investments and of other business transactions cannot be completely separated from issues of civil and political rights. There are at least two problems which a business may have with dictators like Idi Amin or Bokassa: such despots either may easily change their mind, or they may be overthrown.

Moreover, in the post-Cold War world, as we have already mentioned, most human rights violations do not occur in strong, stable states like, for example, the former Soviet Union, its Eastern European allies, Chile, Paraguay or Argentina under military dictatorships, which were able to guarantee the stability and order (though at the expense of justice and human rights) necessary for businesses. Currently, in most states where gross and massive human rights violations occur, there is neither justice nor order. Suppression of human rights is not leading to an unjust order, but is contributing to the increase of unjust chaos. Pinochet's success story (I do not know whether in this context to use quotation marks or not) will hardly be repeated. As *The Economist* aptly points out, 'If dictators made countries rich, Africa would be an economic colossus'.[41]

On the other hand, there does seem to be a positive, though not absolute, and somewhat controversial correlation between economic development and political freedoms. There are studies which confirm that, other things being equal, an improvement of one mark in civil and political freedoms raises annual growth per head of roughly a full percentage point.[42] And, *vice versa*, economic growth has been followed, at least in some important cases, by political liberalization (for example, in South Korea, Malaysia, Taiwan, Chile). Eric Hobsbawm writes that 'the rapid industrial growth tended to generate large and educated professional classes which, though far from subversive, would have welcomed the civic liberalization of authoritarian industrializing regimes'.[43] 'Authoritarianism works only up to a point', argues Soogil Young, President of the Korea Transport Institute in Seoul. 'It becomes a victim of its own success'.[44] Osvaldo Sunkel writes, of Latin American dictatorships: 'With the exception of Chile, military governments were rather unsuccessful and unpopular, particularly as they were unable to deal with the economic and social crisis that is still largely present'.[45]

It seems that, in countries such as Singapore and Malaysia, their newly prosperous people may soon become tired of the *de facto* one-party rule which has brought them stability and wealth at the cost of political freedom.

This means that businesses, being interested in economic freedoms, may become unexpected and unintentional allies for those who are interested in the promotion of human rights. Certainly, their interest in economic stability is not affected by the limitations on freedom of the press, or by the corporal punishment meted out to young vandals who spray cars with graffiti somewhere in Singapore or Malaysia, especially if such limitations or punishments are not actively protested against or are even supported by the majority of the population at home. However, when authorities use excessive violence to suppress popular discontent, resort to torture or arbitrarily kill opponents of their regime, businesses ought to think twice before investing in such countries.

There are examples which show that some businesses have taken action in support of human rights abroad. At the beginning of 1995, US Federated Department Stores, which owns Macy's, New York's largest shop, declared that it would stop buying clothes made in Myanmar, and the City Council of Berkeley, California, decided not to buy goods produced by companies doing business in that country. Levi Strauss, the clothing giant, had already withdrawn earlier.[46]

Of course, there are many other examples of quite a different kind. Arms producers and dealers are especially notorious for selling their products to the worst human rights violators. However, civilized investors need at least some minimum standard of civilized business conditions. Robert Keohane argues that 'stable property rights require constitutional government, although not necessarily democracy. Hence the desire for economic growth provides a set of incentives for constitutionalism, as can be observed in Korea and Taiwan and perhaps in the future will emerge in China'.[47] However, he also warns that 'these incentives are not necessarily decisive; other favourable conditions have to apply before constitutionalism can be effectively instituted'.[48] To the extent that business needs the stability of property rights which cannot be guaranteed without at least some law and order, business may be an ally of those who are interested in the promotion of human rights (see Chapter Five).

HUMAN RIGHTS DIPLOMACY FOR THE SAKE OF HUMAN RIGHTS

The link between the atrocities committed by the Nazis at home and their aggressive foreign policy was not the only reason for the rapid development of the international – inter-governmental as well as non-governmental – human rights movements after the Second World War. One need not be Jewish to feel deeply shocked by the Holocaust, or Muslim to call for action in order to stop the rape of Muslim women in

Bosnia. There are not only pragmatic but also humanitarian reasons why peoples and states have become concerned with human rights in other countries. Not only religious or ethnic bonds, but simply the fact of belonging to humankind, may be for many individuals and peoples a factor which does not allow them to remain indifferent to the plight of fellow human beings in other countries.

The world is composed not only of states. Other entities, such as non-governmental as well as inter-governmental organizations, and individuals play an active part in world affairs. That is why we have a rather specific branch in international law – international human rights law – whose emergence and development is not only due to the fact that some human rights situations may adversely affect inter-state relations but whose genesis also reflects the increasing role of individuals and non-governmental bodies in domestic and international affairs.

Richard Rorty observes that the last two hundred years of moral progress has brought us to a moment in human history in which it is plausible to say that the human rights phenomenon is a 'fact of the world'.[49] Though Rorty is cautious and writes that this phenomenon may be just a 'blip', he nevertheless believes that 'it may mark the beginning of a time in which gang rape brings forth as strong a response when it happens to women as when it happens to men, or when it happens to foreigners as when it happens to people like us'.[50]

More recently, the so-called 'CNN factor' has brought humankind even closer together, with the result that many people in many countries feel strongly that 'something should be done' when acts of genocide, torture, gross discrimination based on race, ethnicity, religion or gender, as well as other crimes against human rights, take place in far-away places. Mass media and public pressure are often factors inducing the governments of democratic countries to take human rights into consideration in their foreign policy decision-making. The governments of democratic countries would feel rather embarrassed had they remained silent in the face of the atrocities committed against civilians in Bosnia, had they not reacted at all to the genocide in Rwanda or to the persecution of opponents of the military regime in Nigeria.

Of course, since the emergence of the very first international human rights instruments on the protection of certain minorities, human rights issues, as we saw, have been used as an instrument of state policy with quite a large portion of hypocrisy. Thus, in the Cold War era, human rights were often abused as part of the ideological and political struggle between the East and the West. However, in the development of international law, there is a phenomenon which could be called the 'hypocrisy trap'. For example, in the domain of human rights – where morality plays an important role and governments seldom want to be seen as outrightly immoral – some governments, which pay only lip-service to human rights or which try to use the issue as an instrument against their political adversaries, may find at the end of the day that their behaviour has nonetheless led to the emergence of certain norms and even practices which may really start to affect governments' policy. International human rights standards, like many other principles and norms of international law, are not just pieces of paper. They have the capacity to create expectations on the part of individuals and peoples as well as on the part of other governments – expectations which states may find difficult to resist. Louis Henkin is right when he says that

> the development of human rights law may indeed serve as a lesson in the benign consequences of certain kinds of hypocrisy, of the homage that vice pays to virtue. It is important that human rights is the virtue to which vice is impelled to pay homage. Then all states are impelled to accept human rights in principle, making promises to their own people as well as to the world. Repressive states are compelled to deny and conceal, but concealment can be uncovered and lies exposed.[51]

The international human rights movement, whatever its causes and reasons, has acquired its own momentum, and states could stay away from it only by losing further some of their credibility and power to other actors.

CONCLUSIONS

I believe that these examples and arguments show that governments and peoples have a legitimate interest in human rights issues everywhere, at home and abroad. This interest does not depend on whether violations are committed by strong or weak regimes. It is not surprising, therefore, that the planners of the Western European Union are currently drawing up contingency plans for operations on humanitarian relief, peacekeeping and crisis-management. For example, one of the planning exercises in November 1994 concerned a relief mission in an imaginary African country.[52] It is obvious that, if military planners are concerning themselves with the consequences of humanitarian emergencies, the thoughts of politicians should be aimed at how to prevent such emergencies from arising. Human rights situations in many countries may be the indicators of impending instability and an object of serious concern for the world community.

Thus we may conclude that human rights have today become an important part of international diplomacy, because their absence or serious violation can often negatively affect relations between states (an issue which will be discussed in some detail in the following chapters), and also because there is a common bond between most human beings, irrespective of their racial, ethnic, religious or national origin, which allows us to speak of humanity and which sometimes forces governments to act even contrary to the precepts of *Realpolitik*. Luc Ferry is right that 'tant que la politique continuera de sous-estimer l'importance historicale de la naissance de l'amour modern, tant qu'elle ne compranda pas le potenciel extraordinaire de solidarité, de sympathie qui réside dans la sphère privée, tant qu'elle ne fera pas fond sur lui, rien, en elle, ne suscitera l'enthousiasme'.[53]

2 Human rights and international stability

There are various links between human rights and international stability. Domestic and international stability are linked and, since human rights issues have a direct influence on domestic stability, they may also become relevant, at least indirectly, for international stability.

In this chapter, I will begin by analysing some general questions about the interaction between domestic and international stability in so far as this relates to human rights issues, and go on to examine how certain specific human rights situations affect domestic, and consequently, international stability. In this context the absence or neglect of social and economic rights and the interdependency between these rights and civil and political rights will be one of our concerns, as will also be the violation of the rights of ethnic minorities and human rights violations related to religious extremism; both of these are categories of human rights situations which can bear heavily on international stability.

It is not only the absence or violation of human rights that may adversely affect domestic and international stability. Sometimes the initiation of the processes of liberalization and democratization of authoritarian or totalitarian regimes can have a similar effect. Therefore it is necessary to look also at the dangers and pitfalls associated with these processes, and to see how they may affect international relations.

In Chapters Five and Six I will try to outline some possible strategies for dealing with human rights violations in different countries. In this chapter I intend to show how concerns for stability on the one hand and for human rights on the other are often interdependent. The pursuit of one of these concerns may sometimes hinder the achievement of the other; however, in different conditions they may support each other. Much depends on the concrete circumstances.

STABILITY AND HUMAN RIGHTS: INTERNAL AND INTERNATIONAL DIMENSIONS

The UN Charter makes a direct link between human rights and international peace: the promotion of human rights is important for the sake of peace and international security (Articles 1 and 55 of the Charter). As we have seen in the previous chapter, such a correlation may be true in some cases, but not in all. However, it is true to say that in the post-Cold War world, the most widespread threat to international relations does not come from direct cross-border attacks or international armed conflicts which directly breach or threaten international peace and security. It comes from the spread of domestic instability, which is often caused by human rights emergencies, over national borders. Therefore it seems that, currently, the key idea behind the relationship between human rights and international relations is stability.

Human rights and democracy in a country are directly related to its domestic stability in various ways. The relationship is not always positive. It is not necessarily the case that with more democracy and human rights the country will become more stable. As we will try to show, the relationship is much more complex.

How, and in what circumstances, does a human rights situation affect international stability? Does the promotion of human rights enhance international stability? And if it does not, what then?

There may be a conflict between interests in security and stability in the world and concerns for human rights in certain countries. During the Cold War era this conflict between human rights and security interests was, as we will show later, usually resolved in favour of the latter, regardless of whether the security threats were real or perceived.

The Cold War induced some democratic states to support dictators, provided that they were anti-communists. In the post-Cold War era there continue to be tensions between the concern for human rights and other foreign policy interests of states. Take, for example, a situation in which a stable authoritarian regime with a rather poor human rights record, but friendly with and important for Western democracies, is or may be threatened by its equally authoritarian neighbour (e.g., by Iraq in the Middle East). The interests of international or regional stability seem to dictate the necessity not only to close one's eyes to the human rights records of the threatened authoritarian regime, but to cooperate with the latter in building up its military capability. Pushing such governments, which usually resist any efforts at liberalization or democratic reform, too hard on human rights issues could alienate them; or possibly worse still: the introduction of certain reforms could dislodge the lid on oppression and open a Pandora's box which may plunge the country into chaos.

Similarly, there is usually a complicated 'human rights–international stability' relationship between the right of peoples to self-determination, or minority rights, and the requirements of territorial integrity of states. While it may be morally difficult not to support claims of oppressed minorities to independence, the road to realization of most of such claims (usually self-determination is understood by claimants as calls for political independence) may not only generate threats to international stability, but also create new human rights emergencies. The world community is hardly ready to support behaviour in accordance with the maxim *fiat justicia, ruat coelum* (let justice be done, though heaven fall). Or, as Thomas Franck and Nigel Rodley write: 'Nothing would be a more foolish footnote to man's demise than that his final destruction was occasioned by a war to ensure human rights'.[1]

Security concerns are coupled with economic interests, and both frequently seem to speak against showing too much interest in human rights, at least in some countries. Robert Manning, for example, writing on US foreign policy towards China, observes that 'a new three-tier framework of human rights, political/strategic issues, and economic affairs is gradually emerging, and Clinton's new challenge will be to set political priorities to manage these issues and establish benchmarks of behaviour'.[2] However, the recent practice of US–Chinese relations shows that these tiers often seem to work against each other and concerns for human rights are certainly not the issue of utmost priority among them.

Human rights and international stability are not, naturally, synonyms, and stability may often be inimical to justice. The former Soviet Union and South Africa, or even the former Yugoslavia, were examples of rather stable but unjust societies. In these and many similar cases stability may be inimical to other values, including human rights.[3]

On the other hand, without peace and stability, observance of human rights is, at best, difficult. Sometimes the quest for justice (especially if we take into account that justice may be perceived differently by different people and nations) and human rights may destabilize domestic and international relations, which, in turn, is not the best environment for human rights. This rings especially true for multi-ethnic societies where minorities who are suffering from injustices seek justice through separation. Albanians in Kosovo and

Macedonia, Hungarians in Slovakia or Muslims in Kashmir may be examples of such cases. Hedley Bull wrote that, in the international system, 'in which rights and duties are applied directly to states and nations, the notion of human rights and duties has survived but it has gone underground. Far from providing the basis from which ideas of international justice and morality are derived, it has become potentially subversive of international society itself'.[4]

Human rights may be subversive for order in the international system in two respects. The first is what Hedley Bull had in mind: concerns for human rights in international relations undermine the fundamentally inter-state character of these relations. However, human rights may also be subversive for order in the international society by undermining the existing order in some states. It is not accidental that many governments still consider human rights activists as subversive elements. And rightly so, because their claims for human rights and freedoms subvert the order on which the power of these governments is based. Aung San Suu Kyi constitutes a threat to the State Law and Order Restoration Council (the military junta) of Myanmar and, like Chinese dissidents, she undermines the authority of the non-democratic and human rights-hostile government. Wei Jingsheng, who was sentenced in December 1995 for fourteen years of imprisonment for alleged 'conspiracy to overthrow the State',[5] and his 'co-conspirator' Wang Tang were threats to the ageing Chinese leadership. Similarly, Soviet dissidents like Andrei Sakharov and Sergei Kovaljov helped to bring down the communist rule in the USSR. Their efforts, as well as the struggle of *Solidarnosc* in Poland, Charter 77 in Czechoslovakia and other human rights activists, contributed to the chain reaction which is currently transforming Eastern and Central Europe.

These examples show that, though a quest for human rights and justice may have a destabilizing effect on international relations, this is not necessarily a bad thing after all. System transformations are always characterized more by chaos than order, because one structure and order is being replaced by another structure and order. Such a situation is inevitable because order can emerge only from chaos, not from frigidity, which may be stable but which is not amenable to change.

However, justice and human rights are often ephemeral without order and peace. This can be seen by glancing retrospectively at events in Africa over the last, say, thirty or forty years and analysing the changing attitude of some prominent African authors towards the relationship between peace and justice. Ali Mazrui, for example, wrote in the 1960s that 'the prevailing view of the purpose of the United Nations among the richer countries is... the maintenance of peace; the prevailing view among poorer countries, especially among the new states of Asia and Africa, is of the UN as a global ombudsman, protective of the rights of man at large'.[6] Although Mazrui, like some African politicians, may have had in mind not so much human rights as such but a re-arrangement of the existing international order in favour of African and other Third World states, his observation is interesting: justice, rather than order, is the priority for poor countries.

However, recent developments, especially in Africa, have shown that talk about human rights and justice, without peace and order, may turn out to make a mockery of human rights. Though the current difficulties with human rights in many African countries are not due exclusively to the lack of peace and order (the lack of economic and social development being other important factors negatively affecting human rights as well), the absence of domestic peace in many parts of the continent is the major direct cause of most of the human rights emergencies in this continent and in many other parts of the world as well. Therefore, it may not be so surprising that, in the mid-1990s, Ali Mazrui writes that 'only parts of Africa can govern themselves'.[7] Now he is more concerned with order and peace in the continent, than with human rights. He even foresees the possibility and desirability of the establishment of a kind of 'African concert' to police the continent. 'External recolonization under the banner of humanitarianism is entirely conceivable.' And Mazrui continues: 'Although colonialism may be resurfacing, it is likely to look rather different this time around. A future trusteeship system will be more genuinely international and less western than it was under the old guise'.[8]

His fellow-African, Mauritanian diplomat Ahmedu Ould Abdallah, even feels that 'only a form of re-colonisation can save Africa from itself'.[9]

Be that as it may, one thing seems to be clear: a lack of peace, stability and order also means a lack of human rights and freedoms. Without peace, both international and domestic, we may be concerned not so much with human rights as with humanitarian law, i.e., the laws and customs of war, be it domestic or international.

This may all sound like an apology for order and stability at the expense of justice and human rights. However, domestic and international stability may also be rather ephemeral without at least a certain degree of justice, including human rights. If it is true that without internal peace and order one could hardly speak of justice in Liberia, Rwanda or Burundi, it is equally true that the lack of human rights in these countries contributed to the upheavals these countries are facing. And this dependency of order upon justice is especially true in the post-Cold War world, where the discipline imposed by the competing power blocks has vanished. Many Third World dictators whose hold of power was legitimized by external, either Eastern or Western, support are now on their own. Daniel Bach characterizes the new situation in Africa in the aftermath of the Cold War in the following terms:

> It is no longer possible for Africa's ruling elites to take advantage from real or supposed East–West competition to secure financial, diplomatic or military aid which all too often was employed to neutralise internal pressure for change: apartheid South Africa, the MPLA-controlled Angolan government or the francophone states linked to France by defence agreements, have all in their own ways had to face the effects of Africa's global devalorisation. In this respect, the subsequent revival of internal pressure for democratisation owes probably far more to Africa's marginalisation than to the more recent Western concern for extending political conditionality to relations with the 'South'.[10]

Dictators left on their own may constitute a serious threat to the stability of their own countries which, in certain circumstances, may have serious repercussions for international stability as well.

We have seen that some manifestly unjust regimes which seemed to be rather stable, like for example the Soviet Union or South Africa, have collapsed. This happened not because these regimes did not deliver economically: South Africa did rather well in economic terms; but their unjust, human rights-hostile character was an even stronger factor contributing to the eventual fall of these regimes. These, as do other examples, show that though stability is possible without justice, it is unlikely to last, and often, in order to last at all, injustice has to become stronger and stronger, thereby contributing to the inevitable explosion.

Therefore I agree completely with Max Singer and Aaron Wildavski that 'a more profound definition of stability would sometimes require support for change to prevent some drastic upheavals later'.[11] Social stability, be it domestic or international, often calls for changes, and therefore resistance to them and attempts to maintain the *status quo* in such circumstances can only serve as destabilizing factors.

It seems that stability in the world is often like the stability of a bicycle: it does not fall as long as it keeps moving. In this way, the world can be relatively stable, passing of course through periods of instability, while it is constantly changing, and one of the directions of these changes seems to be towards the enlargement of democracy and the promotion of human rights.

Moreover, it is not just a creeping pragmatism which changes the world and sometimes, somewhere, makes it a better place to live in. Often, ideas and idealists are the driving forces behind human progress and liberation. The concepts of human rights and democracy – although very idealistic at first and even divorced from what was then an existing reality – having now taken possession of millions of people, have already become a material force. The hard-nosed realist Henry Kissinger has a point when, writing about the essence of America's political faith, he finds that it 'is at once "naïve" and draws from that naïveté the impetus for extraordinary endeavors'.[12]

The idea of universal human rights, which was, and may still be in the eyes of many, rather naive and idealistic, has by now left few societies unaffected. The rapid development of new means of communication, being the inevitable concomitant of economic and technological progress, further accelerates the dissemination of human rights ideas.

Nowadays it is often the case that the longer and harsher a regime tries to prevent the enjoyment of human rights by its population, the stronger and more disastrous for human rights and international stability is the collapse of that regime. It may result either in leftist extremism (e.g., Cuba after Batista, Nicaragua after Somoza) or religious extremism (Iran after the Shah). Therefore, concern for human rights, expressed either by the international community represented by the UN or other bodies, or by individual states, may help to smooth domestic transformations and avoid destabilization of inter-state relations.

I must disagree with Singer and Wildavski when they write that the US experience in Iran is an example of how harmful a simple-minded commitment to democracy can be. They write: 'We undercut the Shah because he was insufficiently democratic, and his fall produced massive death and suffering, less immediate democracy, great international problems, and quite possibly a setback in Iran's long-term path to stable democracy'.[13]

The reality seems to have been quite different. The fatal blow to Iran's long-term path to democracy was given in 1953 when the US government intervened to topple the relatively democratic Mossadeq government.[14] David Forsythe's interpretation of Iran in 1953 is that a combination of concerns about economic advantage and a perceived national security threat led the United States to engage in a covert

international 'war' against the Mossadeq regime, a regime which was
partially democratic and certainly far more democratic than what
followed.[15] Jack Donnelly even writes that 'long-standing U.S. support
of repressive regimes in Iran and Nicaragua contributed significantly
to U.S. foreign policy problems with the new revolutionary governments in these countries in the late 1970s and early 1980s'.[16] I am not
so sure whether these problems may otherwise have been very much
different, but the support for these authoritarian regimes helped them
to stay in power longer, and to become more oppressive and corrupt
which, in turn, radicalized the opposition to these regimes.

As Sattareh Farman Farmaian, an Iranian who was educated in the
United States and lived in Iran during the Shah's rule, writes:

> The illiterate, apolitical poor could barely make sense of the radio
> speeches given by the Shah and his false-hearted, fancy-talking
> ministers. They were seeking solace and explanations for their
> miseries from the person who, back home in the village, had always
> stood for simple righteousness and God's will, the mullah in the
> Friday mosque.[17]

And she adds: 'The Shah was watering Khomeini like a slow-growing
tree and making him the religious opposition's uncontested cham-
pion'.[18]

Therefore I completely agree with another point made by Donnelly,
that, 'If the United States had not created and then supported the
Somoza family dictatorship over half a century, it might never have
had to deal with a Sandinista government. Likewise, the real cause of
the 'loss' of Angola was the colonial policy of the U.S.-backed military
dictatorship in Portugal'.[19]

These examples, albeit from the Cold War period of international
relations, show that the support of stability while sacrificing justice
may ultimately be detrimental to the realization of the very stability
sought.

It seems that a healthy proportion of the idealism reflected, *inter
alia*, in human rights diplomacy should be an important part of
realistic foreign policy. It is not always the case that the dictates of
Realpolitik, which put the interests of security and stability in first
place, clash with concerns for human rights. And even when they do
clash, or seem to clash, this does not mean that human rights should
always be on the losing side. On the contrary, long-term interests in
international stability should induce governments not to marginalize
human rights concerns when formulating foreign policy.

THE INTERPLAY OF CIVIL-POLITICAL AND SOCIO-ECONOMIC RIGHTS AND INTERNATIONAL STABILITY

Gross and systematic violations of civil and political rights, especially the rights of ethnic or religious minorities, as is shown in other parts of this book, usually have a tendency to affect international stability adversely. Massive violations of the right to life, and to freedom from torture, arbitrary arrest and detention without fair trial (if any trial at all), are usually the human rights violations which cause domestic instability, civil or inter-ethnic wars and refugee flows, and which may eventually lead to threats to international stability. However, in some countries the lack of social and economic rights, which may be tantamount to gross social inequality and injustice, is one of the main causes of violations of civil and political rights and social instability.

Civil-political rights and socio-economic rights are equally important; there are also close links and a certain interdependence between these two categories of human rights. The denial of social and economic rights may be a serious cause of social unrest which many governments often meet by political repression. The underlying situation may not only be caused by ineffective and corrupt economic management. Rapid economic development, if it is accompanied by gross social inequalities and neglect of social and economic rights, may lead to a political crisis. The revolutions in Mexico, Cuba and Nicaragua all took place following a period of economic growth, not stagnation. But the growth was very uneven.[20] The Islamic revolution in Iran in 1978 had many causes, but it is interesting to note that it happened after a decade of rapid socio-economic change which had resulted in an annual *per capita* income of over $2000.[21] As Fred Halliday writes, 'more important for the mass of urban poor, however, were the inequalities and tensions associated with the boom itself: while the gap between rural and urban income began growing in the late 1960s, inequalities in the urban areas themselves began to be increasingly pronounced'.[22] Oil had introduced 'external revenue into the society without any comparable transformation of its socio-economic and productive structures'.[23]

Therefore, for example, the revolt of the peasants of Chiapas in Southern Mexico in 1994–95 should be a warning not only to the Mexican government. It also reveals the string of developments which led to the undermining of international stability: neglect of the interests and rights of the peasants of Chiapas; revolt of the peasants against the government; repressive measures by the government. These factors all contributed to the social and economic crisis in Mexico which, in turn, adversely affected world finances generally and US financial interests in particular.

Since the decline of the overshadowing threat of a global nuclear war, threats of the type described above will likely become one of the most serious problems which the world community has to deal with.

Zebra Arat observes that:

> the decline of democracy and the transition to authoritarian rule in developing countries are attributable to policies that create an imbalance between the two groups of human rights, civil and political rights and socioeconomic rights, by ignoring the latter group. The increasing gap between the two groups of rights...causes frustration and social unrest, which in turn is suppressed by coercive politics.[24]

One may doubt whether there really is such an imbalance in favour of civil and political rights in developing countries, or an increasing gap between these two categories of human rights. It is true, however, that in many developing countries, notwithstanding all the talk about the primacy of economic and social rights over civil and political rights, both categories of rights are equally neglected.

Arat is certainly right in saying that 'the stable democracy tends to reflect higher levels of socioeconomic equality. The neglect of social and economic rights puts pressure on the system and eventually leads the civil and political rights that are ingredients of a viable democracy to draw a declining curve'.[25]

This means that no state, not even a poor one and sometimes especially not a poor one, can completely neglect social and economic rights. Such neglect may undermine domestic stability and eventually constitute a threat to international stability. There are studies which argue very strongly that democracy, meaning the broad implementation of civil and political rights, will prove stable only if serious attention is payed to economic and social rights as well.[26] H. Shue is right to say that 'no one can fully, if at all, enjoy any right that is supposedly protected by society if he or she lacks the essentials for a reasonably healthy life'.[27] Danilo Türk writes that states 'should pay particular attention to the most disadvantaged groups and extremely poor. They should bear in mind that extreme poverty leads to the exclusion of the affected persons and to the consequent inability fully to realize their human rights, including civil and political rights'.[28]

The current tendency of a spreading free-market economy in different parts of the world – a trend which in itself seems to be positive and even necessary – may well call for greater emphasis on the necessity to guarantee social and economic rights. The Committee on Economic, Social and Cultural Rights – a UN body monitoring the implementation of the Covenant on Economic, Social and Cultural Rights – stressed in its statement to the 1993 World Conference on Human Rights:

> The increasing emphasis being placed on free market policies brings with it a far greater need to ensure that appropriate measures are taken to safeguard and promote economic, social and cultural rights. Even the most ardent supporters of the free market have generally acknowledged that it is incapable, of its own accord, of protecting many of the most vulnerable and disadvantaged members of society.[29]

However, such an emphasis on the importance of social and economic rights does not mean that they are more important than civil and political rights. This thesis was propagated by Soviet doctrine and diplomacy. But the very Soviet experience is a textbook example of how the absence of civil and political rights leads to social and economic stagnation and, as a result, social and economic rights suffer as well.

Social and economic rights are largely conditioned by the economic development of a country, and the relationship between economic development, human rights and democracy is a rather complicated one. If the Soviet Union stressed the priority of social and economic rights, some governments today put an emphasis on economic development or the right to development rather than on economic and social rights. Liu Huaqiu, head of the Chinese delegation to the Vienna World Conference on Human Rights of 1993, opined:

> For the vast number of developing countries to respect and protect human rights is first and foremost to ensure the full realization of the rights to subsistence and development. The argument that human rights is the precondition for development is unfounded. When poverty and lack of adequate food and clothing are commonplace and people's basic needs are not guaranteed, priority should be given to economic development. Otherwise, human rights are completely out of question.[30]

But even if it is true (and I believe that in many cases it is) that, for poor developing countries, social and economic development is the most important and urgent task, does this mean that for the sake of rapid economic development it is necessary to sacrifice human rights, especially civil and political rights?

Sylvia Hewlett, in *The Cruel Dilemmas of Development: Twentieth Century Brazil* writes that 'impressive economic performance...in the modern period has depended upon massive poverty and political repression, and it would not have been possible under democratic governments pursuing egalitarian economic policies'.[31]

It is possible that, in certain societies at certain periods of their socio-economic or political development, 'enlightened authoritarian' regimes guarantee higher speeds of economic growth than would a democratic system. Jack Donnelly, analysing the experience of Brazil and South Korea, finds that 'some repression is likely to be "required" (or at least extraordinarily difficult to avoid) in pursuit of what can be called *the structural task* of removing institutional and sociocultural barriers to the development and *the political task* of assuring conformity to development plans'.[32] But I would emphasize that Donnelly makes here a subtle distinction between repression being politically unavoidable and it being economically necessary. He concludes that it is not economic necessity but rather the characteristics of ruling elites which necessitate the use of repression.[33]

Though there is some truth in assertions that, in many cases, trade-offs of human rights for the sake of political stability and maximization of investment go hand-in-hand with rapid economic development, this is true only for the lower stages of social and economic development. Even here it is hazardous because, instead of guaranteeing the stability necessary for development, it could contribute to undermining that stability if it is sought through repression.

It goes without saying that certain kinds of gross and systematic human rights violations (for example, torture, disappearances, arbitrary arrests) have nothing to do with the speed of development. So-called 'developmental repression', which is often tantamount to the massive violation of civil and political as well as socio-economic rights, does not contribute to domestic and international stability and, as some authors have shown rather convincingly,[34] is not even necessary for economic growth.

It is important to note that in several cases a return to democracy and political liberalization has accelerated economic growth. In Chile, a country which is considered by many as an example of a case where political repression (under General Pinochet) went hand-in-hand with economic growth, the economy started to develop more quickly after the restoration of democracy than before. Table 1, which gives Chilean GDP over the years,[35] illustrates this point rather well.

Table 1 Chile's GDP in millions of US$ for the years 1973–1994

Year GDP		Comments
1973	10,352	Military coup
1974	11,058	
1975	7,218	
1976	9,857	
1977	13,362	
1978	15,400	
1979	20,732	
1980	17,571	
1981	32,644	
1982	25,584	Strong devaluation of local currency
1983	20,199	
1984	19,596	
1985	16,486	
1986	17,123	
1987	20,695	
1988	24,153	
1989	28,204	First free elections, 14 December 1989
1990	30,402	
1991	34,411	
1992	42,749	
1993	45,658	Second free elections, 11 December 1993

These figures seem to refute assertions that authoritarianism is necessary for development or that democracy cannot deliver economically.

From my own point of view, certain limitations of civil and political rights, as well as of economic and social rights, may be difficult to avoid during the initial stages of rapid development. However, these limitations could fit into the permissible limitations provided for by, for example, Article 18 of the Covenant on Civil and Political Rights which stipulates that 'freedom to manifest one's religion or beliefs may be subject only to such limitations as are prescribed by law and are necessary to protect public safety, order, health, or morals or the fundamental rights and freedoms of others'. I believe that excessive limitations, and by the same token moreover massive repression, are not only economically dysfunctional, but may also have a destabilizing effect on society.

MINORITY RIGHTS AND INTERNATIONAL STABILITY

The biggest threat to international stability, among those threats which have human rights violations as factors contributing to the genesis of instability, stems from the violation of the rights of ethnic or religious minorities. Many recent or ongoing conflicts (for example, in Liberia, former Yugoslavia, Georgia) involving serious international repercussions started with or were accompanied by violations of the rights of ethnic minorities. *The Economist* points out: 'In countries such as Liberia and Somalia, rebellion has led to the meltdown of the state. These countries imploded; their societies became atomised; the land was taken over by warlords and gangs. In each, the war began as a protest against a government that had excluded influential ethnic groups. Conversely, the most successful states, like the new post-apartheid South Africa, have inclusive governments that involve as many groups as possible'.[36] As David Welsh writes, 'an important lesson for the management of ethnic conflict is that no salient group should be prohibited from a share of effective power'.[37]

As noted in Chapter One, international concern with human rights started with attempts to protect the rights and interests of certain religious and ethnic groups. Because of the close links between ethnicity and the state, be it a nation-state or a multi-nation one, it is understandable that inter-ethnic frictions or conflicts can easily affect inter-state relations. The future likelihood of civil wars, refugee flows and foreign interventions may to a large extent depend on how governments treat their minorities.

Not all inter-ethnic conflicts are due, however, to the violation of minority rights. Some conflicts have their roots in centuries-old animosities. It is true also that minorities themselves are not always only innocent victims. It is not so rare to find that they (or to be more precise, their political and military elites) contribute on an equal footing with the majority leaders to the development of inter-ethnic conflicts. Zviad Gamzakhurdia of Georgia and Vladislav Arzinba of Abkhazia are not only both to be blamed for the conflict in that part of Georgia, but also depended upon each other in order to boost their authority among their own followers and to consolidate their power.

Often governments in power are either unable to find solutions to minority concerns or deliberately discriminate against minorities. Such policies contribute significantly to inter-ethnic conflicts. A recent report by Human Rights Watch covering fifty-three countries contends that contemporary ethnic violence arises as much from deliberate government policies (i.e., from violations of the rights of minorities) as from traditional communal antagonisms.[38] The 1995 Report of the UN High Commissioner on Human Rights states that 'unresolved problems related to national or ethnic, religious or linguistic minorities are widely recognised as one of the major sources of international and internal conflicts involving widespread human rights violations'.[39]

Repression in a mono-ethnic state (or in a state with relatively small and dispersed minorities) can lead to riots, rebellions or social revolutions. Repression in an undemocratic multi-ethnic state, which usually, if not exclusively, is directed against certain ethnic groups, has a tendency to generate a movement for secession or irredentism. This, in turn, may result in even more brutal repressions or an inter-ethnic war, both of which constitute a major threat to international peace and stability.

Of course, secessionist movements are not alien even to some developed democratic states (for example, Canada, Spain or the United Kingdom). But in the context of dealing with the relationship between human rights and international stability, such cases are of limited interest here, as developed democratic states tend to pose considerably less threat to international stability even when they may break up. Nevertheless, as Conrad Black observes, even 'Quebec's independence would be complicated, costly, and at best an exhilarating and frightening voyage into the unknown'.[40] There are no doubts that even a 'velvet' separation of Quebec from the rest of Canada would adversely affect at least regional economic, financial and political relations.

In democratic states it is easier for minorities to gain independence, but they have less incentive to struggle for it. Extreme nationalists in these countries who often resort to violence usually do not represent a minority as a whole. For example, a 1982 survey indicated that 38 per cent of the Basque population considered members of ETA, a Basque terrorist organization, to be patriots and idealists, while 31 per cent considered them to be fools and criminals. But only 8 per cent of the Basques said that they supported ETA, while 77 per cent were opposed to their activities.[41] It is also interesting to note, as Patrick Brogan writes, that the ETA leadership was particularly concerned to defeat the Spanish government's plan for Basque autonomy: they wanted the Basques oppressed, so that they would rise in revolt and thereby create a new order.[42] Similarly, the Corsican separatists led the violent struggle against the French authorities despite obvious lack of public support.[43] The National Front for the Liberation of Corsica split up, and, recently, different separatist groups have been heavily engaged in fighting each other or have become involved in extortion and drug smuggling as well as in nightclubs, cabarets and restaurants around the island.[44] As for the IRA and its political wing, Sinn Fein, support for the latter in Northern Ireland, even among the Catholic minority, has always been outnumbered by support for the Social Democratic Labour Party (SDLP).[45]

These facts themselves underline the importance of the democratic legitimacy of governments, which is especially difficult to achieve in the eyes of minorities.

Minority problems can raise issues related to the right of peoples to self-determination for three reasons. First, because it is not easy to make a distinction between minorities and peoples; second, because the satisfactory resolution of minority issues may soften or even remove claims for self-determination – often equated with secession; and third, because the complete denial or gross suppression of the rights of minorities may indeed lead to justified claims for secession.

There seems to be an increasing understanding, which has found expression, for example, in the deliberations of the UN Human Rights Committee[46] and in works of academics,[47] that in the post-colonial era, 'peoples', for the purposes of self-determination under international law, can be defined as populations of states, while minorities constitute parts of these populations. The right to self-determination is itself increasingly being seen as an entitlement to democracy and not necessarily involving a right to secession.[48] An example is the third periodic report of Cyprus to the UN Human Rights Committee of 20 January 1995 on the implementation of the Covenant on Civil and Political Rights under Article 1 of the Covenant (on the right of peoples to self-determination). The report states that 'in Cyprus democratic elections are held enabling its people to determine their political status and to pursue in a free manner their economic, social and cultural development'[49] and deals in some detail with presidential, parliamentary and local elections. Equally, the third periodic report of Mauritius of 15 September 1995 reports on the implementation of the right to self-determination in Mauritius about elections, referenda and the judicial control over the fairness of elections.[50] This means that the right of self-determination is understood more and more, not as a principle of exclusion or separation, but as a principle of inclusion, i.e., of inclusion of the whole population of a state in the political process, as a right to political participation.

When a minority is oppressed and discriminated against, it is not only ethnically or religiously distinct from the rest of the population, it also becomes socially, economically and politically different from the majority. I would say that some minorities, owing to the repressive policies of majorities, acquire the characteristics of 'peoples' which are in a sense similar to those of colonial 'peoples': being subjects, they are not full citizens. It may even be that an ethnic or religious minority can only survive, in some cases even physically, independently from the majority.

When a minority is discriminated against, or its identity is threatened, it does not participate with the rest of the population in the political life of the country. This means that the minority can realize its right to self-determination, i.e., its right to be included in the political process and the social and economic development of the country, not together with and as a part of the whole population of the state, but only separately. Thus, secession should not be, in my view, excluded for such minorities.

However, secession could only be an option supported by the international community when a minority, because of the attitude of the majority, is unable to exist and develop its identity in the framework of the existing state; that is to say when its minority rights are denied or grossly violated. John Chipman is right in saying that 'morally, a secession from an existing state may be permissible when numerous conditions are met, including the following: the group in the seceding territory has consistently experienced an infringement of its rights or its culture, and there is no practicable way, short of secession, that those rights can be preserved'.[51] Otherwise, and as a general rule, solutions should be found in the framework of existing states.

The reason for such a conclusion lies not just in the immediate necessity to preserve stability in international relations. It so happens that separations or dissolutions of states do not usually diminish the number of minorities. On the contrary, new minority problems and inter-ethnic conflicts can often arise. There are not less, but more minorities in the new states which have emerged in place of the former Soviet Union. The dissolution of Yugoslavia created, *inter alia*, the Bosnia which we have now. Hurst Hannum is correct when he says that 'individuals and minorities will continue to exist no matter how carefully borders are drawn'.[52]

The close relationship between minority rights and international stability is evidenced also by the fact that, in the OSCE (Organization of Security and Cooperation in Europe) framework, the rights of minorities are not considered as exclusively or even primarily a human rights problem, but as a security issue. The OSCE High Commissioner on National Minorities is seen as an 'instrument of conflict prevention at the earliest possible stage' who should 'provide early warning'.[53] The

High Commissioner has been active in Estonia, Latvia, Hungary, Slovakia, Albania, Romania and Macedonia, and has played a constructive role in mitigating some of the inter-ethnic tension in these countries stemming, if not from direct violation of minority rights, then at least from neglect of the interests and problems of their ethnic minorities.

For example, in the case of Estonia, the High Commissioner, finding that 'there is no convincing evidence of systematic persecution of the non-Estonian population since the re-establishment of Estonian independence',[54] nevertheless made a series of recommendations to the Estonian authorities concerning their legislation and practices in a number of areas, including citizenship, status of aliens, reduction of statelessness and use of languages.

Addressing the Estonian government, the High Commissioner also made an important comment which is of general interest and therefore deserves to be quoted in full:

Against this background [i.e., historical facts, and the demographic and ethnic composition of the country], your government is in my view, at least in theory, confronted with two completely contradictory options regarding the non-Estonian population of your country. The first is to try to assure in various ways a privileged position for its Estonian population. Apart from the fact that such a policy would scarcely be compatible with the spirit, if not the letter, of various international obligations Estonia has accepted, such a policy would, in my view, involve a considerable risk of increasing tensions with the non-Estonian population which, in turn, could lead to destabilization of the country as a whole. In addition, it would have a strong negative effect on relations between Estonia and the Russian Federation.

The alternative policy is to aim at integration of the non-Estonian population by a deliberate policy of facilitating the chances of acquiring Estonian citizenship for those who express such a wish, and assuring them full equality with Estonian citizens. In my view, such a policy would greatly reduce the danger of destabilization.[55]

This statement would be relevant *mutatis mutandis* in many other situations. Though there was not any persecution of the non-Estonian population, their concerns were not being met by the authorities. Restrictive legislation on citizenship led to the emergence of numerous stateless persons, and the law on the status of aliens had to be amended at the insistence of the Council of Europe and the CSCE.[56] But the most important general point is that the mishandling of minority issues increases the danger of destabilization of society which, in turn, can adversely affect international relations.

When the issue of the Hungarian minority in Slovakia created friction between Hungary and the Slovak Republic, the High Commissioner proposed to designate three experts on minority issues who would visit both countries with a view to submitting advice and recommendations to the High Commissioner. The High Commissioner would then decide whether, and in what form, such advice and recommendations would be communicated to the governments of Hungary and Slovakia.[57] This proposal was met with approval by both governments, and a team of experts has visited both countries on several occasions.[58] Their recommendations included, *inter alia*, a proposal to the Slovak authorities that any administrative divisions introduced in the Slovak Republic should respect the rights of national minorities, and the hope that the process of devolution of powers would be implemented in the near future.[59]

How explosive the neglect or mishandling of minority issues can be is shown by the developments in Macedonia (Former Yugoslav Republic of Macedonia, or FYROM) concerning the issue of an Albanian University. The authorities procrastinated with the implementation of their promise to open a pedagogical faculty for training teachers for Albanian-language schools. Marek Jeziorski, Adviser to the OSCE High Commissioner on National Minorities, observes that the failure of the government to act timely gave radical political forces in Macedonia a powerful argument. The Albanian 'university' was inaugurated in Tetovo in December 1994 without the approval of, and proper consultation with, the authorities. Tension rose and led to clashes on 17 February 1995, in which one Albanian was killed. Jeziorski concludes that, 'in this way, educational questions acquired an extremely strong political significance and touched the essence of the problem of the peace and stability in Macedonia and the region'.[60]

The statements and proposals of the OSCE High Commissioner on National Minorities, as well as his very polite and discreet diplomatic dialogue with different governments, may seem to be insignificant in comparison with the inability of the world community to cope with genocide in Bosnia or Rwanda. However, it is important to stress that such preventive measures are helping to pave the road towards a world with less Bosnias and Rwandas.

Therefore, it is not surprising that, besides creating the post of the High Commissioner on National Minorities in the framework of the OSCE, European countries have undertaken additional measures to deal with minority issues.

In February 1995, twenty-two states who were party to the Council of Europe signed the Framework Convention on the Protection of National Minorities, because, as the Preamble to the Convention says, 'the upheavals of European history have shown that the protection of national minorities is essential to stability, democratic security and peace in this continent'.[61]

A specific problem of minority rights with serious security implications has arisen in the territories of the former Soviet Union, as well as in some other places in Eastern Europe. Hungary[62] and Macedonia,[63] for example, have in their Constitutions clauses which claim that it is the right and obligation of these states to take care of the rights and interests of their ethnic brethren living abroad. The Russian authorities currently seem to be much more concerned with the human rights of ethnic Russians living in so-called 'near abroad' countries (territories of the former Soviet republics) than with the rights and interests of Russia's citizens, including its numerous minorities.

In the Autumn of 1993, Marshal Yevgeny Shaposhnikov, the former Commander in Chief of the CIS (Commonwealth of Independent States) forces and Secretary of the Russian National Security Council, wrote an article entitled 'On the Concept of the National Security of Russia'. In the article he stated that 'an acute and painful security problem stems from the implementation of rights and protection of interests of ethnic minorities of Russian origin in the former Soviet republics'; and he considered that one of the threats to the national security of Russia, alongside, for example, armed conflicts on the periphery of Russia, was the threat stemming from 'the violation of human rights and freedoms in neighbouring states and from the resulting migratory processes'.[64]

Constantine Pleshakov, the Director of the Pacific Studies Centre of the Institute of the US and Canada of the Russian Academy of Sciences, makes the point (in the spirit of Zhirinovsky) that 'apartheid is evident in the policy of Latvia and Estonia'[65]. He comes to the conclusion that 'safeguarding the human rights of Russians in the territories of the former Soviet Union has become a matter of national survival for Russia'.[66]

Such a statement is frightening. While not denying that Russia may have a legitimate interest in the plight of its ethnic brethren living abroad, including 'near-abroad', and that the rights of ethnic Russians may have been violated in some of the former Soviet republics, including Estonia and Latvia, I nevertheless believe that more important as 'a matter of national survival for Russia' should be the situation of human rights within Russia. This is even more so because, as the Report of the Commission on Human Rights headed by Sergei Kovaljov, the former Russian Human Rights Commissioner, has stated, violations of human rights, including the rights of ethnic minorities, and especially those of persons belonging to Caucasian and Central Asian nationalities, are rife in Russia.[67]

Such a concept of human rights, linked with such an understanding of matters of national survival for Russia, is especially worrying in the light of Russia's new military doctrine, which claims that one of the main existing and potential threats outside the Russian Federation is 'the suppression of the rights, freedoms and legitimate interests of citizens of the Russian Federation in foreign states'.[68] This doctrine provides for the use of the armed forces of Russia, *inter alia*, for the defence of its citizens abroad.[69] At the same time, Russia insists that the states of the 'near-abroad' accept dual citizenship for ethnic Russians living in their countries. Professor Gregory Morozov writes that no one can deny Russia's right to protect the interests of dozens of millions of Russians in other countries. And he refers, as he says, to the long-existing international practice, above all to that of the United States, on this matter which 'confirms the lawfulness of Russia's concern for Russians who found themselves abroad'.[70] It seems that he has in mind the use of force by the US, for example, in Grenada in 1983 or in Panama in 1989, in which one of the justifications for that use of force was a threat to the lives of Americans in these countries. But quite differently from US practice (which itself is not non-controversial), Professor Morozov is obviously referring not to Russian citizens but to ethnic Russians or so-called Russian-speakers, whose interests Russia is supposed to take care of.

The issue of Russian minorities in other former Soviet republics is a sphere where 'Greater-Russian' nationalism and the nationalism of some of its neighbours feed on each other. Like the components of binary chemical weapons, they become especially poisonous and deadly when merged with each other.

These potentially explosive situations are not limited to the former USSR or Yugoslavia. Similarly, Albania and ethnic Albanians in Kosovo (Serbia) and in Macedonia, and Hungary and ethnic Hungarians in Slovakia, are equations which have potential implications for international stability.

Though under international law a state has special rights to protect only its own citizens in other countries (usually through diplomatic channels, but including in extreme cases, as will be discussed in Chapter Six, the right of intervention to save the lives of its citizens) it would be unrealistic to expect that 'motherlands' or 'kin-states', as they are called, will stand by idly when the rights of their ethnic brethren are being trampled upon in a neighbouring country. However, sometimes this very emotional issue of minority rights is used by minorities in order to gain more and more autonomy, other special rights (for example, by the Russians in Crimea which belongs to the Ukraine, and by Hungarians in Slovakia) or to further their irredentist aspirations. Similarly, 'motherlands' often use their ethnic brethren ('compatriots' as Russia calls them) in other countries to exert pressure on the latter. Russia, for example, tried to link the withdrawal of its troops from the Baltic countries with the treatment of the Russian-speaking population there, threatening to stop withdrawal if alleged violations of the rights of ethnic Russians continued.

Fear of secession is often the main cause of the suppression of the right of minorities not to be discriminated against and, especially, of their right to the preservation and development of their identity (e.g., Kurds in Turkey, Albanians in Kosovo). This leads to even stronger claims and sometimes to armed struggle for secession, which, in turn, is usually met with further repressions. And the vicious circle goes on. In majority–minority conflicts it is rarely the case that only one side deserves to be blamed.

The dilemma of accommodating the conflicting demands for territorial integrity of the state and for autonomy or self-government of ethnic minorities is one of the most difficult issues to be resolved in many inter-ethnic conflicts. On the one hand, governments fear that granting territorial autonomy or self-government to minorities may be a step towards secession; on the other hand, the refusal to satisfy these claims of minorities may really push the latter towards secession.

The reluctance of governments to create separate territorial–political units may be enhanced by the world community's approach to the problem of the territorial integrity of federal states. It seems that after the dissolution of federal states such as the Soviet Union, Yugoslavia and the Czech and Slovak Republic, all of which broke up into their constituent parts, there is a feeling that federal or autonomous units like Quebec, Catalonia or Abkhazia may have a better case in their claims for independence than, say, the Bretons, Australian aborigines or the Kurds, who do not enjoy any territorial autonomy.

However, if there should be any difference between multi-ethnic unitary and federal states in this respect it should be, on the contrary, in favour of the respect for the territorial integrity of federal states which, by granting some autonomy or self-government to ethnic minorities, have undertaken measures in order to accommodate their interests and rights.[71]

The application to breakaway parts of federal states of the *uti possidetis* principle, which states that administrative boundaries become inter-state frontiers after territorial units gain independent statehood, may also have contributed to government fears that it is easier for a minority to break away from a federal state, where administrative boundaries of federal units are usually clearly defined, than from a unitary one. The *uti possidetis* principle had its *raison d'être* in the process of the emergence of new states in Latin America in the nineteenth century, because of the ethnic, cultural and linguistic uniformity of the former Spanish colonies. This principle was voluntarily accepted also by the African leaders in the process of decolonization of the African continent, because of the lack of any other principle which could have worked in this specific context.

Uti possidetis may indeed have become a customary norm of international law, as asserted by the International Court of Justice in its Judgement on the case between Burkina Faso and Mali[72] and confirmed by the Arbitration Commission on Yugoslavia,[73] but there are still serious doubts as to its universal applicability. With hindsight, it seems that Lord Owen may be quite right, not only on the issue of the premature recognition of Croatia and Bosnia-Herzegovina,[74] but also that 'the unwarranted insistence on ruling out changes to what had been internal administrative boundaries within a sovereign state was a fatal blow in the attempted peacemaking in Yugoslavia'.[75]

It may be that in the process of the decolonization of Africa no better principle could be applied: *uti possidetis* was the lesser evil when compared to any other possible way of untying the Gordian knots of territorial delimitation in post-colonial Africa. However, even here we see that the current political, ethnic and cultural structure of the continent is contributing to constant territorial and ethnic conflicts. Is it not at least partially because, as Herbert Ekwe-Ekwe writes:

> the overwhelming majority of Africans still do not live their every day normal lives as Senegalese, Nigerians, Zairians, Kenyans, Chadians, Rwandans or whatever names these disarticulated creatures of 'nation-states' call themselves. Instead, they live their lives as Wolf, Aerobe, Ibo, Nape, Backing, Baluba, Kikuyu, Asante, Eritrean, Fante, Yergam, Ewe, and so on. After thirty years of Africa's post-colonial restoration of independence, the principal sites of the continent's intellectual and cultural creativity remain

located in the crucibles of these ancient nationalities, and they will remain there forever.[76]

One may doubt whether this is so everywhere in Africa, and whether it will indeed remain so forever, but there seems to be at least some truth in the words of Ekwe-Ekwe.

However, if granting autonomy or self-government to ethnic minorities may really threaten the territorial integrity of a state, denying it may be equally dangerous. Will Kymlicka is right to say that, since claims to self-government and autonomy are here to stay, we have no choice but to try to accommodate them, because rejecting them in the name of common citizenship will simply promote alienation and secessionist movements.[77] In addition, recent surveys show that self-government arrangements reduce the likelihood of violent conflict, while refusing or rescinding self-government rights may escalate such conflicts.[78] Gamzakhurdia, the first President of Georgia, in annulling the autonomy of Ossetia and Abkhazia, thereby invited the trouble which continues to haunt Georgia. The abolition of autonomy for Kosovo by the Serbian authorities contributed immensely to the tension in that province.

Human rights violations against ethnic or religious minorities, even if committed as a reaction to the illegal secessionist claims of minorities, may seriously undermine the stability of a state using repressive methods. In this way, the Russian authorities, responding with excessive force (which was used indiscriminately against the civilian population of Chechnya) to the Dudayev regime's declared secession from Russia, succeeded in transforming the legally dubious secessionist attempts of the regime into the Chechen nation's struggle against the Russian bear on the prowl. Russian atrocities in Chechnya have turned many formerly loyal Chechens into nationalists for the Chechen independence cause.[79]

There are no universal recipes to cure such simmering or already exploding inter-ethnic conflicts; however, one can offer two pieces of advice which those who are directly involved in such conflicts will certainly find difficult to accept: authorities and majorities have scrupulously to observe minority rights, including their right to the free development of their identity, while minorities have to refrain from secessionist claims. It is not by accident that the Framework Convention on the Protection of National Minorities contains not only an enumeration of the rights and freedoms of minorities which states have to guarantee through their legislative or administrative measures; it also states that nothing in the Convention 'shall be interpreted as implying any right to engage in any activity or perform any act contrary to the fundamental principles of international law and in particular of the sovereign equality, territorial integrity and political independence of States'.[80]

Unfortunately, many societies are still very far from such an accommodative way of resolving minority problems. Canada's experience with Quebec, Belgium's ultra-sophisticated arrangements to accommodate its minorities and the latest Anglo-Irish efforts to disentangle Northern Ireland's problem fall into stark contrast with what is going on in this domain in many other parts of the world. Though these situations in Belgium or Canada, considered by themselves, may be rather unpleasant and difficult to resolve, they seem to be quite positive when compared with other inter-ethnic problems and conflicts. This comparison also shows that democracy and respect for human rights is a necessary precondition for the civilized resolution of the problems of ethnic minorities.

RELIGIOUS EXTREMISM, HUMAN RIGHTS AND INTERNATIONAL STABILITY

One of the phenomena which constitute a threat to both human rights and international stability is the rise of religious extremism in different parts of the world.

This rise is often a part of the fundamentalist revival in many religions. Protestantism, Catholicism, the Russian Orthodox Church, Sunni and Shi'ite Islam, Hinduism and Judaism, all have rather strong fundamentalist trends.[81] Religious fundamentalism is always reactive (though not always reactionary) to processes of modernization and change, because 'fundamentalists begin as traditionalists who perceive some challenge or threat to their core identity, both social and personal.... They react, they fight back with great innovative power.'[82]

It seems that, though religious fundamentalism may play different roles, including positive ones, in all its forms it inevitably has some problems with human rights, especially with requirements of equality between men and women or the freedom to choose one's religion. As fundamentalism is about fighting back it always has an enemy against whom it has to fight. This in itself creates an atmosphere which is not conducive to human rights. Donald Swearer writes about Buddhist fundamentalism in Sri Lanka: 'The threat to identity may come from different quarters – in the Sri Lankan case, British Christendom or Tamil Hindus. The fundamentalist response to the threat is couched in terms of rhetoric of persecution aimed to produce a sense of unity against a common enemy'.[83]

Often religious fundamentalism takes a form of militant religious extremism. For example, it is astonishing at the end of the twentieth century to read words such as those uttered by Sardar Angre, an advisor to Rajmata Vijayaraje Scindia, one of the founders of the extreme right-wing, pro-Hindu Bharatiya Janata Party (BJP): 'The Muslims must be made to understand that they must be proud of Hindustan.... If the Muslims followed the Hindu ideology there would be no more trouble.... They should accept our common culture and unite with us in the name of god'.[84]

This is precisely a recipe for an inter-religious conflict and, consequently, for gross human rights violations with possible international repercussions. Recent clashes between Hindus and Muslims in different parts of India show that the policies of Hindu extremists are as dangerous as those of any other religious extremism.

However, Hindu extremism, like some other religious extremisms, is confined on the whole to one country, albeit a very large and populous one at that. This is not the case with Islamic extremism. Paul Kennedy observes:

> Far from preparing for the twenty-first century, much of the Arab and Muslim world appears to have difficulty in coming to terms with the nineteenth century, with its composite legacy of secularisation, democracy, laissez-faire economics, transnational industrial and commercial linkages, social change, and intellectual questioning. If one needed an example of the importance of cultural attitudes in explaining a society's response to change, contemporary Islam provides it.[85]

Francis Fukuyama points out that 'part of the current, fundamentalist revival is the strength of the perceived threat from liberal, Western values to traditional Islamic societies'.[86] Abdulaziz A. Sachedina writes that

> the support lent to the dictatorial and at times oppressive governments by the Western nations convinced many ulama and educated Shi'ites of Iran, Iraq, and Lebanon that modern secular ideologies imported from the West or the East were not only inadequate for providing them with solutions to their identity crisis; they were also incapable of correcting the socio-political injustices endured by the downtrodden in those countries.[87]

Islamic extremism, though continuing to create serious trouble for many particular countries and for the world community as well, is hardly likely to become a global threat which would lead to a new split of the international system on a scale similar to that of the Cold War division. The reason for this lies not only in the fact that in by no means all Muslim countries are religious extremists in power (and that most countries of the world are non-Muslim). Another important reason which speaks against Islamic extremism becoming a global threat, replacing the Soviet Union in its capacity as the 'evil empire', lies in the fact that extremist Islam – like, for example, fundamentalist Catholicism was in the Middle Ages – is a brake on the economic and social progress of any society, and such progress is ultimately the basis of technological or military competitiveness. Islamic extremism, like any other religious or ideological extremism, seems to lead into a social cul-de-sac. In a sense, the Soviet Union was a fundamentalist and extremist state where the words of the founding fathers of Marxism–Leninism constituted a holy book which, in the words of Vladimir Lenin, was such a perfect edifice that no brick could be taken away from it. Its ideological fundamentalism created a stifling atmosphere which made the collapse of the Soviet Union inevitable.

Yet another reason why Islamic extremism will not be able to compete with liberal democracies lies in its confusion about which domains belong respectively to Caesar and to God. Priests or mullahs are not always the best politicians or administrators. But this would be a relatively minor problem. However, an ideologue, philosopher or cleric would lose his holiness and immunity from criticism if he started to deal with mundane issues. It is easy to imagine what would have happened to the Papacy had the Pope also been the Prime Minister of Italy, for example, in the 1990s. There are signs in Iran that many within the Shia hierarchy believe that the incompetence of Iran's political leaders has hurt the country's religious base. Some assert that 'the rise of the technocrats is an irreversible trend in Iran' and that there is 'definitely a feeling among the Iranians that they have to run the country better if they want to survive'.[88]

Further, Islam is divided into moderate and extremist regimes, into shi'ites and sunnis, and also into countries which have different geopolitical and national interests. Moreover, as Fred Halliday aptly observes, 'while the Islamists are not short of their own rhetoric of denunciation and demagogy, much of the language and practice of confrontation comes not from the Islamists at all but from those opposed to them, or who find in them a convenient scapegoat – be it Orthodox Christians in Serbia and Greece, or right-wing parties in France, Germany, Holland or Denmark'.[89] Similarly, Russian military and ultra-nationalists, trying to justify the presence and behaviour of Russian armed forces in Tajikistan or Chechnya, use Islam as a scarecrow or scapegoat.

Nonetheless, gross human rights violations and terrorism, which in our interdependent world necessarily transcend state boundaries, are almost inevitable concomitants of any religious or ideological extremism. Therefore, Islamic extremism will remain, at least for some time, a serious threat to regional and even world stability, and it certainly undermines the very essence of human rights in societies where Muslim extremists are in power (e.g., Iran, Sudan) or where they exert significant influence on the social and political life of the country.

In this book it is impossible to enter into the details of a comparison between Shari'a law and universal human rights standards. This topic has been covered extensively by other authors,[90] including those who are familiar with Islam from within.[91]

Consideration of periodic reports on Sudan and Iran by the UN Human Rights Committee revealed serious inconsistencies between Islamic laws and practices as applied in these countries and the International Covenant on Civil and Political Rights. These occurred primarily in three areas: equality of men and women; freedom of conscience and religion; and prohibition of cruel treatment and punishment.[92] The report on human rights in Iran by Galindo Pohl, former Special Representative of the UN Commission on Human Rights, referred in particular to the high number of executions, cases of torture and cruel treatment or punishment, and the discriminatory treatment of certain groups of citizens, notably the Baha'is, by reason of their religious beliefs.[93] The situation in these crucial areas inevitably leads to violation of other rights, such as, for example, freedom of association.

Abdullahi Ahmed An-Na'im writes that 'by granting women and non-Muslims a lower status and sanctioning discriminatory treatment against them, Shari'a denies women and non-Muslims the same degree of honour and human dignity it guarantees to Muslim men'.[94] Cruel forms of punishment are provided for in some countries under Shari'a and apostasy is held to be a capital crime. These are some of the other practices which are manifestly contrary to universal human rights norms.

Certainly, it is not realistic to get rid of such deplorable practices overnight. But on the other hand, though these practices have some roots in religion and customs they are no longer any more unreservedly accepted by all Muslims in the world. In Spring 1993, in Bangkok, 110 NGOs from Asia and the Pacific region, where many Muslim countries are to be found, called on all governments of the region to ratify basic UN human rights instruments and especially the Convention on the Elimination of All Forms of Discrimination against Women (CE-DAW), and to withdraw reservations, particularly those applying to CEDAW and to the Convention on the Rights of the Child.[95]

Are not such views, from the countries where these particular violations of human rights take place, the strongest indicators that the world community can no longer accept references to cultural or religious peculiarities as an excuse for these practices?

During consideration of the Iranian report to the UN Human Rights Committee the Iranian representative, Mr Mehrpour, claimed amongst other things that women themselves wished to wear traditional clothing, including the veil. There is no doubt that many women do really wish this. But as members of the Committee rightly put it in questioning this assertion: 'However, that desire must be very moderate in the extreme if the authorities needed to resort to death sentences and raids by militia in order to secure women's compliance with that requirement'.[96] They also emphasized that 'women who did not wish to change [their dress or lifestyle] should not be forced to do so, but it was quite wrong to threaten and penalise those women who were desirous of change'.[97]

It is certainly true that if certain standards of behaviour are rooted in traditions, be they religious or cultural, and these standards correspond to the interests, perceptions and wishes of the population, it is not necessary for the authorities to enforce such traditions by means of draconian measures. Hammed Shahidian is right observing that

> The experience of the past fourteen years [in Iran] has shown that sex-segregation is not a matter of choice, but one of imposition. It is the men, not 'the Islamic feminists', who decide who should be confined to which quarter. The cultural relativist approach, which wanted to avoid an imperialistic imposition of values, ended up apologizing for the abhorrent treatment of women . . . [98]

Fundamentalism may become a threat to the very religion of which it is an emanation, since religion, in order to survive, has to accommodate itself to changes in the life of society. An-Na'im correctly points out that 'toleration of unorthodoxy and dissent is vital for the spiritual and intellectual benefit of Islam itself'.[99] And he continues:

> It is my conviction as a Muslim that the public law of Shari'a does not represent the law of Islam which contemporary Muslims are supposed to implement in fulfilment of their religious obligation. I

also strongly believe that the application of public law of Shari'a today will be counter-productive and detrimental to Muslims and to Islam itself.[100]

The truth in these words is confirmed by the experience of different societies where efforts to implement the 'back to basics' idea as a way out of a crisis have ended with failure. The Iranian leadership has become more pragmatic in order to cope with economic and social problems.

Speaking of Islam and human rights, it is necessary to emphasize that Islam, like practically any other religion, can be 'the vehicle both for political protest against undemocratic regimes and for the repression meted out by such regimes'.[101] Ayatollah Taleghani wrote that 'the most dangerous of all forms of oppression are laws and restrictions forcibly imposed on people in the name of religion', and that 'any group that wants to restrict people's freedom, [the freedom] to criticise, protest, discuss and debate does not comprehend Islam'.[102] In contrast, Ayatollah Khomeini asserted that 'What they call human rights is nothing but a collection of corrupt rules worked out by Zionists to destroy true religions'.[103]

Such varying approaches reveal the different potentials of Islam. Most importantly, one should not forget that, behind references to Islam, there are very often interests of power, and political, social and economic aims. In most Muslim countries people are trying to claim more freedom, an open society, and human rights. As Fred Halliday writes, if these wishes are not allowed to come out into the open, 'it is in part because the Islamic state has available to it instruments and practices of an eminently secular and modern kind to suppress them',[104] and 'behind claims to transhistorical and divinely sanctioned legitimacy lie projects for the acquisition and maintenance of political power in the late twentieth century'.[105]

Unfortunately, in many Muslim countries governments trying to suppress the revival of religious fundamentalism are grossly violating human rights. The Algerian authorities at the beginning of 1992 used undemocratic ways and means to prevent forces that they considered hostile to democracy from coming to power through democratic processes. As a result of these measures, thousands of people have been killed during violent clashes, and hundreds of militants have been sentenced to death. These measures have, in turn, led to the slaughter by Muslim extremists of foreigners, journalists and other intellectuals in Algeria. Governmental repression has given rise to yet further militants. Chechen separatists, too, who are fighting Russian forces in the Caucasus, are becoming more determinedly Muslim, as they are squeezed into a smaller space, and Shari'a law is supposedly in force.[106]

These experiences, taken together with those in some other Muslim countries, show that the use of repression in the violation of human rights is not the way one should deal with religious fundamentalism. It can lead to a new spiral of violence which inevitably undermines basic human rights in the society as a whole. Here, the Jordanian experience (where King Hussain has sought to co-opt Islamic parties into the political system) of dealing with religious fundamentalists who were outvoted in national, and even more so in local, elections has been much more successful. It is also necessary to point out that fundamentalists have much stronger positions in countries where governments are ineffective and corrupt. Often the rise of religious fundamentalism is a response, not only to the penetration of 'Western' ideas or practices, but also and foremost to the corruption of and repressions by local authorities. It may well be the case that some societies have to go through a long and painful process of fundamentalist rule in order to understand the inevitability of the failure of the call for 'back to basics'. Suppression of religious fundamentalism by brute force may only prolong the agony of such societies, thereby inevitably contributing to the destabilization of international relations.

PROCESSES OF THE LIBERALIZATION AND DEMOCRATIZATION OF SOCIETY AND INTERNATIONAL STABILITY

Practically all states have been authoritarian, if not totalitarian, at one time or another in their history, at least from the point of view of contemporary standards of democracy and human rights. Quite a number of them have by now become democracies where the whole range of human rights is rather well protected. Usually this has taken years and years, during which many trials and errors were made. The process has usually been painful, has often destabilized the societies undergoing the changes, and has not always been beneficial for the stability of international relations. The War of American Independence (1775–83) of the thirteen colonies from British rule brought about not only the Declaration of the Rights of Man of 1774, it also discredited George III's government, weakened France financially, and served as an inspiration for the French Revolution and for revolutions in the Spanish colonies in America. The French Revolution, in turn, gave France not only the Declaration of the Rights of Man and the Citizen of 1789, but also the Napoleonic wars which shook Europe for a decade.

As a rule, democratic changes and the introduction of human rights have occurred as the result of developments and events, including fierce struggles between different forces in society, which have had mainly domestic roots.

Today, because of the closeness of the world and the example of states which are democratic and affluent, many societies embark upon processes of liberalization and democratization. Paradoxically, we find that, not only the absence of human rights, but also their quick introduction into some societies, may be a cause of domestic and international instability.

The process of *perestroika* and *glasnost* in the Soviet Union not only led to greater freedom, they also resulted in armed conflicts between Armenia and Azerbaijan over, and in, Nagorny-Karabakh; fighting in Georgia and in Tajikistan; tension between Russia and the Ukraine over the Crimea; conflict in the Trans-Dniestr region of Moldova; and other, similarly negative, events. It is not necessary to remind the reader of what happened in the former Yugoslavia after the communist regime started to collapse in that country.

Jason Abrams, writing about Burundi, makes an interesting point in his observation that 'the recurring violence demonstrates that while Burundi's system of ethnic apartheid is not sustainable, it is difficult and dangerous to reform it'.[107]

Processes of changing or dismantling authoritarian regimes are like operations in mine-clearing. You cannot live with a mine under your own or your neighbour's house, but the removal of the mine runs the risk of blowing up all of the houses. Therefore the issue of pitfalls and dangers, including threats to international stability, in the process of liberalization and democratization of non-democratic, authoritarian and human rights-hostile states deserves serious attention.

On the whole, democratic states seem to be externally less aggressive, and internally more stable, than undemocratic states. Their governments have, as a rule, stronger legitimacy. Therefore the more we have of such states, the better it will be for international stability. Here, I should stress once more the point which was made in Chapter One (see p. 26): really stable states are 'mature' democracies and not 'barely participatory' states. It is not enough simply to have regular multi-party elections. Equally important is the observance of other civil and political rights, as well as a sufficient level of social and economic development without gross social inequalities.

However, not only 'mature' democracies but also many authoritarian regimes are rather stable (though their stability can be sometimes likened to that of a powder keg waiting to explode). The biggest threats to domestic and international stability often emerge in the process of transformation of a stable, non-democratic state into a democratic and human rights-friendly one. Edward Mansfield and Jack Snyder write that 'in fact, formerly authoritarian states where democratic participation is on the rise are more likely to fight wars than are stable democracies or autocracies'.[108]

The democratization of multi-ethnic states, like the former USSR or Yugoslavia, may be an especially painful process. The dissolution of multi-ethnic states, resurrection of suppressed nationalism and violation of minority rights are dangers which may arise when oppressive regimes start to fall apart.

The process of democratization of free market authoritarian regimes may be smoother than the democratization of totalitarian command economies, because the latter have also to face painful market reforms. 'Pushing nuclear armed great powers like Russia or China toward democratization', write Mansfield and Snyder, 'is like spinning a roulette wheel: many of the outcomes are undesirable'.[109]

Studying the correlation between democratization and war, Mansfield and Snyder exclude civil wars from their analysis.[110] It seems that there is an even closer link between processes of democratization and violent domestic conflicts than there is between such processes and international wars. If a lack of democracy, oppression and other human rights violations may, as we saw, lead to armed rebellions or civil wars, processes of liberalization and democratization may open the way for inter-ethnic wars or other civil disturbances.

Even if the governing elites of a democratizing state do not choose to use foreign adventures to channel nationalistic sentiments (which, as the contemporary evidence shows, often go hand in hand with rising democracy), there is still a danger that destructive forces released by the processes of democratization are too difficult to harness. Mansfield and Snyder observe that 'governing a society that is democratizing is like driving a car while throwing away the steering wheel, stepping on the gas, and fighting over which passengers will be in the driver's seat'.[111]

Nationalism, economic chaos, rising crime rates and, above all, the resistance of the forces in society which lose their power and privileges in the process of democratization (for example, the Khmer Rouge in Cambodia; attachés or tonton macoutes in Haiti; the military in most authoritarian regimes; former elites in practically all countries undergoing processes of democratization) are the forces which may try to overthrow fledgling democracies and plunge a country into chaos.

However, these dangers do not necessarily mean that liberalization and democratization should not take place. The experience of the dissolution of the USSR and Yugoslavia, and the resulting difficulties and threats, should not be seen as warnings against the liberalization and democratization of totalitarian or authoritarian regimes, but rather as lessons to be learnt about what to do and what to avoid. The fact of the matter is that, when the time is ripe, authoritarian or totalitarian regimes will, as a rule, fall, often destabilizing not only their own countries but adversely affecting international relations as well. During the Cold War, some states were kept stable by outside interference (for example, Haiti, Iran and Nicaragua by the US; Ethiopia by the USSR; Somalia by both superpowers at different times). Now such support of dictators is hardly possible. In many cases it would appear that the earlier reforms start, the better for these countries, and for the world as a whole. Therefore, encouragement and sometimes even pressure to introduce democratic reforms should be the policy of the world community.

At the same time, it has to be remembered that democracy cannot be imposed from outside. Brad Roberts writes:

> Democracy cannot be imposed. The twentieth century provides an abundance of evidence to suggest that the only stable political institutions and values are those that arise from the historical circumstances unique to each political community. Democracy and respect for human rights have emerged in so many countries because they fulfil, better than any other political form, the pragmatic need for effective governance, as well as basic human aspirations.[112]

However, if it is true that democracy and human rights cannot be imposed from outside, democratic reforms can be encouraged and promoted by outside forces, especially if there are internal forces which are ready to fight and work for democracy and human rights. Outside forces can play an important role in the prevention of anti-democratic forces from achieving their comeback in countries which are making the first steps towards democracy and human rights. This holds true not only in obvious cases such as Haiti, which without the UN-sanctioned intervention would have certainly been ruled now by a military junta. There is little doubt that Eastern and Central European countries and the Baltic states could not succeed in their democratic reforms without Western 'interference'.

One of the lessons which has to be learned from the recent Soviet and Yugoslav experience is that, when the reforms were unleashed, the leadership often found itself lagging behind the course of events.

Leaders quickly became obstacles for reforms, thereby making the process of reform even more painful. Had Milosevic in Autumn 1991 agreed to some form of a loose confederation, it is quite possible that events in the former Yugoslavia would have taken a very different turn. It is doubtful whether the dissolution of the USSR could have been avoided in any case. But had the reaction of the Centre to the demands of the Baltic republics at the end of the 1980s been more adequate, and had Gorbachev not started to play the card of minorities against majorities in some recalcitrant republics, trying to hold together the Union, there could certainly have been fewer painful problems later.

It may be inevitable that some multi-ethnic states break up in the process of liberalization or democratization (for example, Eritrea broke off from Ethiopia). While such break-ups should by no means be encouraged, the world community should be ready for the possibility.

Though the former Yugoslavia, the former Soviet Union and Burundi are in many respects very different cases, they have at least one important commonality: the collapse of communist dictatorships in Yugoslavia and the USSR, the end of colonialism in Africa, and the end of the rivalry between East and West in the continent, are all developments which in general have been positive and have been aimed at the liberation of peoples and individuals, but which have, at the same time, led to some horrible events. Equally, economic modernisation, progress in health care, or elimination of illiteracy, while bringing well-being to many peoples, have also contributed to many problems and have had a destabilizing effect on entire regions. However, these negative side-effects should not be seen as a warning against changes which, as a rule, are inevitable, but should be taken as lessons to be learnt about governing these processes.

CONCLUSIONS

States are not marbles which differ only as to their size, while moving and occasionally colliding on the playground of world politics. Their internal characteristics, such as their level of economic and social development, political regime, cultural and religious traditions differ, influencing their foreign policy and thereby international relations. Domestic factors often spill over into the international system and can directly affect other societies. Similarly, international issues increasingly penetrate the thinning veil of state sovereignty. Human rights is one of the issues constantly moving between the international system and the domestic affairs of states, affecting inter-state relations and influencing internal developments, having a stabilizing or destabilizing effect on international relations and domestic societies. Therefore, states cannot afford to ignore human rights issues in either their domestic or their foreign policy.

Having analysed the relationship between human rights and international stability and having also discussed how particular human rights situations may have a stabilizing (or, *vice versa*, destabilizing) effect on international relations, it is time now to turn our attention to the various factors which the world community and individual states have to take into account in exercising their human rights diplomacy.

3 The role of cultural factors, societal development and power interests in the human rights discourse

In order to be able to outline some of the possible responses of the world community or individual states to serious human rights situations, it is necessary to reveal the main root causes of systematic human rights violations. Why are human rights trampled upon in some countries and not in others? Why are dictators in power in states A and B, and not in C or D? Why do some human rights violations affect international peace and security while in other cases a complete lack of human rights may not raise any concerns over international stability? Responses to these questions may help to determine future strategies for human rights diplomacy.

ON THE UNIVERSALITY OF HUMAN RIGHTS AND CULTURAL RELATIVISM

Practically all UN human rights documents, directly or implicitly, proceed from the assumption of the universality of human rights, their indivisibility and equal importance. The Universal Declaration of Human Rights of 1948 sets as a goal the securing of 'universal and effective recognition and observance of all rights and freedoms enshrined in the Declaration'.[1] The Vienna Declaration and Programme of Action, adopted on 25 June 1993 by the World Conference on Human Rights, referring to the UN Charter and other UN instruments relating to human rights, reiterates that 'the universal nature of these rights and freedoms is beyond question', and that 'human rights and fundamental freedoms are the birthright of all human beings'.[2]

However, the implementation of these rights and freedoms varies greatly from society to society. Although there may be no human rights paradise in the world, there are quite a few human rights 'hells' where none of the rights and freedoms solemnly proclaimed in UN documents are applied in practice.

Often the obvious cultural diversity of the world is given, if not as an excuse or justification, then at least as an explanation of the absence or violation of human rights in some societies. It is asserted that human rights are a Western concept which does not fit well with societies based on different values and traditions. Such voices come most often from the non-Western world, but interestingly enough, similar views are held by a number of people in the West as well.

In 1947 the 'Statement on Human Rights' published on behalf of the executive board of the American Anthropological Association,[3] and submitted to the UN Commission on Human Rights, emphasized the Western cultural bias of the draft UN Declaration on Human Rights:

> It will not be convincing to the Indonesian, the African, the Indian, the Chinese, if it lies on the same plane as like documents of an earlier period. The rights of man in the Twentieth Century cannot be circumscribed by the standards of any single culture or be dictated by the aspirations of any single people.[4]

Recently, Bilahari Kausikan, a senior Singaporian diplomat, similarly questioned the values behind international human rights standards: 'But what institutions and which values? The individualistic ethos of the West or the communitarian traditions of Asia? The consensus-seeking approach of East and South-East Asia or the adversarial institutions of the West?'[5]

Do differences of values and traditions really constitute an obstacle to the universality of human rights? If so, then to what extent? And are these traditions and values as different as they are sometimes asserted to be?

Obviously, there are no simple answers to these questions. Yes, there are different cultures which have different values. But at the same time, there is more similarity in different cultures than a perfunctory glance would disclose. As Michael Walzer writes: 'every human society is universal because it is human, particular because it is a society'.[6] One of the most important and difficult questions in the domain of the international promotion and protection of human rights is the question of the relative influence of factors which are common to various societies, on the one hand, and factors which are different, on the other hand. To answer this question, one must examine the particularities of each culture, and the impact that its history, traditions, religion and economic development have on the perception and acceptance of international human rights standards.

Although the idea of human rights as such emerged in the West, there were early precursors of human rights in different concepts of human dignity which can be traced, both in Eastern and Western thought, as far back as 2000 years BC. As Arthur Henry Robertson and John Merrills wrote: 'The idea of individual worth can be found in the work of sages, philosophers, prophets and poets from different countries and many faiths in all continents, including India, China, Japan, Persia, Russia, Turkey, Egypt, Israel, several countries of black Africa and pre-Columbian civilisations of South America'.[7] In this chapter, I will try to show that cultural, religious or other traditions are not insurmountable obstacles for a universal acceptance of basic human rights and their implementation. This objective must be prefaced with the notion that cultures and values can change, and with this flexibility comes the possibility for a universal approach.

Culture is capable of changing, although these changes occur more slowly than changes in the economic and political structures of society. Francis Fukuyama notes that 'we see evidence of cultural change all around us. Catholicism, for example, has often been held to be hostile to both capitalism and democracy... yet there has been a "Protestantization" of Catholic culture that makes differences between Protestant and Catholic societies much less pronounced than in times past'.[8]

Moreover, societies themselves change. As Eric Hobsbawm observes, 'in the 1980s, socialist Bulgaria and non-socialist Ecuador had more in common than either had with the Bulgaria or Ecuador of 1939'.[9] A similar comment could be made about many states. For example, human rights were previously an unfamiliar concept in most Asian societies. Today, the peoples of Asian states are taking human rights more and more seriously.

Contemporary human rights standards are not immutable values, inherent only to Western countries. This can be illustrated by the fact that Western countries themselves, and others as well, came to the acceptance of these values through a long historic process. David Selbourne traces back the historic widening of claims-to-rights in liberal-democratic civic orders:

> From claims made by seventeenth-century property owners to the concomitant political rights to which they believed themselves entitled by virtue of their ownership; to claims made by non-property-owners in the nineteenth century to a variety of civic rights which should owe nothing to wealth or position; to claims made by all citizens (and even non-citizens) in the twentieth century to rights of protection from the consequences of misfortune, including the

consequences of unemployment, old age, homelessness, and sickness.[10]

It is also asserted that some religions which are Western-based, for example Christianity and Judaism, contain more human rights roots than those based in the East, especially Islam.

Although international human rights standards protect the freedom of religion, and different religions or individual clergymen have quite often contributed to the protection of human rights, there is no religion which has always been conducive to human rights or which has not had any pernicious effect on human freedoms and dignity. The Spanish Inquisition was probably the most violent example in Europe of how a religion can be used for inhumane purposes. Torquemada, the Grand Inquisitor, torturer of Moors, Jews, Protestants and others who were called heretics, was a fruit of Christianity.

Even in a liberal church such as the Church of England the decision to allow the ordination of women, which from a human rights point of view is quite natural, was adopted in 1993 far from unanimously and has alienated many followers of that Church. Arthur Schlesinger Jr quite rightly observes:

> As an historian, I confess to a certain amusement when I hear the Judeo-Christian tradition praised as the source of our concern for human rights. In fact, the great religious ages were notable for their indifference to human rights in the contemporary sense. They were notorious not only for acquiescence in poverty, inequality, exploitation and oppression but for enthusiastic justifications of slavery, persecution, abandonment of small children, torture and genocide. Religion enshrined and vindicated hierarchy, authority and inequality.... [11]

One may not be surprised at a finding, made by Adamantia Pollis, that in Orthodox theology 'woman is considered morally inferior' or that Pollis's 'inexorable conclusion ... is that individual human rights cannot be derived from Orthodox theology'.[12] What should be more surprising is the underlying idea that human rights may be derived at all from a particular religion. Fred Halliday is right that 'no derivation from any religion is ultimately possible'.[13] Will Durant's comparison of two branches of Christianity in the *Age of Faith* is rather different from that of Adamantia Pollis: 'While Western Europe was shrouded in darkness, misery and ignorance of the ninth and tenth centuries ... the Greek Church drew strength and pride from the revived wealth and power of the Byzantine state.... To the Greeks of this age the

Germans, Franks, and Anglo-Saxons of the contemporary West seemed crude barbarians, an illiterate and violent laity led by a worldly and corrupt episcopate'.[14]

Therefore, while it is hardly possible to anchor contemporary human rights in any particular religion, practically all religions contain premisses upon which human rights ideas and practices can be built. There are traditions, including religious ones, in all nations which can be supportive of the acceptance of human rights ideas.

It seems that sometimes it is rather the format, wording or details of international human rights standards than their substance which sounds Western. For example, Article 14 of the International Covenant on Civil and Political Rights contains detailed rules of fair trial. The terminology of the Article is certainly Western, but the logic of these rules is rather simple and universal: to guarantee, as far as possible, that no innocent person is behind bars, or worse still, executed, and that there is no unnecessary suffering for those who may have committed crimes.

Jack Donnelly correctly observes that, while human rights – the inalienable entitlements of individuals held in relation to state and society – have not been a part of most cultural traditions, or even of the Western tradition, until quite recently, there is a striking similarity in many of the basic values of most cultures that today we seek to protect through human rights. This is particularly true when these values are expressed in relatively general terms: 'Life, social order, protection from arbitrary rule, prohibition of inhuman and degrading treatment, the guarantee of a place in the life of the community, and access to an equitable share of the means of subsistence are central moral aspirations in nearly all cultures'.[15]

In June 1995, *The Independent* published a table which showed the attitude of different religions (the Church of England, the Roman Catholic Church, Judaism, Islam, Hinduism, Buddhism), as well as today's secular consensus, to issues such as blasphemy, non-observance of religious events, murder, adultery, theft, lying, pre-marital sex, homosexual practices, divorce, masturbation, suicide and cruelty to animals.[16] The attitudes were categorized in terms of 'sin', 'wrong', 'harmful', 'permitted', 'not a sin', 'not harmful', 'accepted', 'not mentioned'. Some of these practices (murder, lying, adultery, theft) were considered either as a sin, wrong, or harmful by all religions and were condemned by secular morals. Others (e.g., pre-marital sex, homosexual practices, suicide, blasphemy) were considered wrong by all or most religions. Generally, the overlap in attitude between religions was considerable. And it is also necessary to mention that, even if some practices are not considered to be wrong or sinful, especially by today's secular morals, they are often tolerated rather than encouraged or considered completely normal by the majority of people in different societies.

These comparisons prove that there is much more in common in different societies than cultural relativists usually assume.

At the same time, one can hardly deny that there are cultural differences and historical or religious traditions which may make the implementation of at least some human rights problematic in certain countries. The equality of men and women and the freedom to choose or change one's religion are obvious examples of rights which are difficult to realize in some, particularly Muslim, societies. Nor are historical traditions always supportive of the acceptance of the basic assumption of democracy – the one person, one vote principle.

Therefore it would be wrong to ignore cultural or religious traditions when speaking of human rights in a particular country, and these differences should be kept in mind by individual states and international organizations when trying to promote human rights. We must equally admit that not all human rights, even those which are enshrined in various UN instruments, are universally accepted by or even equally important for every society. There may be periods in a given society when certain rights become particularly important, either because they are manifestly violated (like the right to life or the freedom from torture in Uruguay or Argentina under the military dictatorships), or because at a certain level of societal development and implementation of basic rights people start to pay more attention to other rights and freedoms.

In societies where people are arbitrarily killed, like in Rwanda or Bosnia, it may not be an issue of priority whether accused and convicted persons are kept together or separately in places of detention, or whether victims of ethnic cleansing have the right to leave any country, including their own, respected. In such a case, the right of refugees to return to the places from which they were evicted becomes most important. Even the importance of this right is conditioned by the observance of the right to life and the right to liberty and security of person if the refugees return.

It may well be that difficulties rooted in the cultural or religious traditions of some societies inhibit the full and immediate implementation of international human rights standards. Furthermore, for some countries, a significant time period would be needed before full compliance with human rights standards could be achieved. Deeply rooted traditions, even when they are inexcusable from the point of view of international human rights standards, cannot be eradicated overnight. India, for example, has not yet succeeded in completely ridding itself of such vestiges of the past as the 'dowry death' (where a wife is killed because of the insufficiency of her dowry) or sati (where a widow is expected and even encouraged to commit suicide after the death of her husband). The latest figures on crimes against women in India show that nearly 6000 women were killed in 1993 for failing to produce sufficient dowry.[17] However, the government is certainly undertaking legislative and administrative measures aimed at overcoming these practices.[18]

What is important, rather than the immediate insertion of the whole range of human rights into an unprepared soil, which sometimes may lead to social unrest, is a gradual effort by governments to implement universal human rights standards.

The arguments of those who deny the very possibility of the existence of universal human rights in the multi-cultural world overstate their case. I would agree, for example, with the Foreign Minister of Singapore, Wong Kan Seng, who in his statement at the World Conference on Human Rights in Vienna said that 'universal recognition of the ideal of human rights can be harmful if universalism is used to deny or mask the reality of diversity'.[19]

But is it? Does the recognition of the universality of human rights really mean that it is necessary to reject the obvious cultural diversity of the world? Wong Kan Seng, as an example, stated that 'Singaporeans, and people in many other parts of the world do not agree, for instance, that pornography is an acceptable manifestation of free expression or that a homosexual relationship is just a matter of lifestyle choice'.[20] The problem with Mr Seng's example is that he compares the values of his own society, not with universal human rights standards, but with the values of some other societies. Neither the freedom to distribute pornography nor equality between homosexuals and heterosexuals in all domains are universal human rights norms. The 1923 Convention for the Suppression of the Circulation of and Traffic in Obscene Publications[21] and Protocol to amend the said Convention of 1947[22] are still in force, despite falling to desuetude. Indeed, there are many controversial issues such as the death penalty, euthanasia, abortion, pornography, homosexuality, etc., which touch upon deeply rooted moral and religious sentiments and are considered differently in various societies. Although these issues may be closely related to human rights, there are no universal standards guaranteeing or prohibiting such acts.

The most important human rights and gross and massive violations of them are not culturally conditioned. Genocide, other mass killings, torture (except, probably, some forms of cruel punishment which may amount to torture), arbitrary arrests, and racial discrimination belong in this category. The experience of such culturally different countries as Nazi Germany, Democratic Kampuchea, Bosnia, and Rwanda shows that there is no specific genocidal culture in the world. To put it another way, acts of genocide can be committed by people whose culture, traditions or religion differ widely. Most nations have had institutions such as slavery, serfdom, legalized social inequality, like the caste system in India or social stratification in Medieval Europe (which was a kind of social apartheid). The precise forms which such social structures have taken have been different and dependent, *inter alia*, on cultural factors. However, their substance has been culturally irrelevant.

Moreover, universal human rights standards are not rigid rules whose interpretation and application cannot be adapted to different cultural traditions. Although this is not always possible, there are many cases in which apparent contradictions can be reconciled. International human rights standards are rarely as detailed as domestic laws on the subject. Often they are framework norms which leave room for states to adjust their implementation to the peculiarities of their domestic legal systems.

There is often room for what, in the context of the European human rights system, is called the 'margin of appreciation'. At the universal level this margin is even bigger. For example, Article 25 of the Covenant on Civil and Political Rights provides for free, regular elections by universal and equal suffrage and by secret ballot, and stipulates that everybody should have the right to participate in the conduct of public affairs and to have access, on general terms of equality, to public service in the country. However, states may have different electoral systems (majoritarian or proportional); they may even have unelected heads of state like monarchs. The margin of appreciation in issues concerning rights of ethnic and religious minorities is especially great. The reason for this is because similarities between individuals in different societies and their basic needs and interests are significantly greater than similarities between minorities and their needs in different countries. Some of such minorities are small, while others comprise millions; some are dispersed, while others live compactly, and so forth. Even in the same country different minorities do not have similar needs and claims. For example, the problems of Gypsies and Hungarians in Slovakia differ substantially. For these reasons, the European Charter for Regional or Minority

Languages contains a special undertaking which provides that each state, at the time of ratification of the Charter, undertakes to apply a minimum of thirty-five paragraphs or sub-paragraphs chosen from among the provisions of Part III of the Charter. This means that states can, in principle, accommodate their own interests and capabilities as well as the interests and demands of minorities, though in practice it may not be so easy to accomplish.

Most international human rights instruments also contain clauses of permissible derogations which try to balance different interests. For instance, several articles of the International Covenant on Civil and Political Rights contain a clause which provides that no restrictions may be placed on the exercise of the rights contained in the Covenant 'other than those imposed in conformity with the law and which are necessary in a democratic society in the interests of national security or public safety, public order (*ordre public*), the protection of public health or morals or the protection of the rights and freedoms of others'.[23] Although these clauses are open to abuse and, therefore, should not be easily resorted to, they show that there is often quite a large 'margin of appreciation' for states to take care of interests of public health and morals (which really can differ significantly from society to society), national security and the rights and freedoms of others. Moreover, in exceptional cases of public emergency which threaten the life of the nation it is possible to suspend temporarily the application of certain rights.[24] Article 4 of the Covenant on Civil and Political Rights, which provides for derogations in cases of public emergency, also stipulates that under no circumstances can governments suspend: the right to life; the right to freedom from torture, slavery, servitude and imprisonment on the ground of inability to fulfil contractual obligations; the right to be recognized as a person before the law; and the right to freedom of thought, conscience and religion. States must not also pass criminal laws with retroactive effect (except laws which may be beneficial for the accused).

There are two recent intergovernmental documents, one regional and the other of universal character, which try to strike a balance between the universality of human rights on the one hand, and differences in cultural and historical traditions in their implementation on the other. One of them is tilted more towards cultural relativity, the other emphasizes more the universality of human rights. The Bangkok Inter-Governmental Declaration on Human Rights, adopted in Spring 1993 at the regional conference of official representatives of countries of Asia and the Pacific region (one of the preparatory conferences for the World Conference on Human Rights in Vienna), recognizes 'that while human rights are universal in nature, they must be considered in the context of a dynamic and evolving process of international norm-setting, *bearing in mind the significance of national and regional particularities and various historical, cultural and religious backgrounds'* (emphasis added).[25] A somewhat different version of the relationship between the idea of universality and cultural relativity has found its expression in the Vienna Declaration and Programme of Action, adopted at the World Conference on Human Rights in Summer 1993. After stressing that 'all human rights are universal, indivisible and interdependent and interrelated', the Declaration admits that 'while the significance of national and regional particularities and various historical, cultural and religious backgrounds must be born in mind, it is the duty of States, regardless of their political, economic and cultural systems, to promote and protect all human rights and fundamental freedoms'.[26]

These statements, by their words, do not really differ much. It seems that the emphasis is only placed in a slightly different way: the Vienna document emphasizes more the universality of human rights, while the Bangkok declaration stresses the necessity to take into account national and regional particularities as well. But in order to understand the meaning of this slight difference in emphasis, one has to know what is behind these seemingly innocuous and, when taken *in abstracto*, even quite correct wordings. Behind such statements and policies which emphasize the necessity to bear in mind national or regional particularities and historical, cultural or religious traditions when dealing with human rights are often attempts to justify human rights violations caused by political, economic or other interests. Jack Donnelly aptly observes that 'while recognizing the legitimate claims of self-determination and cultural relativism, we must be alert to cynical manipulations of a dying, lost, or even mythical past'.[27] The cultural and historical traditions of practically all societies tend to support inequality between men and women, and to discriminate on the basis of race, religion or ethnicity. Does this mean that we should respect such traditions? Does this mean, for example, that Western societies, which had traditions which discriminated against certain categories of persons, are now free to discriminate against Muslims or immigrants?

It is also necessary to clarify what is meant by saying that, despite the universality of human rights, they must be considered in the context of dynamic and evolving norm-setting, and that regional and national particularities have to be born in mind in the implementation of universal human rights standards.

The Bangkok NGO Declaration on Human Rights, adopted by 110

NGOs in the Asia and Pacific region on 27 March 1993, just a few days before the adoption of the above-mentioned inter-governmental Declaration, confirmed that it is not just cultural differences in societies which give rise to human rights violations in their countries; such violations largely take place as a result of the specific political interests of the ruling circles in some of these states. The Declaration further stressed that 'cultural practices which derogate from universally accepted human rights, including women's rights, must not be tolerated'.[28] It should be noted that this concern is not on this occasion being voiced by Western NGOs. Similarly, Aung San Suu Kyi, the Nobel Peace Prize winner of 1991 from Myanmar, writes that 'when democracy and human rights are said to run counter to non-Western culture, such culture is usually defined narrowly and presented as monolithic. In fact, the values that democracy and human rights seek to promote can be found in many cultures'.[29]

Experts and human rights activists from all over the world must engage in frank and open dialogue in order to clarify whether it is necessary, for example, to limit political or civil rights in order to promote economic and social ones, and to what extent genuine concerns for political stability or the stability of inter-ethnic relations require restriction of certain rights, such as the freedom of the press and the like. Serious and concerted efforts are needed in order to separate those deviations in the implementation of international human rights standards which may be genuinely caused by cultural, historical or religious peculiarities and which are generally supported by society, from abusive references by elites to these peculiarities in order to justify repressions caused by their interest in power. Such a 'dialogue between cultures can seldom if ever be conducted as a dialogue between governments – if only because some governments just do not like human rights and other governments can't make them'.[30]

There are still some traditional practices occurring in the world today which can never be reconciled with universal human right norms, e.g., death for apostasy in some Islamic countries, or the caste system and sati in India. These practices, however, are no longer widely accepted, even in Muslim or Hindu societies. Thus they are not only condemned from the point of view of other value systems and universal human right standards, but they do not find wide support in their own culture. Ann Elizabeth Mayer comes to the conclusion that 'the common forms of oppression by Middle Eastern regimes are not just objectionable by Western standards but are perceived by people within these societies, especially the members of the educated elite, to be impermissibly harsh in their impact on society and culture'.[31]

Roger Scruton may take a view which is too absolute when he observes that 'in argument about moral problems, relativism is the first refuge of the scoundrel'.[32] However, it is true that, for many scoundrels, relativism is a convenient excuse for the rejection of human rights allegedly as an alien phenomenon. The rejection of cultural relativism in arguments about human rights does not mean that cultural traditions do not matter at all in the human rights discourse, or that all human rights can be applied immediately in every society. When motivated by the ideal of human rights, one must maintain a realistic approach in the implementation of international human rights standards in culturally different societies.

International human rights norms, by gradually helping to eradicate inhuman practices, do not undermine the cultural foundations of the Asian or African societies in which such practices still occur, or impoverish them. In the same way, they did not undermine and impoverish the cultural foundations of Western societies when these societies rid themselves of the court of inquisition, death by hanging or guillotining, or imprisonment for inability to fulfil contractual obligations. On the contrary, the introduction of human rights ideas and practices, often adjusted to local conditions, helps to make them more humane. The acceptance of the universality of human rights certainly does not mean that the reality of cultural diversity is to be rejected.

HUMAN RIGHTS AND INDIVIDUALISM VERSUS COMMUNITARIANISM

Another aspect of the arguments of cultural relativists is the suggestion that, since human rights stem from, are inherently linked with and are virtually an extension of, individualism, they are not applicable in societies with different, that is to say, communitarian, traditions. However, it seems that references to communal or collectivist traditions to justify human rights violations also often miss the point. In addition, such references can be, and sometimes are, simply used to mask systematic violations of human rights in the interests of ruling elites.[33] Donnelly has noted that 'communitarian rhetoric too often cloaks the depredations of corrupt and often Westernized or deracinated elites'.[34]

After the dissolution of the Soviet Union and the collapse of communism, it has become clear for practically everybody, even in the former socialist countries, that references to the supreme interests of the collective, be it a state, society or party, were simply used to keep in power the communist elite – or the new class, as Milovan Djilas called it.[35] Such a policy in the USSR, though probably helping to mobilize the population for the initial industrialization (an industrialization which coincidentally was achieved at quite inhumane costs), eventually led to the stagnation of society and the collapse of the whole economic, political and social system. Collectivist ideas were manipulated by the leaders in order to subordinate everybody to the interests of the Communist party.

However, it is even more important to stress that not all collectivist or communitarian ideologies are inherently hostile to human rights. Respect for the rights of individuals does not necessarily mean that one needs to neglect families (even the most extended ones), larger communities or society as a whole. Nor does it even call for disrespect towards authorities (especially if respect towards them is deserved). In fact, unbridled individualism may be as unfavourable a soil for the promotion of human rights as excessive communitarianism.

Although individualism, as a philosophical doctrine, and human rights are linked in their genesis, this does not mean that the Western person is inherently individualist or that Western society has always been and will necessarily remain individualistic. Both individualism and human rights ideas were aimed at liberating human beings from oppression by the state and church and at getting rid of feudal hierarchies which not only kept individuals in shackles but also stifled the development of society as a whole. Yash Ghai writes:

> The 'communitarian' argument suffers from at least two weaknesses. First, it overstates the 'individualism' of Western societies and traditions of thought. Even within Western liberalism there are strands of analysis which assert claims of community (e.g. Rousseau); and second, most Western human rights instruments allow limitations on and derogations from human rights in the public interest, or for reasons of state. Western courts regularly engage in the task of balancing the respective interests of the individual and the community.[36]

Currently in the West we hear more and more criticism about excesses of individualism, abuse of rights and the erosion of communitarian bonds. Amitai Etzioni and the communitarian movement in the United States have called for the restoration of a civil society and have criticized 'a major aspect of contemporary American civic culture: a strong sense of entitlement – that is, a demand that the community provide more services and strongly uphold rights – coupled with a rather weak sense of obligation to the local and national community'.[37] The former US Ambassador to the United Kingdom, Raymond Seitz, speaking of the US and the UK, said recently: 'If a democracy becomes only a matter of asserting rights – merely an excuse for licence – then society can rapidly become a *mêlée* of self-indulgence'.[38]

There is a serious call in the West to think more about the duties of citizens. David Selbourne, in his book entitled *The Principle of Duty*, writes:

> For it is only on the basis of a reciprocity of obligation, in accord with the ethic of the civic bond and the principle of duty, that 'commodious and peaceable living' is possible in the civic order; that civic disaggregation can be arrested without recourse to draconian measures; and that life, health, and true liberty of the individual can be preserved.[39]

In this regard, it is interesting to note that in November 1994 the Council of Europe convened a meeting of experts on the topic of 'Citizens' Responsibilities'. Different views were expressed during the meeting, and the majority of experts rightly rejected the idea of any legally binding or even declaratory document emanating from the Council which would call for the implementation of citizens' duties. However, the meeting concluded also that 'modern democracies cannot survive unless their citizens assume active responsibility in their day to day lives, and in terms of participation'.[40] Some experts called for drafting a reference document emanating from the Committee of Ministers which would highlight the values of morality, responsibility and participation.

Speaking at the end of 1995 of a future Bill of Rights for the United Kingdom, Jack Straw, the UK's Shadow Home Secretary, made a strong point about dangers of the 'me-first society', of over-emphasis on rights to the near exclusion of duties and responsibilities. He concluded by saying that we 'need to break out of the language of dutiless rights, and begin insisting upon mutual responsibility. Rights and duties go hand in hand'.[41] The recent report of the Commission on Global Governance also stresses that 'rights need to be joined with responsibilities' and that 'the tendency to emphasize rights while forgetting responsibilities has deleterious consequences'.[42]

However, the concern in the West with excessive individualism by no means supports the views of those who endorse communitarian ideas in countries where the absence of rights and freedoms of the individual, and not excessive individualism, is the problem. Reminders that without duties and responsibilities, the civic bonds of society could be damaged to such an extent that there may be the threat of a kind of authoritarianism which would restore these bonds, are not especially relevant for societies where individual rights are absent. Amitai Etzioni writes: 'The people of China, Eastern Europe, and Japan for that matter may well need to move in the opposite direction: to make more room for self-expression, to slash excessive government control, and to roll back severely enforced codes that suppress creativity and impinge on individual rights'.[43]

In short, societies need what they lack, and different societies lack different things. Human beings, however, need rights and liberties to protect them from the state, which has a tendency to encroach upon individuals' freedoms. Also, human beings need protection from society or its sometimes rather intrusive sub-structures (trade unions, local councils or the neighbourhood watch). Similarly, they need healthy and cohesive societies and good governments. Without these stable institutions there would be an 'anarchy-easily-turned-into-dictatorship' situation. Hamish McRae, who writes that it is difficult not to feel that both North America and Western Europe 'have put themselves at an economic disadvantage by their quest for individual freedom', concludes: 'Maybe the real message is that all modern industrial societies have to find a way of striking a balance between individualism and social control, and that somehow the democratic process has to maintain that balance, making the costs and benefits clear'.[44]

Therefore the argument put forward by some authors and politicians, that Asian or African values, based on communitarian ideas, are incompatible with individual human rights, is simply false. The West has had its own communitarian phases of development and communitarian ideas and practices can be still found in some sectors of Western society. Seymour Martin Lipset, for example, writes that 'Canada's five significant political parties remain committed in varying degrees to an activist government, to communitarianism'.[45] Francis Fukuyama rightly observes that 'the countries of medieval and early modern Europe were in many respects highly communitarian societies, with a large number of overlapping sources of communal authority – princely, ecclesiastical, seigniorial, and local – constraining the behaviour of individuals'.[46] And currently, many people in the West are thinking of how to put some limits on individualism, which, while being necessary for human liberation and economic development, may become excessive and indeed constitute a threat for both liberty and economic development. Therefore it may even be the case that the realization of some so-called Asian communitarian values would be conducive to the development of human dignity and rights in Western societies. Asian and other developing societies, participating in the process of the promotion of human rights, are not only on the receiving end. Their experience and ideas on human rights and human dignity, like their ideas and practices in the domain of economics, will inevitably enrich the whole human rights discourse. For example, in the domain of the promotion of human rights, non-confrontational, non-adversarial approaches which are based on what, in UN parlance, is called constructive dialogue, are in many cases preferable to adversarial or accusatory approaches to the promotion of human rights. Often it is more fruitful for the human rights cause in a particular country not to accuse the government of human rights violations, but rather to try to become engaged in a dialogue and to use different incentives in order to achieve progress on human rights. Here, like in some other areas, the experience of Asian societies may be useful.

HUMAN RIGHTS AND LEVELS OF SOCIETAL DEVELOPMENT

Besides some cultural practices which may influence the perception and implementation of human rights, there is another factor which is sometimes confused with the cultural or historical traditions of a given society and which, in my view, provides a more realistic explanation of different human rights situations around the world. This factor is the level of its societal development, including its economic, social, political and cultural aspects.

The concept of human rights is not an immutable or ahistorical concept which always existed somewhere, only waiting to be discovered by some advanced thinkers. The West, where the idea of human rights and its practical implementation emerged, arrived at this concept and such practices through a long, historical development. In ancient Greece, both Aristotle and Demosthenes expressed the view that torture was the surest method for obtaining evidence.[47] In Western countries, women were discriminated against (and in some of them they still are), and in many European countries heretics were burnt at the stake. In Spain the inquisition was abolished only in 1834,[48] and in 1925 in Tennessee, US, a school teacher was condemned by a local court for teaching Darwin's theory of the origin of species.[49] In Denmark in 1770, King Christian VII's personal physician and minister, Struensee, introduced the freedom of speech by an Order of the Cabinet.[50] However, without any tradition supporting this declared freedom, the Order caused chaos and a smear campaign against Struensee himself (alleging his intimate relations with the Queen). After Struensee was executed in 1773, the freedom of speech, not yet ready to be the order of the day in Denmark or anywhere else, did not last very long.

It took Christians 1800 years to come to the conclusion that slavery was not a natural situation for some human beings.[51]

As to the punishment of crimes, Western European countries have moved from such cruel forms of execution as hanging or the guillotine to the complete abolition of the death penalty during peacetime. How people are executed (hanged, stoned, or guillotined) or tortured may, to a great extent, depend on the specific culture. Whether people are executed or tortured at all depends more on the stage or level of societal development.[52]

In traditional societies (be they in the East or the West) the individual could realize his or her human dignity only according to his or her position in society. The very notion of the autonomy of the individual was absent. Most non-Western cultural and political traditions, like the pre-modern West, lacked not only the practice of human rights but also the very concept. It was the emergence of the modern state and the market economy which called for liberal concepts of human rights and respective practices.[53] The emergence of the market economy made individuals autonomous, not only *vis-à-vis* each other as owners, vendors or buyers, but also *vis-à-vis* society. This means that a degree of autonomy of the individual *vis-à-vis* the state was also needed. But the state has always had, and still has, a propensity to encroach upon the autonomy of the individual, especially in the absence of guarantees of such autonomy in the form of human rights and freedoms. Therefore, a modern state and human rights, as entitlements of the individual *vis-à-vis* the state, are mutually conditioned.

Today, in practically all societies, modern states have emerged with certain attributes – police, army, secret services, bureaucracy, etc. For the purposes of our analysis, it is not especially important whether some countries have accepted these attributes from Western societies or have developed them on their own. What matters is whether, having introduced institutions which have the tendency, in the absence of proper guarantees in the form of human rights, to suppress not only individual freedoms but also to subordinate the whole society to the state apparatus, leaders of these states are free to leave human rights aside.

Rhoda Howard uses a different reference point. She writes that 'a comparison of human rights in Africa in the 1980s with human rights in the Western world at similar stages of national consolidation and economic development [i.e., a couple of hundred years ago] is, then, much more appropriate than a comparison of Africa with contemporary Western societies'.[54]

Although this argument is generally correct, there is one rather serious problem. Contemporary African societies, even if their levels of economic development and other societal characteristics are comparable to those of European ones some hundreds of years ago, are not isolated from contemporary European, American or Asian societies and are influenced by them in a variety of ways. Although the *per capita* GDP of some African countries may be comparable to that of medieval England, their human rights situation cannot simply be judged by the yardstick of seventeenth-century Europe. And though not all of the standards applied by the European Court of Human Rights may be easily applicable in today's Africa, the Africans themselves would hardly be content with human rights yardsticks drawn from Europe of the seventeenth, or even the nineteenth century.

Humankind, while remaining heterogeneous not only culturally, but also (and this is even more important from the point of view of the promotion of human rights) in terms of the level of societal development (including the economic, social, political and cultural aspects of development) in different countries, is becoming at the same time closer and closer.

Although the world has always been diverse, it has never been so close. Today, post-industrial and feudal societies not only coexist on the same planet, they closely interact with and influence each other. This inevitably creates strain: on the one hand, there is a trend towards greater homogeneity (especially in the economic and technological spheres) and interpenetration of different cultures; on the other hand, we face the continuing, and in some cases even widening, hiatus between the levels of development of different societies. The interpenetration of cultures also leads, as a counter-reaction, to an even stronger search for cultural identity and resistance to what is perceived as alien cultural challenges.

This situation is a major challenge for many societies and for human rights as well. Eric Hobsbawm writes that 'perhaps the most striking characteristic of the end of the twentieth century is the tension between this accelerating globalization and the inability of both public institutions and the collective behaviour of human beings to come to terms with it'.[55]

The closeness and interpenetration of societies create a pull towards the universalization of human rights, while the developmental gap and emphasis on historical and cultural traditions is an obstacle for the acceptance of this universality. At the same time, the world today has become too small and interdependent to expect that only missile technology, computer hardware and software or narcotic drugs can transgress state boundaries. The Soviet leadership tried hard to close its society from outside influence: not only human rights, but also computers and photocopying machines (as potential tools for the distribution of 'alien' ideas, including those of human rights and fundamental freedoms) were considered dangerous for the regime and were kept out of the reach of ordinary Soviet citizens. This inevitably led to the stagnation of Soviet society. If in a closed society it is possible to produce more steel than anybody else, it is impossible to compete in a world where success depends not so much on how many millions of tons of steel is produced by a country but on the knowledge and information held by its citizens.

The Soviet authorities could restrict the distribution of foreign publications, but they were only partly successful in jamming Western radio stations. The BBC, the Voice of America, Radio Liberty and Free Europe carried news to millions of listeners in the Soviet Union and Eastern Europe. It has been rightly observed that electronic media had contributed to the fall of communist power in the Soviet Union.[56] Currently the Internet is raising fears throughout the Middle East and Asia that their closed societies may be opened up to heretical ideas which threaten their governing cliques. The *Sunday Times*, speaking of Saudi Arabia, observes that 'the Internet creates a poignant dilemma for the oil-rich kingdom. On the one hand it vaunts its capitalist and high-technology credentials, vital in the modern marketplace. At the same time the country is desperate to restrict access to the interloper from cyberspace with its seditiously irreverent ethos'.[57] The same problem is haunting other Arab autocracies, and Iran and China.

Ideas and practices such as human rights, a market economy or the Internet, Western discoveries which came at a certain level in the development of Western societies, touch all societies including those which have not yet come to these ideas, let alone practices, on their own.[58] They may affect these societies like a medicine: while some of them may be cured, and made healthier and stronger, other societies, and especially their leaders, may be rather allergic to injections of human rights, market economy or the Internet. As we have already discussed at the end of Chapter Two (see p. 26), the rapid introduction of human rights into such societies may sometimes make them rather ill, and certain forces, whose power base is threatened by the ideas and practices of modernity, including human rights, may become even more active and influential. Ideas of human rights, as we discussed above, have always been and still are subversive ideas in societies which are not based on those ideas.

In the contemporary world we have not so much a clash of civilizations[59] as a clash of epochs, and this clash is taking place not only between different societies but within many of them as well. Human rights and democracy are playing an important part in these clashes, which often revolve around such notions. At the same time, the idea of human rights is used and abused as a tool in these conflicts.

I believe that human rights in the contemporary world are conditioned by three types of factors: anthropological, societal and international. These factors are not immutable in time or space. While societal factors, that is, factors pertaining to the characteristics of a given society, have exercised the strongest influence on the content of the rights and freedoms of members of society, international factors are of more recent origin, but their influence is rapidly growing. Some rights, like the right to life, the right to freedom from torture and the right to found a family, may be said to be of an anthropological nature because they are closely related to the physical needs of human beings, even though (similar to other rights) they can exist only in society. For instance, Robinson Crusoe could have had neither rights nor obligations before the appearance of Man Friday.

It seems that the natural law approach to human rights, which asserts that all human rights are the birthrights of every human being and are immutable in time and place, is simply wrong. The Virginian Bill of Rights was authored by George Mason, a slave-owner, who did not find that slavery contradicted what the Bill found self-evident – that all men were endowed by their creator with certain inalienable rights. This understanding of 'all men' by progressive thinkers of the eighteenth century would be considered today an example of extreme bigotry. Therefore, it is not possible to assert that there is such a thing as immutable human nature from which to draw rights and freedoms corresponding to that nature. Richard Rorty is right that 'since no useful work seems to be done by insisting on a purportedly ahistorical human nature, there probably is no such nature, or at least, nothing in that nature that is relevant to our moral choices'.[60] Human rights, as Philip Windsor writes, should be seen not in terms of 'being' but in terms of 'becoming'.[61]

Usually this 'becoming' is driven by endogenous factors, though exogenous forces are becoming more and more important. Rorty emphasizes two factors which play an important role in the spread and development of human rights: security and sympathy. He writes:

Foundationalists [Plato, Aquinas, Kant] think of these people [bad people who do not respect human rights] as deprived of truth, moral knowledge. But it would be better – more specific, more suggestive of possible remedies – to think of them as deprived of two more concrete things: security and sympathy. By 'security' I mean conditions of life sufficiently risk-free as to make one's difference from others unessential to one's self-respect, one's sense of worth. These conditions have been enjoyed by Americans and Europeans – the people who dreamed up the human rights culture – much more than they have been enjoyed by anyone else. By 'sympathy' I mean the sort of reaction that the Athenians had more of after seeing Aeschylus' *The Persians* than before, the sort that white Americans had more of after reading *Uncle Tom's Cabin* than before, the sort that we have more of after watching TV programmes about the genocide in Bosnia.[62]

Rorty's view – that security and sympathy usually go together – makes sense. The tougher things are, the more you have to be afraid of, the more dangerous your situation, the less you can afford the time and effort to think of what things might be like for people with whom you do not immediately identify. Sentimental education only works on people who can relax long enough to listen.[63] When life is a constant struggle for survival, the sufferings of others cease to be of interest. As Paul Abramson and Ronald Inglehart have shown, higher levels of economic development bring a shift from 'materialist' to 'post-materialist' values – that is, less concern with economic and physical security and more with freedom, self-expression and the quality of life.[64]

And it is not surprising that, for Rorty, and probably millions of other men and women, Harriet Becher Stowe's *Uncle Tom's Cabin* is a more important contribution to moral philosophy than Kant's categorical imperative.

The growing interdependence of the world as a whole and the transparency of most societies mean that international factors, not only through the purposeful efforts of individual states, international organizations and human rights NGOs, but also through the interpenetration of cultures, ideas and knowledge, are influencing the perception of human rights concepts as well as the practices in different societies. It seems that no government is able to stop this process indefinitely. *The Economist* comments that 'the Saudi royal family – and lesser rulers in the area – have already watched with alarm as their south-eastern neighbours in Yemen played with democracy. As education spreads, oil revenues shrink and Islamic fundamentalists become bolder, they have enough to make them nervous without anyone else trying the same game'.[65] Michael Freeman is right when he says that 'the human rights culture is no longer Western. It is no longer a matter of agreement among state élites. It is a global politico-cultural movement'.[66]

However, this spread of human rights does not and should not lead to the cultural uniformity of the world. Neither does this mean that all societies develop and change in the same manner, or that they inevitably pass through similar stages of development. It means that there are some things which human societies need because they are human, while remaining different as societies.

One of the rational points among the ideas of realists' approach to international relations seems to be that states, out of necessity, have to become more and more similar to each other in different (though not in all) respects, taking over those characteristics and features which make some societies more successful than others. Kenneth Waltz writes that 'one has to be impressed with the functional similarity of states and, now more than ever before, with the similar lines their development follows. From the rich to the poor states, from the old to the new ones, nearly all of them take a larger hand in matters of economic regulation, of eduction, health, and housing, of culture and arts, and so on almost endlessly'.[67]

Societies which self-isolate (e.g., Albania until recently) or obstinately try to retain traditional ways of life which inhibit development or attempt to go back to basics (e.g., Iran, Sudan) are doomed to fail in the eternal worldwide competition. Therefore, as Fred Halliday writes, 'as a result of international pressures, states are compelled more and more to conform to each other in their internal arrangements'.[68] That is why Halliday, in studying international relations, rightly pays considerable attention to what happens within states and societies, and examines the interaction of international activity with domestic legitimacy and stability.

Human rights as a historical and evolving phenomenon have become an important part of the concept of development. In some rapidly developing parts of the world (for example, in Asian countries such as South Korea, Taiwan or Thailand[69]), positive changes in the field of human rights are coming about not so much because the West, or international bodies which are 'infected' with Western views on human rights, is pressing for changes, but because domestic constituencies developing alongside the economic growth are starting to demand not only the bread and butter, and more of it; they are also demanding a say in the distribution of that bread and butter. Francis Fukuyama writes that it is, of course, possible for a capitalist economy to coexist with an authoritarian system, as in the PRC (People's Republic of China) today or as previously existed in Germany, Japan, South Korea, Taiwan and Spain. But, as he points out, 'in the long run, the industrialization process itself necessitates a more highly educated population and more complex division of labour, both of which tend to be supportive of democratic political institutions'.[70] William Brands makes a strong point, reiterating that 'the key factor in the political evolution of Asian countries will be the efforts of the people in the countries themselves rather than the actions or non-actions of the United States or other external powers'.[71] While this may be true, external efforts may not be altogether superfluous.

One of the factors negatively affecting human rights is extreme poverty. It is not often recognized in the West that, in certain cases, poverty may really be the most important cause of the absence of human rights. A poor democratic country with a high degree of observance of human rights is simply an oxymoron. Yash Ghai is right to say that 'poverty is a great cause of the denial of human rights. The international system refuses to accept this reality – for largely political reasons'.[72] However, the recognition that poverty destroys human dignity does not, of course, mean that all rich countries (there are some rich under-developed societies, like the oil-rich Arab states) are democratic and human rights-friendly. Neither does it refute the thesis that some poor countries are poor, at least to some extent, because of their corrupt authoritarian regimes, and accordingly due to the lack of democracy and human rights.

As mentioned previously, human rights are conditioned by three types of factors (anthropological, societal and international). In addition to that, it seems that the spread of human rights is conditioned by two different pairs of factors. The first pair is internal and external factors. As I have just shown, though internal factors may be predominant, it would be wrong to ignore the influence exerted on human rights by external factors in our interdependent world. The second pair consists of ideas of human rights and democracy on the one hand, and economic, social and political conditions, on the other. These conditions either facilitate the acceptance and development of human rights ideas in society, or they inhibit this process.

Although economic, social and political conditions, as we have tried to show, exert great influence on the human rights situation in a country, and human rights are even one of the indicators of the development of society, it is necessary to admit that ideas about human rights are also very important. They can become a material force when held and supported by millions.

However, it is not enough to have ideas. As has been mentioned, there were precursors to human rights in different faiths and philosophies. Wherever there were oppressed human beings, there were often also ideologues who, instead of dreaming of changing places with the oppressors, dreamed of getting rid of the very oppression. But ideas need material conditions for their development and realization.

Ideas and dreams about liberty, freedom and human dignity could indeed be found in different cultures. But what the West had earlier than anybody else was the market economy and the modern state, which not only gave a push for the development of these ideas but also created the conditions for, and even necessitated the realization of, ideas of human rights and freedoms. Ideas, struggle for rights and freedoms, and material conditions in the form of the market economy and the modern state were necessary and sufficient preconditions for the emergence of human rights.

Therefore I tend to agree with Robert Bartley that 'the dominant flow of historical forces in the 21st century could well be this: economic development leads to demands for democracy and individual (or family) autonomy; instant worldwide communications reduce the power of oppressive governments; the spread of democratic states diminishes the potential for conflict'.[73]

All of the above seems to indicate that the receptiveness of different societies to international human rights standards is less conditioned by the cultural peculiarities of a given society than by the level of its social, economic and political development.

IS THE NORTH–SOUTH DIVIDE ON HUMAN RIGHTS REPLACING THE EAST–WEST ONE?

The end of the Cold War has considerably changed the context of human rights diplomacy. On the surface, it may be seen that the North–South confrontation on human rights has been substituted for the East–West one. In Spring 1995, during the fifty-first session of the UN Commission on Human Rights, there was a rather clear-cut division between developed and developing countries in voting on most sensitive issues. For instance, the draft resolution presented by Western countries criticizing the Chinese human rights record was narrowly defeated by 21 votes to 20, with 12 abstentions;[74] and the draft resolution critical of the situation in Nigeria was rejected by 21 votes to 17, with 17 abstentions.[75] No Third World country voted to condemn human rights violations in Nigeria,[76] and of these countries only Nicaragua and Guinea-Bissau voted for the resolution on China. At the same time, the draft resolution, 'Human rights and universal coercive measures', presented by Cuba, alleging that some countries abuse their dominant position in the world economy and continue to intensify the adoption of unilateral coercive measures against developing countries – measures which, the draft says, clearly contradict international law (such as trade restrictions, blockades, embargoes and the freezing of assets with the purpose of preventing those countries from exercising their right to fully determine their own political, economic and social system) was adopted by 24 votes to 17, with 12 abstentions.[77] It goes without saying that it was mainly the developing states which were in favour of this resolution, while developed countries voted against it.

However, the current North–South divide is not at all a mirror image of the Cold War era East–West clash over human rights. The East–West confrontation, as it related to human rights, was about two alternative ways for the development of humankind (liberal democracy and Marxism–Leninism), both of which emerged in the framework of Western social thought and practice. It was a dispute between two incompatible ways (market versus planned economy, state totalitarianism versus democracy, privileges for conformism versus human rights) for society to proceed. At the end of the day, one had to lose. Communism lost, not just because of its ineffective economic system, but also because it did not satisfy the needs of men and women for human dignity and freedom.

In the new dispute, human rights once again play a substantial role. The current dispute is basically between societies which are at different levels of societal development. Therefore, it is not only, and not so much, about whether humankind has to go to the left or to the right, or whether it can choose a middle way. To some extent the dispute is now about whether to go at all or to stay where one stands, or even to try to find a way back (e.g., the call of religious fundamentalists or extreme nationalists is usually 'back to basics'). In the East–West dispute the question was: how to modernize? Now the essential question for some societies seems to be whether to modernize at all.

The East–West struggle over human rights was a struggle between the natural development of society, including the development of human rights and freedoms, and an artificial one, imposed according to the Marxist–Leninist social theory. The communist system, which was the result of an attempt to put into practice a social theory, was the only widespread artificial social system that has ever existed in reality. It is not surprising that it brought about violence, and that it finally failed. One could hardly squeeze the rich tapestry of societal life into the procrustean bed of any social theory without violence.

The divide on human rights between the North and the South is one which exists, to a great extent, between those societies which have reached the stage of societal development where human rights and freedoms can be guaranteed and those where conditions for the acceptance of human rights could be said to be still rather embryonic.

This divide is not an artificial one which could be overcome by pulling down an imaginary 'Berlin Wall' (though even the cleaning up of the debris of the real Berlin Wall will take time and is not an easy task). Human rights situations in most countries which belong to what is called the South can be significantly improved only as a part of a larger societal change, including the eradication of poverty and the management of inter-ethnic relations, as components of social and political reforms. The root cause of many current human rights emergencies is not so much that something, somewhere, has gone badly wrong, but that in some societies nothing is going on, while other societies are rapidly developing.

These considerations should be taken into account when choosing responses to human rights problems in different societies. However, at the same time one should not forget that, in some cases, it is not so much cultural differences or even low levels of societal development (which may, of course, constitute a breeding ground for all kinds of warlords and dictators), but the thirst for power, which is at the basis of certain human rights emergencies.

POWER INTERESTS AND HUMAN RIGHTS

One of the reasons for serious human rights violations in many societies is the thirst for power. Human rights are trampled upon because those in power hate to relinquish that power. In democratic countries this quest for power is tamed by the rules of the democratic game, democratic traditions and safeguards for those who are not in power.[78]

In authoritarian states, such safeguards are usually non-existent. The winner takes all, the loser may be deprived even of his life. Therefore not only the economic well-being, but the very physical existence, of power-holders often depends on their hold on power. Although authorities which violate human rights make references, as a rule, to the interests of the people or to the need to consolidate the nation in the face of external or internal threats, their real concerns are often only their own interests and the consolidation of their own power. There are few leaders who violate human rights out of pure pleasure; most of them do it out of what they see as necessity. Repression and terror are often the only means which can keep some rulers in power. External pressure may sometimes alleviate the plight of the population under such rulers, but real progress is possible only after a change, not only of rulers, but often also of the underlying conditions which are the power-base of such rulers.

Previously, we analysed the role of ethnic and religious factors which may negatively affect both human rights and international stability. However, it is necessary to emphasize that these factors are often used by unscrupulous politicians as a cover or mechanism in order to facilitate the achievement of political aims. Communists-turned-nationalists, like Milosevic of Serbia, Tudjman of Croatia, or Kravchuk of the Ukraine, have all used the ideology of nationalism in order to further their political power. In Rwanda, the genocidal ideology was nurtured and unleashed by the Hutu-led authorities to consolidate their hold on power, to scapegoat the Tutsis for economic failures and to stall democratic reforms. President Ja'far Nimeiri of Sudan, a leftist ruler after the seizure of power in 1969, turned to Islam in 1983 in order to consolidate his increasingly unpopular regime.[79] Saddam Hussein, the dictator of Baghdad, who Fred Halliday calls 'an eminently secular leader, who has suppressed the independent clergy inside Iraq, and draws his ideological inspiration from European fascism and a little Leninism', and whose dispute with Kuwait was not about Allah, but about more secular matters: oil, debt, frontiers, prestige,[80] turned to Islam and even appealed for the solidarity of the Muslim world after the US-led coalition had come to the assistance of Kuwait. In the mid-1930s, when China's population was victimized by famine, civil war and Japanese aggression, Chang Kai-shek launched a national campaign advocating Confucianism – called 'The Movement of New Life' – which aimed to distract people from real interests and which ended in complete failure.[81]

Therefore one should regard with caution allegations that it is ethnic and religious factors which are at the basis of some internationally destabilizing human rights emergencies. It is often only a half-truth being exploited by politicians whose only real aim is power. As has been mentioned, 'it is also legitimate to investigate what reasons other than religion may lie behind the policies, particularly where the policies serve the interests of the powerful groups already enjoying privileged positions'.[82] At the same time, the reality of the ethnic or religious dimensions of many conflicts cannot be denied. Even if ethnic or religious communities are, as they are sometimes called, only 'imagined',[83] their importance is no less real. Conflicts in Rwanda, Burundi, Bosnia or the Caucasus are as much about ethnic or religious issues as they are about power.

CONCLUSIONS

There are various causes and preconditions for human rights violations or for the complete absence of human rights in some societies. Differences in culture and in levels of societal development may often explain the dissimilarities in human rights situations in different countries. Extreme nationalism and religious extremism often result in human rights violations. Thirst for power is frequently behind the suppression of rights and freedoms in many countries.

It is necessary to attempt to clarify the reasons for gross and massive human rights violations or their complete denial, and to try to separate them from the pretexts, justifications and excuses often put forward by the governments of states where such violations take place. Sometimes, even when difficulties are real, they are not the cause, or at least not the only cause, of human rights violations, but, like economic crises or underdevelopment, may form an environment which tends to be conducive to human rights violations. At the same time, governments often try to hide behind such difficulties and use them as a shield in order to justify their poor human rights record which has different causes.

Often such governments simply deny that acts which constitute a violation of international human rights standards occur at all. In that case they frequently try to hide behind the concept of non-interference in internal affairs. But sometimes it is not so much the denial of facts, but references to specific difficulties or cultural and religious peculiarities, which are put forward in justification of certain practices constituting violation of international human rights standards. It is important to know, on the one hand, where the difficulties are real and may constitute an obstacle for the implementation of universal norms, notwithstanding efforts undertaken by the government, and, on the other hand, where references to economic difficulties or cultural and religious peculiarities serve as an excuse for authorities which often have a vested interest in a situation in which human rights are violated.

Human rights diplomacy has to take into account all the factors discussed above and distinguish between the difficulties which some societies objectively face in trying to implement international human rights standards, and the excuses and justifications used to cover the real interests of political leaders.

Before turning to issues of contemporary human rights diplomacy, the next chapter will address some of the lessons of Cold War human rights diplomacy.

4 Some lessons of Cold War human rights diplomacy

Human rights had played a certain role in inter-state relations long before the Second World War. One may recall Great Britain's anti-slavery diplomacy at the beginning of the nineteenth century. It had abolished the slave traffic in its colonies in 1807 and induced France to agree to cooperate in abolishing the slave trade. There was condemnation of the slave trade at the Congress of Vienna of 1815, and later in the century several treaties aiming to put an end to the slave trade were concluded.[1] Different authors have argued about the reasons for the abolition of the slave trade: whether it was done for humanitarian reasons or whether it had become unprofitable.[2] George Scelle wrote:

> The struggle against slavery, the protection of the bodily freedom of individuals begin in international law only then when it became clear that the slave labour had economic drawbacks and the progress of modern technology allowed such a labour to be replaced.... This proves that moral convictions do not override the necessities of economic life in the formation of legal rules.[3]

Probably, both factors played a certain role in the development of legal rules on the abolition of slavery and the slave trade, in the same way as both material factors and ideas have generally influenced the development of human rights law.

We have seen earlier (Chapters One and Two) that minority rights had influenced diplomacy of many states before and after the First World War. We also saw that not humanitarian concerns but strategic issues were usually paramount when states intervened on behalf of religious or ethnic minorities.

Labour rights, which had already become an international issue before the First World War, received a boost with the creation in 1919 of the International Labour Organization (ILO).[4] Humanitarian reasons, the struggle of trade unions and the interest of industrialists in equal labour conditions were all present in the development of international labour standards. Louis Henkin writes:

> Even the ILO conventions, perhaps, served some less-than-altruistic purposes. Improvement in the conditions of labour was capitalism's defence against the spectre of spreading socialism which had just established itself in the largest country in Europe. States, moreover, had a direct interest in the conditions of labour in countries with which they competed in a common international market: a state impelled to improve labour and social conditions at home could not readily do so unless other states did so, lest the increase in its costs of production render its products non-competitive.[5]

This confirms what we saw in Chapter One, that it has been a mixture of idealism, pragmatism and even cynicism which has been a driving force behind the international human rights movement. However, human rights as a comprehensive set of the rights and freedoms of all individuals became an issue of practical diplomacy only after the Second World War, which means that this occurred, to a great extent, in the Cold War context. Although human rights diplomacy of that period was not exclusively determined by Cold War imperatives, it was certainly rather heavily tainted by the ideological and political clash between the East and the West. Jack Donnelly even writes:

> In a world in which major adversaries see themselves locked in an irreconcilable ideological and political conflict, there is little room for the pursuit of human rights concerns. In fact, there is small reason to believe that the language of human rights will be used for any purpose other than to attempt to gain political advantage. Such a situation prevailed throughout the 1950s and 1960s in the East–West (especially US–Soviet) relations.[6]

If this is an overstatement, then it is only a rather slight one. Although human rights issues were not always used exclusively for political purposes, this was certainly the case in many instances. The Soviet Union used human rights exclusively as an instrument for its ideological and political struggle with the West, as a propaganda tool, even when in its criticism of Western states and especially its arch-rival, the US, it may often have been right. Professionalism and the success of Soviet diplomats in UN human rights bodies were assessed not in terms of rights promoted or protected but whether they had succeeded in trading off resolutions against the Soviet Union or its friends.

Western human rights diplomacy was not always different. The US had its own friendly dictators whom it had to protect from justified attacks (Somoza, Reza Pahlavi, Papa and Baby Doc Duvalier, and many others). Therefore trade-offs were possible. Richard Bilder wrote:

> where political conflict lurks in the background, a certain scepticism as to the sincerity of the asserted human rights motivations of the governments involved may well be in order. One may even suspect that such governments might prefer that their enemies continue human rights denials, thus exposing them to continued propaganda attack.[7]

However, there were also some positive developments on human rights at the international level during the Cold War. The 'international bill of rights', comprised of the Universal Declaration on Human Rights, the Covenant on Economic, Social and Cultural Rights, the Covenant on Civil and Political Rights and its Optional Protocol, conventions against genocide, against racial discriminations and on the rights of women, along with many other international instruments on human rights, which are not outdated in the post-Cold War world, were elaborated and entered into force for hundreds of states during the Cold War.

Although the effectiveness of these instruments may be questioned, they undoubtedly contributed to the emergence, and became an important part, of the global human rights movement.

The system of human rights protection in the framework of the Council of Europe has been fairly successful. It has been rightly argued that the European Convention on Human Rights and Fundamental Freedoms has been one of the success stories of post-1945 human rights developments.[8] The Convention has had a considerable effect upon the national law of the contracting parties. It has served as a catalyst for legal change that has furthered the protection of human rights and has, in so doing, assisted in the process of harmonizing law in Europe.[9]

The inter-American instruments and mechanisms relating to the protection of human rights have also made certain contributions to the improvement of the human rights situation in the Americas. It may be expected that processes of democratization taking place in Latin America will increase the role of the American Convention on Human Rights as well as that of the Inter-American Court and Commission on Human Rights. However, the Cold War environment created a great deal of human rights rhetoric because the issue of human rights was one of the central themes of the ideological struggle between the East and the West. Therefore, if in the future we will hear less on human rights from some governments, it may also be that what is lost is the rhetoric and not the substance.

When speaking of human rights diplomacy during the Cold War period, it is necessary to try to separate those patterns which were, if not completely dictated, then at least distorted by Cold War imperatives, from the patterns which were determined by different concerns. Comparison of the human rights diplomacy of our not so distant past, its modest achievements and failures, with recent changes and emerging tendencies, will help us see better the future of human rights diplomacy.

HUMAN RIGHTS DIPLOMACY OF THE WEST *VIS-À-VIS* THE COMMUNIST STATES

Western democracies had a more or less common front in their human rights approach towards communist countries. There were, of course, many differences as well, and some states were more active than others, but there was a common belief in the West that human rights in communist countries were grossly violated and that these transgressions should not be left unnoticed; this belief affected the foreign policy of Western democracies towards the countries of the Communist bloc. Soviet laws and practices concerning freedom of expression, the right to leave one's own country as well as the persecution of dissidents and the use of psychiatry for political purposes, were issues which were raised in bilateral diplomacy as well as in international bodies.

Concrete modalities of this policy depended on concrete circumstances, and were often linked to other foreign policy issues which were usually more important than human rights. Economic interests and security concerns were, of course, paramount.

As the West and the East were not very interdependent economically, economic levers to influence the Soviet human rights record were rather limited. It was possible for the West, and especially for the United States, to exploit with some success the interest of some Communist bloc countries in MFN (Most Favoured Nation) status, or in access to new technology for the promotion of human rights. However, even here, possibilities for the West to influence events in the East, and especially in the Soviet Union, were rather limited.

For example, in April 1973 US President Nixon proposed a comprehensive Trade Act that would have extended MFN status to the Soviet Union, as part of the linkage between trade and Soviet foreign policy restraint. However, Senator Henry Jackson and

Representative Charles Vanic proposed an amendment which pre-cluded the extension of the MFN status to the Soviet Union as long as the latter continued to restrict Jewish emigration.[10] It appears likely that the Soviet leadership would have liberalized its immigration policies towards Jews (they promised to grant 45,000 visas per year, which was well beyond previous practice) but Jackson went too far, insisting that the Soviet Union permit no less than 100,000 visas per year and that, not only Jews, but also Baltic nationals, Baptists and others be included.[11] At the end of the day the USSR repudiated the whole agreement. As Cathal Nolan writes, 'Jackson–Vanic proved counterproductive in almost all regards and from the point of view of nearly all its backers'.[12] This linkage between trade and human rights did not lead to any significant improvement of the human rights situation in any of the target states.

The Cold War adversaries, constituting the biggest security threat to each other, were at the same time security-interdependent. Soviet security concerns could be used to a certain extent by the West to extract concessions from the USSR on human rights matters. There was, for example, a linkage between disarmament negotiations and human rights in the Soviet Union, and between the first (political and security issues) and the third (humanitarian questions) baskets of the Helsinki process,[13] where the Soviet Union was ready for some rather significant, normative, but not so important in practical terms, concessions on human rights issues in order to have the inviolability of existing borders in Europe recognized by the West.

The Soviet leadership, by signing the Helsinki Final Act[14] in 1975, behaved most hypocritically and arrogantly. The Final Act was published in *Pravda*, the official newspaper of the Central Committee of the Communist Party of the USSR with a circulation of more than 11 million copies. However, the Kremlin relied on 'safety clauses' in the Helsinki document, such as the statement in the preamble of Basket III that cooperation in the field of humanitarian affairs 'should take place in full respect for the principles guiding relations among participant states' (i.e., ten principles, including the one on non-intervention in internal affairs, which was, in the eyes of the Soviet diplomacy, a proper counterbalance to the principle of the respect for human rights). Another example of these 'safety' clauses was a reference in the preamble of the sub-chapter on human contacts that 'the questions relevant hereto must be settled by the States concerned under mutually acceptable conditions'.

Although the Soviet leadership may not have miscalculated very much, in the sense that it was not going to change significantly its laws and practices on human rights because of its signature under the Final Act (and only significant changes would have guaranteed the conformity of Soviet and other Eastern bloc countries' human rights records with the Helsinki requirements), it is undeniable that the Helsinki process had some influence on the Soviet (as well as those of other Soviet bloc countries) internal practices and, most importantly, it was a basis for the creation of human rights movements in the USSR and Eastern European states. These were famous Helsinki monitoring groups which played an important role in the preparation of these societies for the changes which started in the second half of the 1980s. The Soviet Human Rights Committee, headed by Andrei Sakharov and Sergei Kovaljov, Charter 77 in Czechoslovakia, and other groups, were to a great extent children of the Helsinki process.

But even in this context, the character of the interdependency put strict limits upon the ability of the West to influence the human rights policies of the East. The West was no less interested in its own security than the East, and being the Cold War adversary of the East, it could not considerably increase the East's sense of security (e.g., by reducing American forces in Europe or cutting unilaterally its nuclear arsenal), even for the sake of the promotion of human rights in the East, without undermining its own security.

In this regard I have some doubts as to the correctness of the distinction made by some authors between the concerns expressed by both West and East during the Cold War over human rights and the maintenance of peace. Antonio Cassese, for instance, wrote that 'for the Socialist countries, protection of human rights is one of the ways of promoting the maintenance of peaceful relations among states',[15] while 'for the Western countries, the need to ensure respect for human dignity is always pre-eminent'.[16] As I see it, for the socialist countries (primarily the USSR), human rights were an instrument in the global ideological struggle and, therefore, could have had only a rhetorical relation to the maintenance of peace. Equally, some Western states (primarily the US) often showed little concern for ensuring respect for human dignity, when they sacrificed human rights and supported repressive regimes in different parts of the world when it was deemed to be necessary to counter the threat of communism. The Cold War was rather an inhospitable environment for human rights.

However, the most serious limitation on the West's ability to influence human rights in the East was not the lack of adequate leverage but the fact that any significant changes in the human rights situation in any of the Communist bloc countries would have required, not only a change of leadership, but also a change in the very social, economic and political system of these countries. Radical changes of the human rights situations in their countries would have been a much bigger security threat to incumbent regimes in the Communist bloc states than a military threat from NATO. The communist countries could not comply with the human rights clauses of the Helsinki Final Act, or with the UN Covenants on human rights, without ceasing to be communist countries. One could not sentence dissidents without violating the freedom of expression; or have a one-party regime and comply, at the same time, with the requirements of free and fair elections or freedom of association. Therefore, it should be clear that Western pressure could not radically change human rights situations in Eastern bloc countries.

Nevertheless, it could hardly be said that the human rights policy of the Western countries towards the Soviet Union and its allies was completely in vain. It is important to remember that any progress in the protection of human rights can be achieved only incrementally, and it is not always immediate and easily recognizable. Moreover, in certain cases of improvements in the human rights situation in, let us say, the USSR or Romania, it was not always easy to trace them back to Western pressure, because even when there was a causal link between such pressure and positive changes (for example, some dissidents receiving milder sentences or immigration rules being eased), the leadership of the target countries, naturally, never admitted that this was due to Western human rights policy.

However, the greatest significance of the Western human rights policy towards the Soviet bloc countries, I believe, does not lie in minor improvements in the policy of cynical accommodation (although these should not be completely neglected, either, because when we are speaking of violations of fundamental rights, every improvement may be important). It lies in the fact that, otherwise, the spark of human rights in these countries could have been extinguished altogether, plunging them into an even deeper morass. The feeble idea of and belief in human rights was kept alive, to a great extent, thanks to this outside interference and pressure. And of course, without such interference, the West could now hardly have any moral right to speak about human rights in other countries.

I believe that without Western pressure on the USSR and its satellites, without the activities of human rights NGOs such as Amnesty International, Helsinki Watch and many others, without the attention given to the human rights situation in these countries by the mass media (especially Radio Liberty, Free Europe, the BBC and Voice of America), there would not have been such personalities as Andrei

Sakharov, Sergei Kovaljov, Larissa Bogorad, Vaclav Havel, Pavel Bratinka, Arpad Goncz, Bronislaw Geremek, Yuri Orlov, Vladimir Bukovski, Hristo Zhelev and many others, who have played or are continuing to play an active role in the processes of transformation in Russia, Central and Eastern Europe.

Moreover, it is not only the responses of governments, especially their immediate responses, which are important. It is also important how international concern or pressure for human rights affects the population of a target state, or is perceived by the latter. If a population, which suffers at the hands of a bloody dictatorship, is simply left alone with its oppressors, there is little hope for the civilized development of such a society.

Therefore, I believe that Western human rights diplomacy *vis-à-vis* the Soviet Union and its allies served a positive role, though its main impact was felt not so much during the period of totalitarian dictatorship, but in the process of dismantling these regimes and in the creation of the foundations for democratic societies.

HUMAN RIGHTS DIPLOMACY OF THE WEST *VIS-À-VIS* THE THIRD WORLD

The responses of Western democracies to human rights problems in other, mainly Third World, countries were less coherent than their responses to human rights violations in the Communist bloc countries. We find here a rather sharp distinction between the US approach, on the one hand, and that of European countries such as Sweden, Norway, Denmark and the Netherlands, on the other. In this respect, Canadian or Australian human rights policy seems to be closer to the European one.

The US, with a few exceptions (especially during the Carter administration), made a rather clear distinction between violations by leftist (oriented usually towards the Soviet Union), and rightist (oriented, as a rule, towards the West) authoritarian regimes. Jean Kirkpatrick, the US representative to the United Nations under the Reagan administration, theorizing on the issue, distinguished between totalitarian regimes which could not be expected to change and authoritarian regimes which, by contrast, were susceptible to reform and were thus proper recipients of United States support.[17] Although such a distinction may have had some *raison d'être*, it did not bear on human rights and, as we saw in previous chapters, neither leftist nor rightist dictatorships could be reformed without getting rid of dictators and making other deep changes in the social and political structures of society. The only real difference was that, while totalitarian states had complete control over the economy, so-called authoritarian regimes allowed some market freedoms. As mentioned above, the absence of market relations creates additional problems for the processes of liberalization and democratization.

Leftists regimes were always criticized in the strongest terms, while rightists usually enjoyed US support. As leftists (for example, Cuba, Nicaragua, Angola) belonged to the Soviet *de facto* sphere of influence, the US did not have much leverage in order to change the human rights situations of these countries, apart from providing assistance in attempts to overthrow or undermine their governments (for example, the attempt of anti-Castro forces supported by the US government to land in the Bay of Pigs in 1961, or the support given to Nicaraguan contras in the 1980s). In some cases of rather moderate leftist regimes (Mossadeq, Arbenz, Allende), these attempts were successful, but they brought to power significantly more repressive governments than the ones they helped overthrow. As discussed in some detail in Chapter Two, in some cases the US support for unpopular authoritarian governments (the Shah of Iran, Somoza of Nicaragua) may have contributed to the coming to power of anti-Western human rights-hostile regimes.

There are studies which suggest that the worst human rights violators were often the receivers of the largest amounts of US security and economic assistance. The statistics analysed, for example, by Stohl, Carleton and Johnson indicated that under 'Presidents Nixon and Ford foreign assistance was directly related to levels of human rights violations, i.e. more aid flowed to regimes with higher levels of violations, while under President Carter no clear statistical pattern emerged'.[18]

It seems reasonable to conclude that such patterns were due, at least partially, to Cold War realities, and perhaps even more to the exaggerated perceptions of and over-reaction to these realities by American policy-makers. The global role of the United States, its leadership and responsibilities in the fight against the communist threat, put severe restrictions on its human rights policy, not only abroad but even at home.

Yet the situation was not so simple either. There certainly were, and still are, American politicians and diplomats who were in principle against the inclusion of human rights issues in foreign policy. Henry Kissinger, the former Secretary of State, believed that 'it is dangerous for us to make the domestic policy of countries around the world a direct objective of American foreign policy.... The protection of basic human rights is a very sensitive aspect of the domestic jurisdiction of...governments'.[19] However, this was only one trend. Even when the US did not cut off economic or security assistance for some human rights-hostile but US-friendly regimes in a number of countries, and even continued to publicly support these regimes (for example, President Carter, obviously contradicting his own human rights policy, in December 1978 praised the Shah of Iran as a strong advocate of human rights[20]), this did not always mean that Washington completely closed its eyes to human rights violations by friendly allies. There is reliable information available that different US administrations tried to induce, by means of quiet diplomacy, governments, such as those of Iran (under the Shah), Brazil, Argentina, Indonesia and South Korea, to improve their human rights records.[21]

There were even some improvements, but the problem was that often these regimes, like the communist ones, could stay in power only by suppressing any opposition to their rule. Therefore improvements could be only cosmetic and not substantial. But even these cosmetic improvements should not be brushed aside as not deserving any attention. First of all, they sometimes concerned hundreds, or even thousands, of human beings whose plight was thereby eased. For instance, American diplomats have reported that, under quiet pressure by the Carter administration, the Shah publicly ordered an end to torture, allowed certain SAVAK (secret police of the Shah) officials to be charged with criminal excess and punished, and ordered a large number of prisoners either to be freed or remanded for trial with defence lawyers provided.[22] The former American Ambassador to Indonesia, David Newsom, writes that pressure from the US and other Western countries in the years 1975–78 contributed to the release of prisoners who were detained after the 1965 failed *coup d'état* and the following massacre.[23] Second, the presence of an external eye often kept some authoritarian regimes from falling into complete lawlessness and helped those who contributed most to democratic reforms to survive. And, third, minor improvements can pave the way for major reforms.

The policies of those European countries which had a distinctive human rights diplomacy as a component of their foreign policy were quite different from those of the US. Not being great powers, let alone superpowers, their ability to influence events in other countries, and, consequently, their ambitions and rhetoric, were much more modest. If the United States placed the emphasis almost exclusively on civil and political rights, European countries such as Sweden, Norway, the Netherlands and Denmark, as well as Canada and Australia, paid equal, if not greater, attention to economic and social rights. Jan Egeland writes that an important issue in Norwegian human rights policies, like those of some other like-minded governments (Sweden, Denmark and the Netherlands), has been the 'advocacy of international socio-economic rights... and of increased development aid from the industrialized nations'.[24]

The basic instrument through which human rights policies were encouraged and implemented was developmental assistance. The pressure on target governments was not in the form of sanctions or the threatened cut-off of aid, but mainly an engagement in dialogue and reward for improvements. As cutting off aid would have hurt, first of all, those whose rights were being violated, in cases of continuing human rights violations by a government, channels were used which, if possible, bypassed governments and reached people more directly.[25]

European democracies were much more even-handed between leftist and rightist dictatorships and had better fine tuning as well. For example, the Dutch governments, in deciding their human rights policies, have 'distinguished three main violation patterns in the developing nations: historical and cultural repression of women, ethnic groups, castes, and minorities; repression of political rights for the sake of general economic progress by regimes which tried to break down existing privileges and inequities; and repression by a privileged elite which abused its power to maintain or strengthen its own position'.[26] Different patterns and root causes of violations called for different responses and remedies.

The means used by Western democracies to influence human rights situations in other countries varied from quiet diplomacy to exposing violations in international fora; voting for the creation of investigative bodies and appointing special rapporteurs; and cutting off military supplies or even developmental aid. These means have depended on specific contexts, including existing ties with a target state.[27] The US human rights diplomacy tools under the Bush administration, when the Cold War distorting lens was being lifted, included praise and criticism, economic and political assistance programmes, and the granting or withholding of MFN status and other trade benefits. Carothers writes that 'with respect to Romania, for example, the Bush administration attempted to pressure President Iliescu in a pro-democratic direction by conditioning the renewal of MFN status on the holding of free and fair elections and by funding assistance programmes for the Romanian political opposition'.[28]

QUESTIONS OF THE EFFECTIVENESS AND COLLATERAL DAMAGE OF HUMAN RIGHTS DIPLOMACY

There are two important questions to be asked. How effective were these measures? Did they jeopardize other foreign policy aims, such as economic interests or national security?

As already indicated, it is often impossible to measure the effectiveness of human rights diplomacy in concrete terms. John Vincent distinguished three different kinds of reaction of target states to the human rights policy of the United States: contempt, cynicism, and accommodation.[29] As instances of contemptuous reaction, he cites the Argentine and Brazilian reactions to the Carter administration's decision to cut military aid to these countries because of their human rights records. These governments not only considered that the US policy constituted interference in their internal affairs, but also responded by rejecting the aid which had already been appropriated.[30]

However, I would not qualify these apparently negative responses as a complete failure of US human rights diplomacy. Every such act of pressure obviously hurts the pride of national leaders and therefore the immediate reaction is often negative. Moreover, US human rights policy lacked consistency, and its double standard was often obvious, which also negatively affected its efficiency. But more important than the immediate reaction are long term developments. In Argentina and Brazil the latest developments have been rather positive, and there is no doubt that the attention paid to the human rights situation in these countries and the pressure exerted on them by individual states and by the world community as a whole was instrumental in bringing about positive transformations.

There is no doubt also that international efforts contributed to the collapse of the apartheid regime in South Africa. For too long the Western, and especially the US, policy towards apartheid in South Africa was rather ambiguous. John Dugard writes that 'South Africa gained support from many Western governments for its insistence that its racial policies fell within its exclusive domestic jurisdiction'.[31] Although the General Assembly adopted resolutions in every year, beginning in 1962, calling upon states to adopt various measures (for example, the interruption of diplomatic relations, the the boycott of South African goods, the closure of ports to ships under the South African flag, etc.), Britain, France and the US consistently vetoed harsher measures against South Africa in the Security Council.[32] However, 'gradually international opinion changed as apartheid became more brutal, South Africa more intransigent, and decolonization more widespread'.[33] In 1977 the Security Council, acting under Chapter VII, imposed an arms embargo against South Africa.[34] In 1986, the United States finally passed the Comprehensive Anti-Apartheid Act which in, section 310 (a), provided that 'no national of the United States may, directly or through another person, make any new investment in South Africa'.[35] As Les de Villiers, a former South African diplomat, concludes, American sanctions were a major force for political change in South Africa and they significantly dictated the form, substance, timing and pace of reforms.[36] Ultimately, the consolidated efforts of South Africans themselves and the world community at large finally succeeded in dismantling the apartheid regime in the African continent.

Let us for a moment imagine that there had not been any criticism raised in different international fora or by individual states in their bilateral diplomacy concerning human rights, for example, in the Soviet Union or South Africa. Although it is probably impossible to tell what may have happened in these countries in the absence of any attention to their internal politics, two scenarios seem to be quite plausible: either the communist and apartheid regimes would still be in place, or there would be armed struggle going on in both of these countries.

There is no evidence that the concern expressed, or even the pressure exerted, by countries which have active human rights diplomacy has adversely affected the vital interests of such countries. The Foreign Minister of Australia, Gareth Evans, said in May 1989 that in the previous twelve-month period the Government had raised over 400 human rights issues with sixty-eight different governments on a consistent and non-discriminatory basis, and that

> there was no evidence that Australia's activities in the human rights field had adversely affected Australian interests in other areas: although Australian complaints over human rights had been met with resistance, and sometimes hostility, on the part of individual interlocutors, there had been no identifiable instance where a country had retaliated in economic or other unrelated areas to human rights criticisms.[37]

Cyrus Vance, speaking of the US human rights concerns expressed during the negotiations on SALT (the Strategic Arms Limitation Treaty), and of Gromyko's threat to link the progress in arms control to non-interference in Soviet internal affairs, concluded that though the US human rights *démarches* had undoubtedly irritated the Soviets, the latter 'were much too pragmatic to let their deeper security interests be jeopardized by matters that were only an irritant'.[38] This observation by the former US Secretary of State shows, on the one hand, that human rights diplomacy usually does not negatively affect the achievement of other foreign policy objectives. However, on the other hand, it also implies that human rights diplomacy, especially when a target state is an important actor in international relations, has rather limited effects. Otherwise, it would not have remained no more than an irritant for the Soviets.

Other views have been expressed as well. David Forsythe, for example, writes that 'international attention to a state's human rights situation may create considerable conflict – including violent conflict'.[39] But examples given by him of violent conflicts which were allegedly created by the concern for human rights – the US invasions in Grenada and Panama in the 1980s – are not very convincing. There were other reasons for these invasions which overshadowed humanitarian concerns.[40]

However, it is not usually the attention or reaction to human rights violations, but the violations themselves, which cause a threat to international stability. Was it, for example, the Iraqi attack against Kuwait which created a major conflict, or the response of the UN Security Council and the actions of the Coalition on the liberation of Kuwait? Notwithstanding all the efforts of Saddam Hussein's propaganda, there are few people who believe today that the conflict started with the response to the Iraqi attack on Kuwait and not with the attack itself. Was it the US military operation, authorized by the Security Council, which threatened stability in Haiti and in that region, or was it the human rights situation in Haiti which prompted the Council to perceive a threat to international peace and security and to authorize the invasion by US armed forces? I believe that the military coup in Haiti in 1990, which overthrew the democratically elected President Aristide, and the behaviour of the military junta, were factors which triggered the crisis, rather than the response of the world community.

Although, in the abstract, it is possible to imagine a situation where one could say that a violent conflict was created not by human rights violations but by a reaction to them, in practice there have not been such cases, and there can hardly be expected to be any. States have always been, and continue to be, quite cautious (often rightly so) in their human rights diplomacy. It seems that there is still a lot of room for human rights diplomacy before one may expect any significant boomerang effect for those countries engaged in such diplomacy. In Chapter Six I will analyse several cases of foreign intervention in which humanitarian concerns played some role in triggering those interventions. Here, suffice it to say that, if humanitarian concerns were not simply a pretext for an intervention which in fact was triggered by different reasons, it was real humanitarian emergencies or catastrophes (like those, for example, in Eastern Pakistan in 1973 or in Uganda in 1979) and not responses to them. which played the most important part in the genesis of those conflicts.

There is an Asian view which sees a threat to international peace and security in the concern for human rights. Kishore Mahbubani writes that, 'as the experience of South Asia demonstrates, commenting on internal affairs can lead to conflict in less developed states'.[41] Although he provides no references to concrete expressions of this experience, the author concludes that 'one essential reason why no war has broken out among ASEAN states over 25 years is precisely because they adhere to the principle of non-interference in internal affairs'.[42]

Does this mean that the Second World War broke out because of the excessive concern expressed by Western democracies for human rights in Nazi Germany? Or maybe that the conflict in the former Yugoslavia started because other countries showed too great an interest in how Serbian and Croatian nationalists violated the rights of ethnic minorities, thereby paving the way for bigger crimes against humanity? It seems that in many cases non-interference has not only been morally wrong but has contributed to the conflagration of violent conflicts. On the other hand, though Western European countries have created rather intrusive regional human rights procedures and mechanisms, there have not been any wars between these countries since these mechanisms and procedures became operative. Moreover, the very purpose of the creation of European human rights instruments, mechanisms and procedures in the aftermath of the Second World War was to avoid the recurrence of new conflicts on the continent.

CONCLUSIONS

The Cold War put rather serious restrictions on the human rights diplomacy of Western countries, and it certainly distorted, and to a certain extent even discredited, this noble policy. At the same time, in spite of its rather low efficiency rate in terms of the correlation between effort spent and results gained, the human rights diplomacy of Western countries during the Cold War played a certain positive role in the improvements which we now see in many countries, and it did not induce any significant negative repercussions for the countries involved in active human rights diplomacy.

Although democratic reforms in Eastern and Central Europe, in the former USSR, in Latin American countries, as well as in South Africa, had mainly domestic roots, and although their success or failure will depend overwhelmingly on the efforts of the peoples of these countries, it would be wrong to underestimate the role of external factors in internal reforms. Equally, though humanitarian calamities such as those in Rwanda, Somalia, Liberia and the former Yugoslavia were created not by somebody's action or inaction from outside but by the policies of local leaders, it is becoming increasingly clear that mistakes made and opportunities lost by other states or by the world community as a whole have sometimes been very costly.[43]

The post-Cold War world lacks the Cold War period's certainty and predictability. The international system is passing through one of its stages of turmoil and relative chaos. As Richard Falk, in his report to the World Order Models Project, observes:

> Great visionary opportunities for the enhancement of the human condition are contained within the fluidity of circumstances that make this period of history turbulent and fraught with contradiction and surprise. Such opportunities coexist with the most appalling spectacles of human tragedy and mass suffering visually disseminated by television and on the information superhighway, and coupled with dire prophesies of even darker times ahead.[44]

As we discussed in Chapter Two, order hardly ever comes out of disorder without purposeful efforts, and the character of an emerging order will depend on the nature and direction of these efforts. Human rights issues are only one, and may be not the most important, area where the international community should concentrate its efforts. Economic development, ecological concerns, the proliferation of weapons of mass destruction, terrorism and drugs, are all issues of great importance for the future of the world. However, the neglect of human rights will not only be detrimental for human rights, it may negatively affect many areas of international relations as well. Because of its fluidity and relative malleability, this seems to be one of those times in the history of humankind when the slogan *carpe diem* (catch the moment) is especially pertinent. The future depends more than ever on who will catch the moment.

5 A new era
What should, and what can, be done?

As the previous chapters have shown, most countries cannot ignore human rights when it comes to their foreign policy. There are moral, legal and practical–political reasons sufficient to induce sometimes even reluctant governments to take a stand on human rights issues in other countries.

As I have tried to emphasize, the end of the Cold War has considerably changed the environment in which human rights diplomacy takes place. No longer is it the direct threat to security, especially in the traditional – military – sense, which preoccupies most countries most of the time; it is the amorphous challenges, and the instability that they may provoke, which are the focus of concerns today. How should the world community respond to these changes? What will be the place of human rights diplomacy in the foreign policy of democratic countries in the future?

Some possible answers to these questions have already been suggested in previous chapters. To deal more fully with them, however, requires us to consider now the issue of general or differentiated approaches to human rights diplomacy. Similar human rights violations may, depending on the context in which they are committed, have different causes as well as different effects. For example, political repression in a poor, underdeveloped country with a corrupt and ineffective regime which can stay in power only by oppressing any popular discontent may, on the surface, be rather similar to political repression in a rapidly developing country where the government is able to deliver economically, but, for the sake of social and political stability, or in order to guarantee a high level of investment, suppresses any discontent with its policies and especially any discontent with the unequal results of its developmental policy. These repressions, similar on the surface, occur in different political and social contexts and have different causes (though one cause probably coincides: both governments are eager to stay in power and therefore deal harshly with any dissent). How should such situations, which are similar and dissimilar at the same time, be approached? They may be similar, for example, in the light of the Covenant on Civil and Political Rights, but quite different if one looks at them through the prism of the existing social and political realities of these countries.

In this chapter I shall also consider the issue of the legitimacy of governments in the light of their human rights records and democratic credentials, and try to distinguish between governments which deny their population human rights and those which violate the human rights of their people. Finally, I shall compare the potentials of bilateral and multilateral human rights diplomacy, and look at how they can work together to enhance each other's potential.

GENERAL RECIPES OR DIFFERENTIATED APPROACHES?

If, under the legal systems of democratic countries, all individuals are equal before the law, similarly, under international law, all states are deemed to be equal. The principle of the sovereign equality of states stands first in the UN Charter, 1970 Friendly Relations Declaration, and in the 1975 Final Act of Helsinki. It seems to be a cornerstone of the current international legal order; therefore, from both legal and moral points of view, a principled approach under both legal systems – domestic and international – demands that like cases should be dealt with similarly.

There are millions of subjects of law in the domestic sphere, and law and politics could hardly take into account the characteristics and specific problems of every individual or corporate entity. Law acts as an average measure of freedom, and also defines its limits. The blindfolded figure of Themis, the goddess of justice, characterizes well this feature of law. But could a blindfolded Themis also be a symbol of international law?

In contrast to any domestic legal system, there are not more than 200 nation-states in the international system, including such giants as the United States or China and mini-states like Andorra or San Marino. One of the important differences between cases under international law and under domestic law is that, under international law, almost every case is relatively much more unique than cases under domestic law. Wars not only occur less frequently than thefts, burglaries or murders, but they are also much more unique as to their causes, characteristics and outcomes. Therefore international law and politics can, and should, be more individualized, paying much more attention to the specific characteristics of the actors. It may be that blindness could be dangerous for Themis in the international legal system.

It seems to me that a principled approach in international law should be one which takes account not only of relevant principles and norms and their context but also of the consequences, or at least the potential or foreseeable results, of the application of these principles and norms to unique situations. In the international legal system the issue of what measures to undertake should depend not only on the violated principle or norm, but also, and often foremost, on the reasons for deviation from the requirements of international law, the characteristics of the violator and even of its place in the international system.

This means that, when dealing with serious human rights situations, individual states and international bodies have to take into account not only the content of violated principles and norms, but also their own potential to influence events in other countries, as well as the characteristics of those countries.

Sometimes the application of certain measures to enforce compliance with international law may become counterproductive to the achievement of the intended objectives, though in other cases it may work well. Human rights violations, for example, in China or Haiti, which may in many respects be identical (they may, for example, consist of violation of the freedom of expression, the right to fair trial or persecution for political views), cannot be cured by identical means. Whereas a humanitarian intervention may, indeed, restore hopes for democracy in a small island where there are internal forces ready to fight for or, more importantly, work for democracy and human rights, any attempt to push China out of Tibet by force would not only be vetoed in the Security Council, but would be fraught with serious consequences for world peace. Or, to take another example, the people of Saudi Arabia, like the people of North Korea, lack the basic human rights. However, the autocracy in the one, whose legitimacy is based to a great extent on religious and historical traditions as well as on its rich oil resources, is quite different from the communist tyranny in the other, whose lack of practically any legitimacy has to be compensated for by naked force. This means that the possible scenarios for change in these countries are inevitably different.

But does not such a differentiated approach mean that there will be the inevitable double standards in human rights diplomacy against which we spoke in the previous chapter? Probably a threat of double standards remains when human rights violators are treated differently, and that treatment depends not so much on the character of the violation than on the character of the actor who violates. But it seems that there are at least two different kinds of double standard.

Although, under domestic law, courts take into account the characteristics of offenders, their approach to this matter is usually quite different. They are not supposed to be soft with big and strong guys and stricter with the small fry. In the international system, states which violate international law are often treated differently, not because some of them are first-time offenders while others may be recidivists; reaction depends, more often than not, on the strength and importance of the violator-state than on what it deserves. This is what is usually called a 'double standard' in international law and relations. Though there is nothing to be admired in any double standard, it seems to me that in international relations and law there is an objective or inevitable (or at least very difficult to avoid) double standard, and subjective or avoidable (though also in practice sometimes difficult to avoid) double standards.

Individual states, or even the world community as a whole, are limited in their ability to change events in other countries in a positive direction. They inevitably have to choose and to be selective. One needs a superman, not a superpower, to change things at the same time in Bosnia, Rwanda, Burundi, East Timor, Chechnya, Tadjikistan, Kashmir, and a multitude of other places. States and international organizations also have to decide what is possible and what simply is not. This necessitates an objective or inevitable double standard

However, often a double standard is dictated not by these rational, prudent and inevitable calculations of one's ability to change the course of events, but rather by a subjective attitude towards violators. There are friendly and unfriendly dictators; those who kill innocent people, bomb civilian targets or hijack airplanes are not always called terrorists; some of them are called freedom fighters. The end of the Cold War has curtailed the field of application of such double standards, but it has not abolished them completely. For example, while President Milosevic of Serbia was treated rather harshly by the West (and rightly so), the dictatorial and territorial ambitions of President Tudjman of Croatia were condoned, and ethnic cleansing in Krajina went practically unnoticed. This kind of double standard in principle can and must be avoided.

In the domain of human rights, such a double standard can be, if not completely avoided, then at least alleviated, providing the world community and individual states react to all serious human rights violations, while the modalities of that reaction may be different, taking into account, *inter alia*, the characteristics of the violators and the reasons behind the violations. In such a case, there would not be a double standard in the sense that some human rights violators are condemned while others are condoned. At the same time, there would be multiple standards as to the character of reaction to violations, and the main criterion for the choice of reaction would be its potential effectiveness.

One should not forget that, though the practical results and consequences of the enforcement of the principles and norms of international law have to play an important role in human rights diplomacy, of equal importance is the upholding of the authority of international law. And it is well known that every derogation from and violation of its principles and norms, especially if such a derogation remains unrectified, undermines the authority of international law.

How should the world community, in the light of these considerations, respond to human rights violations in different countries, especially to those violations which may constitute a threat to international stability? What should be done when a possible response may itself put international stability at risk? Is intervention by force to stop egregious human rights violations an adequate remedy?

THE LEGITIMACY OF GOVERNMENTS AND HUMAN RIGHTS

In order to answer these questions we have to consider the issue of the legitimacy of governments, because, first, the issue of legitimacy is closely linked with human rights and, second, the higher the degree of legitimacy of the government the more stable a country usually is. Likewise, insufficient legitimacy of a regime may be a cause of domestic instability which, in turn, may lead to a threat to international stability.

A government is legitimate if it is considered as such by the population of the state. As Seymour Martin Lipset wrote: 'Legitimacy involves the capacity of the system to engender and maintain the belief that the existing political institutions are the most appropriate ones for the society'.[1] In the contemporary world, however, the legitimacy of a regime may also depend on external factors. Entities such as the Turkish Republic of Northern Cyprus or the Republic of Srbska may have legitimacy in the eyes of their populations, but the lack of international recognition or legitimation has inhibited them from acting as subjects of international law. This means that we can speak of domestic and international sources of the legitimacy of governments.[2]

Certainly a government which is democratically elected and has a good human rights record is seen as the legitimate authority, both by the population of the state and by the international community. Max Weber spoke of three alternative claims to legitimacy: the authority of 'eternal yesterday', which is like the traditional domination exercised by the patriarch; the authority of the extraordinary and personal gift of grace (charisma); and finally, domination by virtue of legality.[3] Nowadays, only a government with moral and legal authority, including its democratic credentials and its human rights record, can govern 'by virtue of legality'.

Sometimes the lack of democratic credentials coupled with a poor human rights record may be compensated for by domestic sources of legitimacy, such as historical and religious traditions, specific ideology, the personal charisma of a leader, functional efficiency of the government, the presence of rich natural resources, or by international recognition and support. This means that a regime, notwithstanding its poor human rights record, may nevertheless be considered legitimate by the majority of the population and may therefore be quite stable. Consequently such a regime will not usually constitute at least an imminent threat to international peace and stability, in the sense of the 'spill-over' effect. Neither, as a rule, will it have any incentive to seek foreign adventures in order to consolidate its hold on power.

In the Cold War period, some repressive regimes compensated for their lack of legitimacy and poor human rights records by receiving external support from one of the two superpowers. Nimeiri of Sudan, Mengistu of Ethiopia, Siad Barré of Somalia, Karmal and Najibulla of Afghanistan, as well as all the rulers of the Eastern European socialist countries, could only rule thanks to external support. After the withdrawal of this support they all fell, and many of them left behind an appalling legacy. Currently, there are yet more autocrats on the waiting list to be overthrown.

It seems to be possible to generalize that, in the light of the legitimacy factor, which is an important aspect of the internal stability of a state and which therefore has its impact on international stability, we should distinguish two categories of states, both of which have serious problems with human rights.

The first category comprises countries where the denial of human rights goes hand-in-hand with certain historical and religious traditions which facilitate such a denial. For example, in Saudi Arabia or Kuwait, in some other Arab countries, and to a lesser extent in the former Soviet Central Asian republics of Uzbekistan and Turkmenistan, certain historical and religious traditions facilitate the denial or limitation of the civil and political rights of the whole population. I would call the situation in such states not so much a violation of human rights as their denial or absence. Governments in such countries usually do not use, and it is not necessary for them to use, massive repression in order to keep the population in obedience, because the population does not actively claim its rights.

The situation is different in countries where such traditions are absent, but where governments which do not have any popular support nevertheless try to stay in power (for example, military dictatorships, formerly in Latin America or currently in some African countries). In such countries, authoritarian regimes have to resort to massive repression against those who oppose their rule and often actively claim their rights and freedoms.

Of course, there are some situations where we have a rather mixed picture. For example, in the former USSR communist ideology was not the only, or even the foremost, thing which kept the population in obedience and which, to a certain extent, legitimized the regime, not only in the eyes of a substantial part of the population, but even in the eyes of quite a lot of people in the West. The massive repression under Lenin and, especially, under Stalin had created a situation where it was no longer necessary to use wide-scale repression for the absence of rights and freedoms to be accepted by the majority of the population. Similarly, as we saw in Chapter Three, in many Muslim countries, historical and religious traditions which are contrary to human rights are not accepted voluntarily by quite large parts of the population, and the authorities resort to harsh measures against those who do not comply with these traditions.

However, in most cases the distinction is relevant and has to be taken into account when the international community or individual states are considering possible approaches to serious situations of human rights violation.

In both types of case we have either the massive violation of human rights, or their denial. But these two categories of situation have to be dealt with differently, and one of the reasons for such a conclusion is that they differ significantly as to their impact on international stability.

The human rights situation in the first-mentioned category of undemocratic and human rights-hostile states does not, as a rule, constitute an imminent threat to international stability. If the absence of human rights is accepted by the majority of the population, usually because this absence is compensated for by historical and religious traditions, there are no human rights emergencies which would immediately threaten international stability. It may even be that, as argued in Chapter Two, attempts at the immediate introduction of human rights into such unprepared soil would cause serious risks to stability.

However, this does not mean that inequality between men and women, or the absence of the right of political participation, even if not protested against by the majority of the population, should remain without any reaction from outside. In many cases these and similar practices are not accepted voluntarily at all, but nor are they actively protested against, because any attempt to counter them would entail rapid and severe punishment. Moreover, it is necessary to bear in mind that human rights ideas find their way through even without direct prompting on the part of other states or international bodies, and attempts by undemocratic governments to counter human rights ideas may often lead to outright repression – a sure way to social instability.

There is serious doubt whether the legitimacy and stability of regimes such as Saudi Arabia, Morocco and the Gulf Emirates will last, like diamonds, for ever. David Forsythe writes that:

> There are governing arrangements, especially in the non-Western world, whose legitimacy stems in important if partial ways from tradition. But these arrangements are increasingly unstable. The traditional political culture emphasizing authoritarian rule is increasingly challenged by contemporary values of political morality.[4]

The US State Department Country Reports on Human Rights for 1994 informs us that human rights abuses in Saudi Arabia included the torture of prisoners, incommunicado detention, prohibitions or restrictions on the freedom of speech, press and religion, systematic discrimination against women, and strict limitations, and even suppression, of the rights of workers and ethnic and religious minorities. However, the Reports emphasizes also that the Government's legitimacy is based on its adherence to the Shari'a law, and upon the consent of the governed, who are obliged to obey the ruler as long as he continues to govern according to Islamic law.[5]

But the defection to the West in 1994 of a group of Saudi diplomats who revealed gross human rights violations by the governing dynasty,[6] the imprisonment of fifteen university professors for anti-royal activities and the banning of about sixty others from travelling because they had expressed views critical of the government,[7] and the creation – and the banning – of the Committee to Defend Legitimate Rights,[8] are all indications that not everything is stable in the Saudi Kingdom. Emerging economic and financial difficulties[9] may undermine even further the regime whose legitimacy is based not only on historical traditions and religion, but also on its rich oil resources. As Michael Binyon, the diplomatic editor of the Times, writes, 'the threat new to the oil-rich sheikdoms is internal: almost all face rising popular discontent, an economic squeeze, Islamic fundamentalist agitation and potential revolution born of thwarted expectations and stunted political progress'.[10] And the newspaper concludes in its leading article that it is precisely because the partnership of Western democracies with Arab states is valuable that 'the West must impress upon the rulers of all Gulf states the virtues of a more liberal domestic order'.[11]

In the case of such societies the world community's approach should be directed at the gradual improvement of the situation with human rights. Quiet bilateral diplomacy, encouragement to ratify international human rights instruments and consideration of human rights situations in such countries by specialized universal human rights bodies are adequate measures.

In contrast to the first category of undemocratic states, the second category of countries, home to regimes with insufficient legitimacy and which have to resort to massive and usually bloody repressions in order to stay in power, may constitute an imminent threat to international stability.

Governing regimes as well as opposition movements in several Third World countries (for example, Somalia, Liberia, Zaire, Angola, Afghanistan) faced severe legitimacy crises after the withdrawal of external support and recognition. These regimes did not have much, if any, domestic sources of legitimacy. Such countries, many of which were either clients of one of the two superpowers or arenas of the superpower contest, now cause the most serious security problems, which stem, at least partly, from their human rights records.

The fact that a government has to use massive repression in order to stay in power does not only show that it is lacking legitimacy in the eyes of at least some important parts of the population of the country. It may also mean that there are political forces in the country which are pressing for a change. In such circumstances the world community, interfering (not necessarily intervening) for humanitarian and security reasons, may facilitate positive changes at least in some countries. In many of such societies the alternative to gradual liberalization, democratization and the introduction of basic human rights would be either an outright and brutal repression or a rise to power of religious extremists. This would mean quite possibly that the vicious circle would simply repeat itself.

However, in by no means all cases where power-holders repress the rest of the population can one find among the repressed a political force which would itself be committed to human rights, democracy and fundamental freedoms. It is not always that those who fight against tyrants are fighting for freedom and democracy (for example, in Liberia, Afghanistan, Angola). What one can realistically hope to achieve in such cases is, probably, the end of violence and excesses, but not an immediate movement towards democracy or a human rights-friendly society. The priority would be order and the absence of systematic and massive repressions. When this is achieved it may be possible to start gradually to promote other human rights as well. Angola and Mozambique are examples of countries which probably need to go through a process of this sort: the establishment of some degree of order and stability through compromises and balances; the gradual liberalization of the regime; and the introduction of elements of democracy and human rights. Outside interference, in the form of providing assistance or creating stimuli, could in some cases be rather important, though this would only be in addition to the prerequisite need for change felt internally.

It seems that in some societies it is possible or even necessary to push for the gradual introduction of basic human rights without trying to open immediately the floodgates of democracy. Stable authoritarian regimes may be in some instances, and for the time being, preferable to weak governments, even if the latter are freely elected. It has been rightly observed that US officials (not only they, of course) 'extol an election with little attention to the more complex realities of actual political participation. They will herald a new Parliament while knowing little of the actual relations between the Parliament and citizenry'.[12] Elections do not in themselves herald any real progress on the road to democratization. When quick elections, organized and monitored by the UN or other international bodies, are followed by a quick withdrawal, a quick regression is also to be expected. The post-election events in Haiti, Angola and also in Cambodia have shown that elections are only one, and not always the most important, step forward.

This means that in some cases the world community's attention should be focused not so much on free and fair elections as on the observance of the basic human rights, such as the right to life, freedom from torture and physical security of the person. In countries such as, for example, the former Soviet Central Asian republics, it is more realistic to achieve a measure of progress in the observance of basic human rights than it is to have regular free and fair elections (which presumes unhindered activity of opposition, freedom of the press and the right to associate freely). All of these republics, by the way, have had presidential as well as parliamentary elections, but they could hardly be called free and fair. Opposition has been heavy-handedly suppressed, if not actively prosecuted, and the media is completely under governmental control.

Charles Mayenes has a point when he writes that calling for winner-takes-all democratic elections cannot solve problems in countries which have serious ethnic conflicts: 'Indeed, elections may even trigger a conflict, as in Bosnia, where the West foolishly encouraged a referendum on independence that the Serb population boycotted'.[13]

Certainly, democracy and human rights are closely linked, and it is impossible to imagine a human rights-friendly non-democratic state. It also may well be, as Thomas Franck suggests,[14] that an entitlement to democracy is really emerging as a human right. However, it may also be the case that in certain circumstances (e.g., in the presence of strong historical or religious traditions or inter-ethnic tension) the introduction of basic human rights, including, for example, minority or religious rights, should precede the processes of democratization and be part of the process of liberalization. Sometimes attempts to democratize a poor, socially and politically underdeveloped, ethnically or religiously divided society may lead to instability and civil war instead of democracy. Virginia Page Fortna, writing on the Angolan elections of 1992 which were supervised by the UN and which did not succeed in putting an end to the conflict in the country, emphasizes: 'Because of the winner-take-all nature of the elections, each side's preference for peace was conditional on its expectation that it would win the elections. This electoral structure was a crucial flaw in the peace agreement because it gave the loser no stake in the peace and therefore no incentive to cooperate'.[15]

The report of the Commission on Global Governance emphasizes that the winner-take-all system of parliamentary democracy, which may be successful in some countries, has clearly failed in others to ensure the rights of minorities or preserve national cohesion through conciliatory approaches.[16] The report refers to the experience of some countries in Francophone Africa (Benin, Congo, Madagascar, Mali, Niger, Togo) which have recently developed the practice of holding national conferences in which all major political parties and forces are brought together to determine the political destiny of the country. Power-sharing arrangements and the inclusion of all political forces seems often to be preferable to Western-style democracy.

It seems that, in some countries, authoritarian and non-democratic governments (i.e., those which are non-elected or, even if elected, then through elections which are not free and fair at least by Western standards) are simply inevitable in the foreseeable future. Historical or religious traditions may be one of the reasons of such inevitability. This certainly means that rights and freedoms which are directly linked to fair elections, such as the freedom of expression or association, are also restricted or practically non-existent. At the same time, it is impossible to agree that gross and massive violations of the basic human rights (such as the right to life, to freedom from torture and other forms of inhuman and degrading treatment, to the prohibition of racial discrimination, to liberty and security of the person) are also inevitable. Such human rights violations have their roots in the incompetence and inability of authorities to cope with complicated social, economic and political problems, in the corruption of many dictatorships, and in their desire to stay in power at all costs.

DEALING WITH VIOLATIONS OR ADDRESSING THEIR CAUSES?

In countries where human rights emergencies are caused mainly by low levels of societal development (for example, in many African and some Asian countries) it is hardly possible to achieve significant and sustainable progress on human rights without radical improvement of the economic situation, increases in the level of education and health care, and development of other areas of social life. At the same time, one should not forget that often one of the obstacles to economic growth is a corrupt regime which itself may enjoy all the material benefits of civilization only by repressing popular discontent. Here we see that, in the same way that it is hardly possible to promote respect for human rights and freedoms without radical economic and social development and change, it is equally difficult to achieve the necessary development without changing corrupt and repressive regimes. Usually it is the government which is the main obstacle in the way of development rather than external factors, though the latter may either contribute to development or, on the contrary, hinder it.

In this respect it is interesting to read, for example, the UNDP programmes for Liberia – a country which is currently in the throes of civil war and a humanitarian emergency – prepared in the 1980s. These programmes stressed that the country, which was endowed with considerable natural resources, which had many qualified people among its population, and which had received one of the highest *per capita* aid allocations in Africa, was nevertheless in the midst of a serious economic and financial crisis.[17] The new programmes recommended new economic measures which had been agreed with the government. The 1986 country programme, for example, allocated for these purposes $12,400,000. Alas, as we now know, this did not help either, and the country succumbed to a bloody fratricidal war.

What went so wrong? Why did these financial injections and economic programmes not work? There are, probably, several reasons; but one of the deficiencies of these programmes was that they completely ignored the fact that Dow's regime was bloody, repressive and corrupt, and that therefore no financial injection or even economic reform could change the situation in that country as it stood.

As most serious human rights problems are not simply historical aberrations due to the ill will of an evil leader, but have their roots in the social and political structures of society, it is hardly possible to deal with such human rights violations by means of short-term surgical measures – though, as we will try to show in Chapter Six, such measures may sometimes become necessary.

As the experience of those countries where authoritarian governments have been substituted by democratic or at least democratizing regimes shows, and even where liberalization was initiated by enlightened leaders who had been part of the old regime, it was necessary for new leaders and political forces to come to power. Mikhail Gorbachev and F. W. de Clerk, both Nobel Peace Prize winners and men who really contributed most to the positive changes at the end of the millennium, had just started to put reforms in place when events took over and they both lost their political power. Argentine and Chilean generals had to make way for civilian politicians. Marcos of the Philippines, the South Korean generals, Baginda of Malawi and many other dictators had to go before real changes in the human rights situations in their respective countries were possible. It seems that even such a dictator like Saddam Hussein can, in principle, end all of his programmes for the production of weapons of mass destruction and allow UN monitors to operate freely in the country, or even give plausible guarantees against any Iraqi attack on its neighbours. However, Saddam Hussein cannot loosen the reins of his dictatorship and guarantee even a minimum of human rights for Iraqi citizens, because this would bring about the end of his power.

This raises an important question: is the international promotion and protection of human rights a purely humanitarian matter, as it is often declared to be, or an important political issue? It seems that, in cases of gross and massive human rights violations, purely humanitarian measures are often simply palliatives. Radical changes of the human rights situations in most countries where serious human rights violations take place necessitate deep social and political reforms, though it may be that sometimes the introduction of certain limited rights and freedoms leads to a change of a regime.

One should not expect rapid improvements in human rights situations in countries where historical and religious traditions, a low level of societal development, and vested interests of power-holders all work against the promotion of human rights. As *The Economist* writes of China: 'Nobody expects it to turn tamely into a parliamentary democracy any time soon'.[18] However, without gradual liberalization, these societies are doomed to stagnation and they will also remain sources of at least a potential threat to international stability.

In the light of these considerations I would recommend that, in the determination of human rights diplomacy, serious consideration should be given to at least the following factors:

(a) The characteristics of a society where violations take place, its level of development, historical, religious and cultural traditions (in order not to be misunderstood, I would like to emphasize that these factors should be taken into account not as a justification of human rights violations, but in order to understand their causes and to choose adequate methods of dealing with them).

(b) The concrete causes of human rights violations, which may be conditioned by specific characteristics of a society, but may also be more or less independent from them (for example, inter-ethnic tension, including the reasons for such tension; religious intolerance; the degree of exploitation of these factors for political purposes; suppression of popular discontent caused by economic difficulties or social inequalities, etc.).

(c) The characteristics of human rights violations (whether they occur on a massive scale and in a systematic way and involve practically all basic rights and freedoms, or whether there are violations of just some specific human rights standards). Which rights and freedoms are violated (civil, political or social and economic rights, individual rights or group rights, etc.).

The responses of individual states or international bodies to human rights violations, in order to be effective, have to vary depending on these factors. Though it may not be easy, it is nevertheless also necessary to make a distinction between the genuine difficulties and obstacles which some societies face in their efforts to improve their human rights situation and the pretexts used by some governments to justify their derogations from international human rights standards.

For example, poor prison conditions, or the absence of a legislation on the state of emergency, or deficiencies of Article 114 of the Criminal Code of Estonia (concerning the definition of torture which does not include mental torture) – shortcomings which were highlighted by the UN Human Rights Committee as factors which caused serious concern[19] – may, to a great extent, have been inherited from the Soviet past. There are many positive changes in the laws and practices concerning human rights in Estonia, and the authorities are making considerable efforts in order to improve the situation with regard to human rights in the country. Not everything can be done quickly. However, the most serious problem which was the object of criticism by the Human Rights Committee – citizenship legislation, the law on aliens, and the situation of the Russian-speaking minority generally[20] – is a problem which was created by the nationalistic policies of successive Estonian governments which came to power after Estonia had regained its independence in 1991. The different origins of these problems deserve different approaches to their resolution.

One encouraging tendency seems to be an increasing understanding among decision-makers that, in the new situation, in which human rights issues can be looked at without the distorting lens of the Cold War,[21] it is both possible and necessary to address the root causes of human rights emergencies and disasters. This was a leitmotif of the UN Secretary General's 'Agenda for Peace', as well as of several resolutions of the last (51st) session of the UN Commission on Human Rights. In his Agenda for Peace the Secretary General outlined the UN's new approaches to preventive diplomacy, peace-making, peace-keeping, and post-conflict peace-building. Among the deepest causes of conflicts he named were economic despair, social injustice and political oppression, and he emphasized that 'one requirement for solutions lies in the commitment to human rights with special sensitivity to those of minorities, whether ethnic, religious, social or linguistic'.[22]

The resolution of the 51st session of the UN Commission on Human Rights, 'Human Rights and Mass Exoduses', referring to the statements of the Secretary General, noted that 'humanitarian assistance was essential but must be complemented by measures to address the root causes of complex emergencies'.[23]

Equally, the US State Department's Report on Human Rights for 1994 emphasizes that

with the passing of the Cold War we find ourselves in a new

international strategic environment. The human rights abuses of governments are accompanied by ethnic tension, breakdown of authority, and environmental destruction. As a result, human rights promotion must synthesize familiar forms of pressure and advocacy with *long term structural reform and the support of grassroots movements for change.*[24] (emphasis added)

The new AID (the US Agency for International Development) administrator, who came to this post from the National Democratic Institute for International Affairs, has made the promotion of democracy one of the elements of the Agency's overall strategy of promotioning sustainable development.[25]

Efforts of this kind will take time; but only in such a way is it possible to have sustainable progress on human rights in societies where it is most needed.

BILATERAL PLUS MULTILATERAL HUMAN RIGHTS DIPLOMACY

In human rights diplomacy, like in many other areas of foreign policy, there is a choice between bilateral and multilateral efforts. Human rights situations can be dealt with by individual states applying measures against violators, or, alternatively, human rights issues can be raised in international fora, such as the UN General Assembly, the UN Commission on Human Rights or other universal or different regional treaty bodies, or even in the Security Council if a human rights situation is deemed to constitute a threat to international peace and security.

Bilateral human rights diplomacy will certainly remain an important means for the promotion of human rights, though there should be closer cooperation among like-minded states on measures undertaken against human rights violators.

Human rights issues can and should be raised in bilateral relations because measures applied on a bilateral basis, especially when coordinated with those of other states, may sometimes be more effective than discussions and even resolutions adopted in a multi-lateral forum where those states which have serious problems with human rights, even if they are not in majority, may have at least a substantial voice in the decision-making process. It seems that quiet bilateral diplomacy can sometimes bear more fruit than open condemnation.[26] Measures of encouragement and constructive engagement are usually more effective than punitive counter-measures.

However, the latter cannot be altogether excluded either. Decisions on whether to apply counter-measures should depend on the character of and reasons for violations, as well as on the characteristics of the violator. And they should depend less on the political relations between a violator and the responding states. During the Cold War, as we saw in the previous chapter, the last factor was, unfortunately, overwhelmingly decisive.

The linkage between international trade and human rights does not seem to be particularly effective. International trade relations are usually too important to be sacrificed for a human rights cause, especially as it is often rather doubtful whether trade sanctions have any positive effect on the human rights situation they are meant to change. The American embargo against Cuba has been a complete failure. On the contrary, the current tendency of opening up the country to the outside world may gradually put an end to Castro's regime.

Sanctions often hit those whose plight they are meant to improve. As Lori Fisler Damrosch writes:

> Yet as months stretch into years, the international community has become painfully aware that some programs of collective economic sanctions, begun with the best of intentions, may severely harm the very people they are intended to help. There is the perception, and possibly the reality, that the sanctions, rather than the crises to which they respond, have created humanitarian emergencies.[27]

The policy of pinching the population in the hope that they will rise and rid themselves of their oppressors may not only be immoral, but seems hardly to work. Professor Damrosch, though having doubts as to the effectiveness of economic sanctions and recognizing the damaging effect they may often have on innocent people, nevertheless endorses the trend in the literature which appreciates 'the norm-reinforcing reasons for going ahead with sanctions against violators of international norms, even when there might be little reason to expect the sanctions to achieve their declared objectives in the short term'.[28]

I believe that using economic sanctions or other such heavy measures merely in order to maintain the sanctity of norms, or for norm-reinforcing reasons, without taking into account the factor of the effectiveness (both short-term and long-term) of such sanctions or other measures and their possible 'collateral' damage for the population at large whose rights and freedoms they are deemed to protect, would only undermine the international norms whose sanctity the measures were meant to support.

Let us take as an example the UN sanctions against Iraq. Sanctions against Iraq were not imposed, of course, because of Saddam Hussein's atrocious human rights record but because of its aggression against Kuwait. However, so far these sanctions, which have been in force since 1991, have not succeeded in changing the character of the regime. Instead, they have severely hurt the victims of Saddam's regime. David Keen, writing about the plight of the Iraqi Kurds, observes that 'UN sanctions are deepening the suffering of a people whose access to necessities has already been severely hit by the GOI [Government of Iraq] blockade. They are also inhibiting the rehabilitation of Iraqi Kurdistan and thereby helping to undermine the security they are intended to bolster'.[29]

The report released in September 1995 by the World Food Programme (WFP) stated that 'alarming food shortages are causing irreparable damage to an entire generation of Iraqi children'; that there are 'more than 4 million people, a fifth of Iraq's population at severe nutritional risk'; and that 'the social fabric of the nation is disintegrating'.[30] *The Economist* writes that 'this social implosion could be more of a threat to regional stability and security than the odd new missile or stock of germs that Mr Ekeus may unearth'.[31]

Moreover, it is often economic engagement, not sanctions (which usually lead to the isolation of a target state), which, at least in long term, may bring about political and humanitarian reforms. *The Economist*, for example, believes, and I tend to agree, that economic reforms and liberalization represent the best chance of making China easier to live with, both by creating internal pressures for more political freedom and by strengthening China's interest in getting on with the rest of the world.[32] James Lilley writes that 'through encouraging broadened American involvement in China's economy, the United States fosters democratic forces and enhances human rights'.[33]

This does not mean that human rights and democracy would automatically follow economic growth, or that economic engagement should not be accompanied by criticism of human rights in a country which is being engaged. As the State Department country report on human rights for 1995 emphasizes, trade and rising Chinese prosperity cannot themselves bring about greater respect for human rights in the absence of a willingness by the political authorities to abide by fundamental international norms.[34] Democracy and human rights seldom, if ever, come as the gifts of authorities. It has always been necessary to struggle for rights and freedoms. In the case of China, the world community can support those reformers and dissidents who emerge in the process of economic reforms and development. However, if the reforms fail there is little hope for democracy and human rights in China. Asian experience shows that those countries (Taiwan, South Korea, Thailand) which have carried out successful economic reforms and are rapidly developing, have also become more liberal, while North Korea, Vietnam and Myanmar remain repressive.

Such a negative approach to economic sanctions as a means of dealing with human rights situations does not mean that they should never be used, or that they can never have any positive effect. But, as Louis Henkin writes, 'states are induced, not coerced to comply'.[35] Although this pronouncement corresponds to the basic characteristics of the international system, and therefore rings true in most cases, one should not absolutize it. Coercion can, for example, have a deterrent effect against an aggressor state. Even in certain cases of human rights violations it may be possible to use economic sanctions which target only the regime, without significant adverse effects on the population at large.[36] However, this seems to be rather rare, and appears only to work when there is a clear distinction between a regime and the majority of the population (like there was in Southern Rhodesia and South Africa), or in the case of a completely corrupt regime which pockets all the proceeds from external economic relations.

These conclusions obviously do not extend to arms embargos or to the linkage between the trade in weapons and human rights. Nor do they prevent financial and economic assistance to repressive governments being made dependent on the recipient's human rights record, especially when we take into account the fact that assistance to oppressive and corrupt regimes seldom changes anything in the plight of the population. It may even be that in contradistinction to trade and other forms of economic cooperation which help to open societies, economic assistance may sometimes contribute to their stagnation. Therefore I find quite justified, for example, the decision made on 28 July 1995 by the British Government to freeze the bulk of a new aid programme for Kenya promised in 1994, not only because of President Moi's poor political and economic record but also because of the regime's widespread abuse of human rights.[37]

If economic sanctions seldom have the desired effect in cases of human rights violations, economic incentives can work in more positive ways. Turkey, for example, on 23 July 1995 lifted some of the restrictions on civil liberties which were written into its 1982 Constitution by the military. As *The Economist* observes, though the avowed purpose of these reforms was to increase democratic rights, the real purpose was to hold on to Turkey's chances of joining the

European Union one day. In the Autumn of 1995, the European Parliament had to approve a deal that allows Turkey to enter into a customs union on manufactured goods with the EU in 1996.[38] On 13 December 1995 the European Parliament approved (by 343 votes for, 149 against) a customs union between the EU and Turkey.[39] Though it is always very difficult to predict all possible consequences of such acts, especially as to their impact on democracy and human rights, it seems that more can be achieved by inclusion than exclusion.

However, it is necessary to stress that every human rights situation is unique, and it would be unwise to propose general recipes which would be applicable to all situations. What seems to be clear is that economic pressure for the sake of human rights should be used in a manner which hits violators and not the victims of those violations (otherwise the pressure may be simply counter-productive), and, to be effective, the pressure has to be, as a rule, if not multilateral, then at least coordinated.[40]

Multilateral human rights diplomacy has several advantages over bilateral measures. First, its decisions carry greater legitimacy and are seen to be more impartial than the unilateral acts of states. Second, measures undertaken by international bodies also have a less marked effect on sensitive bilateral relations in other areas of cooperation. The institutionalization of human rights at the international level also gives them additional stability, making them less vulnerable to the inevitable political fluctuations. Finally, though human rights, as we have tried to show, may seriously affect inter-state relations and have, therefore, acquired a steady place in bilateral diplomacy, they are, by their very nature, not a bilateral issue but a universal one, an issue to be dealt with by the world community as a whole.

Human rights violations, especially gross and systematic ones, are *erga omnes* violations of international law which are not committed against a specific foreign state. They are violations which affect the world community of states as a whole and are committed against the interest of all peoples in the maintenance and promotion of the international human rights regime. Therefore, when states individually raise issues of human rights, they are acting on behalf of the world community. That is why the individual acts of states on human rights issues are usually effective only when supported by strong international mechanisms and procedures. Therefore it will be important to give a radical boost to international human rights mechanisms and procedures, especially to those which function in the UN framework and concern all states.

It is undeniable that there has been considerable progress in the domain of what is called in United Nations parlance 'international standard-setting on human rights'. The UN can also take credit for some success in the domain of the promotion of human rights. It has contributed significantly to the promotion of rights consciousness, and has facilitated the adoption of national norms and the establishment of national institutes on human rights in many countries. But the United Nations has been quite weak in the domain of the protection or enforcement of human rights standards.[41]

It seems that several UN human rights procedures, some of which have never been particularly effective while others seem to have exhausted their usefulness, continue to exist simply through institutional inertia. Take, for example, the so-called '1503 procedure', under which the UN Commission on Human Rights and its Sub-Commission on Prevention of Discrimination and Protection of Minorities can consider individual petitions on human rights violations if such petitions help to identify situations involving 'a consistent pattern of gross and reliably attested violation' of human rights. It is difficult not to agree with Philip Alston, who writes of this procedure:

> In general, it would seem [to Alston] that the shortcomings of the procedure are so considerable, its tangible achievements so scarce, the justifications offered in its favour so modest, and the need for an effective and universally applicable petition procedure so great, that it is time to reevaluate its future.[42]

The end of the Cold War has brought about some positive, though still very modest, changes in the UN approach to human rights.

One of the measures in the right direction was the creation in 1993 of the post of UN High Commissioner for Human Rights, who has a mandate to play an active role in removing the current obstacles and meeting the challenges to the full realization of all human rights, and in preventing the continuation of human rights violations throughout the world. The High Commissioner has to engage in dialogue with all Governments in the implementation of his mandate.

The High Commissioner, whose task it is also to coordinate human rights activities within the UN system, has defined his priorities in the report to the General Assembly of 2 November 1995 as follows:

(a) early warning on emergency human rights situations;
(b) field missions by the various special rapporteurs or working groups;
(c) follow-up action of the High Commissioner on recommendations made by special rapporteurs and working groups;

(d) the work of other implementation mechanisms and the provision of advisory services and technical assistance to member states.[43]

One of the positive steps in UN human rights activities has been the transfer of quite a substantial part of the UN's efforts from Geneva or New York to the field where human rights violations occur. In Chapter Six I will deal in some detail with UN field operations, which are often related to issues of international peace and security. Here I would like to emphasize that the High Commissioner himself has visited many areas of human rights emergencies, such as Rwanda and Burundi (between mid-1994 and mid-1995 he payed three visits to both of these countries). Offices of the High Commissioner have been created in Bujumbura (Burundi)[44] and Lilongwe (Malawi).[45] The High Commissioner's special representative visited the Russian Federation, including Chechnya, and the High Commissioner himself discussed the situation in Chechnya with the Foreign Minister of Russia.[46]

While undertaking missions to various countries, the High Commissioner is paving the way for cooperation between governments and the United Nations organs and bodies. Of course, there is a danger that some governments which do not cooperate with the Commission on Human Rights or its special rapporteurs and representatives will try to use the visits of the High Commissioner as a smokescreen. However, the High Commissioner seems to be aware of this danger since, in his report, he emphasizes that his presence in a country does not replace the missions and other activities of competent mechanisms, in particular the visits by the special rapporteurs and representatives of the UN Commission on Human Rights or the activities of treaty bodies.[47] Finding a proper balance between constructive engagement in a dialogue with governments and criticism of them seems to be one of the most difficult and delicate tasks of the High Commissioner.

The High Commissioner has also an important role to play in streamlining and coordinating all UN human rights activities, as well as in feeding human rights issues into the work of the political and developmental bodies of the United Nations.

Even treaty bodies (i.e., bodies which supervise the implementation of human rights treaties) have started to move from Geneva closer to the field. For example, the Committee on Economic, Social and Cultural Rights sent a technical assistance mission to Panama in April 1995.[48] In June 1995 the Special Rapporteur on follow-up of the views of the Human Rights Committee, Andreas Mavrommatis, visited Jamaica at the invitation of the Jamaican Government. Jamaica had had problems with the Committee for a number of years over the death-row phenomenon and the requirement of fair trial (Articles 6, 7 and 14 of the Covenant on Civil and Political Rights). During his visit, Mr Mavrommatis visited five penitentiaries and spoke to numerous inmates. As a result of the visit, the Jamaican Government commuted the sentences of all persons awaiting execution (on death row) who had been sentenced in violation of Article 14 of the Covenant.[49]

There are country programmes of advisory services and of technical assistance on human rights for dozens of countries currently being administered by the United Nations.

The High Commissioner, who has already been active in various crisis situations, should attempt to focus UN attention more on those human rights situations which may eventually lead to humanitarian catastrophes or emergencies and undermine international stability. Currently the various UN human rights bodies, which have multiplied as a result of the adoption of different human rights instruments (there are currently in the UN framework six so-called treaty bodies, which monitor the implementation of respective human rights instruments), often duplicate their efforts and spend time and resources dealing with issues which can be better dealt with at the regional or domestic level. Concentration on the 'routine' monitoring functions over the implementation of UN human rights instruments in a permanently functioning super-committee,[50] and focusing the attention of other bodies and the High Commissioner on human rights situations which can serve as an early warning for humanitarian catastrophes and security risks, should be one of the trends in the development of international human rights mechanisms.

Currently the UN Centre for Human Rights in Geneva, and the various other UN human rights bodies which also function mainly in Geneva, are detached from political and security organs such as the Security Council, the General Assembly or the Department of Political Affairs, which are based in New York. There is a lack of cooperation between New York and Geneva which, as a result, leads to the marginalization of the latter, which means that human rights issues do not find a proper place in the decision-making of the political organs of the United Nations. Of course, such a situation is not only due to faults in the institutional mechanism of the UN. Its origins lie mainly in the fact, observed earlier, that though almost all states engage in human rights diplomacy, it seldom ranks high in their political priorities.

Besides the United Nations there are many other international organizations of universal as well as regional character which focus their attention on human rights issues.

The Council of Europe, basically through the mechanisms of the European Convention on Human Rights and Fundamental Freedoms, has achieved remarkable progress on human rights in Western Europe. The European Social Charter, the European Convention for the Prevention of Torture, and many other instruments adopted within the Council of Europe directly or indirectly related to human rights, have also been rather effective.

The end of the Cold War brought about new activities for the Council in the domain of human rights. Its extension to the East necessitated its attention to human rights situations in countries which formerly belonged to the communist bloc. Advisory services and programmes of technical assistance established by the Council of Europe for the countries of Central and Eastern Europe and CIS member-states have played an important role in constitutional and legal reforms in these countries.

As we have seen in Chapter Two, the Council of Europe has started to pay more and more attention to the problems of ethnic minorities. The adoption in 1992 of the European Charter for Regional and Minority Languages,[51] and in 1995 of the Framework Convention for the Protection of National Minorities,[52] show that the Council of Europe is seriously concerned with minority issues in Europe, and especially in Eastern Europe. Similarly, the OSCE, mainly through the activities of the High Commissioner on National Minorities, is concentrating on minority issues wherever they may threaten the peace and security in Europe.

Though the European Union is not an organization whose aim is to protect or promote human rights, there is no doubt that, because of its attractiveness and economic power, it may have a deeper, though usually a more indirect, effect on human rights in some countries than might many of the specialized human rights bodies. Earlier in this chapter we saw that the desire of Turkey to enter into a customs union with the EU, approved by the European Parliament (which has been rather critical of the Turkish human rights record), prompted the Turkish authorities to initiate changes in the Constitution and criminal laws of the country. In Autumn 1995 the European Parliament threatened to suspend EU assistance to Slovakia and expressed its grave concern at the policies of the Slovak Government which had showed insufficient respect for democracy, human rights and minority rights and the rule of law.[53] The anger of the Euro-MPs was caused by the persecution of opposition politicians by the government of Mr Meciar and by the new Slovak language law which restricted the use of the Hungarian language in areas where the Hungarian minority makes up 20 per cent or more of the population.

In December 1991 the European Community member-states adopted a set of 'Guidelines on the recognition of new states in Eastern Europe and in the Soviet Union'.[54] These guidelines, referring to the traditional criteria of recognition of new states, also established some new criteria, such as the rule of law, democracy and respect for human rights, especially the rights of ethnic minorities. Though the EC member-states did not take these guidelines seriously enough, and relied exclusively on promises made by governments to observe all human rights, the very idea of tying recognition to the observance of at least basic human rights is to be welcomed.

The Inter-American system of the protection of human rights, based on the American Convention on Human Rights adopted in 1969,[55] though not so effective as its European counterpart, has nevertheless contributed to positive changes in many Latin American countries. It is difficult, and may yet be too early, to say anything concrete about the effect of the African Charter on Human and Peoples' Rights which was opened for signature in 1981 and came into force in 1986.[56] However, as John Merrills remarks, 'the African Charter on Human and Peoples' Rights is nevertheless already a milestone in a continent where under-development and undemocratic government are endemic, and progress on human rights an urgent and a pressing need'.[57]

It is an important new development that the international financial institutions have started to pay attention to human rights. The European Bank for Reconstruction and Development (EBRD), created in 1990, enjoys in this respect a special place among international organizations. Being in the first place a financial institution, it has a distinctively political mandate. Article 1 of the Agreement establishing the EBRD requires that the countries in which the Bank operates be committed to the principles of multi-party democracy, pluralism and market economy. The monitoring of adherence to these principles is integrated into the Bank's operations and reflected in the Bank's country strategy papers, which include an assessment of a country's commitment to Article 1. Monitoring democratic reforms and especially minority situations is done in close cooperation with the European Union, the OSCE and the Council of Europe.[58] André Newburg, General Council of the EBRD, writes:

> Underlying these provisions is the conviction that sustained economic development and the operation of a sound market

economy must be rooted in the rule of law, a constitutional order and respect for human rights. The history of economic development has tended to show that without the support of an effective system of civil and political rights, economic investment can take unproductive forms leading to a serious waste of resources. A constitutional order and a sound legal framework are essential conditions for the creation of the climate of confidence that releases the energies of entrepreneurs, attracts foreign investment and fosters the development of a robust market economy.[59]

Though the World Bank, in contrast to the EBRD, does not have any political or humanitarian mandate, it is important to note that its activities are often directly relevant to human rights.

In Chapter Two, where issues related to economic development and human rights were discussed, we saw that in many countries in order to promote human rights (not only social and economic but also civil and political rights) it is necessary to overcome abject poverty. Therefore, the financial assistance of the World Bank, helping to promote economic growth, indirectly contributes also to the human rights cause. However, recent steps taken by the Bank have had a more direct influence on human rights in developing countries.

As the World Bank's financial assistance can be effective only if there is a necessary minimum of political and legal infrastructure in a recipient country, since the beginning of the 1990s the Bank has started to finance programmes with a view to reforming the institutional, legal and judicial systems of such countries. Ibrahim Shihata, Senior Vice President and General Council of the World Bank, writes that 'the Bank's experience has confirmed that successful implementation of fundamental policy changes in the business environment and in the financial sector would normally require fundamental changes in the overall legal and institutional framework'.[60] In 1992 the World Bank made its first loan exclusively for judicial reform, in Venezuela.[61] This was followed by a credit for Tanzania for financial and legal upgrading[62] and for Mozambique for the project called *The Mozambique: Capacity Building, Public Sector and Legal Institutions Development Project*.[63] A similar project for Moldova is based on the conviction of the Bank that, in order to ensure the proper application of new laws which need to be promulgated, Moldova will have to take measures which will ensure the independence of its judiciary, provide the courts with clear and final authority to resolve commercial disputes meaningfully, provide training for its judges, and institute the systematic publication and wide dissemination of judicial decisions and legislative acts and regulations.[64] And as Mr Shihata concludes, 'good governance implies the appropriate management of a country's resources, based upon sound rules which are implemented by effective institutions. It also requires predictability, and due legal process which, in turn, assumes a government of laws and not a government of men'.[65]

The role of an independent and impartial judiciary in securing the stability of commercial, financial or investment transactions is similar to its role in guaranteeing basic human rights, such as the right to liberty of the person and the right to fair trial. There is a close relationship between these two functions of the judiciary. For example, the allocation of oil or gas exploration contracts, not through fair competition, but by using what in the former Soviet Union was called 'the telephone law' (i.e., the party boss called the judge and told him what to do and which way to decide), and the suppression of political opposition to the regime, are two sides of the same coin. In such circumstances, promotion of the rule of law, independence of the judiciary and similar measures have an economic as well as human rights dimension. The remedy against an arbitrary arrest and against an arbitrary breach of contract is, in principle, the same – the rule of law and an independent judiciary. Human rights cannot develop without the necessary infrastructure in the form of relatively well developed market relations, and of institutional, including judicial, and legal prerequisites. International financial institutions can play an important role in the development of these prerequisites. The UN Commission on Human Rights, in its resolution of 24 February 1995, requested the Secretary-General to invite the international financial institutions to continue considering the possibility of organizing an expert seminar on the role of those institutions in the realization of economic, social and cultural rights.[66]

It is difficult to overestimate the role of the non-governmental (both national and international) organizations (NGOs) in the promotion and protection of human rights. Their activity, and the media coverage of some cases of gross and systematic violation of human rights, have helped to create a kind of global 'constituency' for human rights. 'The pointed finger of shame, particularly when directed by an organization with some appearance of impartiality and political independence', writes David Weissbrodt, 'has caused executions to be stayed, death sentences to be commuted, torture to be stopped, prison conditions to be ameliorated, prisoners to be released, and more attention to be paid to the fundamental rights of many citizens'.[67]

In preparation for, and during, the 1993 Vienna World Conference on Human Rights, NGOs saw to it that the Conference did not fail. In all, 841 NGOs were accredited to the Conference and they exerted a significant influence on the content of the Vienna Declaration and the Programme of Action, especially in their emphasis on women's rights and their call for the creation of the post of High Commissioner on Human Rights.[68]

Many human rights NGOs have 'consultative status', under Article 71 of the UN Charter, and regularly participate in the work of different UN inter-governmental or expert human rights bodies, such as the UN Commission on Human Rights or the Human Rights Committee. Although, for example, the NGOs do not have any official standing under the Covenant on Civil and Political Rights before the Human Rights Committee, their contribution to the work of the Committee has been enormous. Amnesty International, the International League for Human Rights, Article 19, Human Rights Watch, the International Commission of Jurists, and many other NGOs, present their material to the members of the Committee, who use them widely, especially in preparation for the consideration of state reports on the implementation of the Covenant. This is true also for other so-called treaty bodies which monitor the observance of other UN human rights instruments. Thanks to its specific status (as a treaty body as well as a subsidiary organ of ECOSOC) and its creative approach to its mandate, the Committee on Economic, Social and Cultural Rights (CESCR) has institutionalized its cooperation with NGOs. ECOSOC's resolution 1987/5 invites NGOs to submit to the Committee 'written statements that might contribute to full and universal recognition and realization of the rights in the Covenant'.[69] Though the CESCR cooperates well with non-governmental organizations, and has even set aside the first afternoon of each of its sessions to hear information from them,[70] most influential NGOs are interested in civil and political rights rather than economic and social rights.

It may, of course, be that human rights NGOs are not always perfect, that sometimes the facts or numbers (for example, of prisoners of conscious or disappearances) they quote may not be terribly accurate (especially if we take into account the fact that governments which violate human rights – and therefore are best positioned to know what is going on – are not eager to reveal this information), or that occasionally some NGOs concentrate too much attention on certain issues or aspects of human rights situations which may distort the overall picture.[71] However, generally it is amazing how well informed and accurate most respectful human rights NGOs are in their criticism and assessment of the human rights records of most countries. The collapse of the Soviet Union, for example, revealed that those NGOs which had been accused by the Soviet authorities as mouthpieces of Western special services (e.g., Amnesty International, the International League for Human Rights, various Helsinki groups) had been quite accurate in their criticism of the Soviet human rights record.

Human rights NGOs are active, and also cooperate with inter-governmental bodies, in field operations during humanitarian crises. Cambodia, El Salvador, Haiti, Somalia, Rwanda, Burundi, Northern Iraq and the former Yugoslavia are only the most prominent examples. It has been claimed, for example, that in Somalia in certain circumstances the NGOs could do work which the UN system was unable to do.[72]

Though states, and even inter-governmental human rights bodies, do not always work on the same wavelength as NGOs, the former, if they are interested in the promotion of human rights in the world, should encourage in any possible way the activities of human rights NGOs and rely on them in their human rights diplomacy. Peter Spiro is right in emphasizing that 'bringing NGOs more deeply into the fold of international institutions – in the United Nations (UN), regional bodies, international financial institutions (IFIs), and the organs of world trade – could enhance the legitimacy of those institutions, as well as promote greater responsibility among the NGOs themselves'.[73] The High Commissioner of Human Rights has also emphasized that the United Nations is strongly interested in close cooperation with non-governmental organizations, as well as in the implementation of its human rights programme through the non-governmental organizations, if their potentials so allow. NGOs are natural partners of the High Commissioner: regular meetings and consultations with them have become an important component of his activities.[74]

CONCLUSIONS

In the contemporary world, various entities – states individually or in coordination with like-minded governments, inter-governmental institutions and NGOs – are engaged in human rights diplomacy. They have different interests, possibilities and mandates. For some states, human rights diplomacy is reduced to efforts to justify their human rights records and ward off any criticism as interference in internal affairs. For example, in December 1995 China's Foreign Ministry spokesman, responding to criticism of the Chinese authorities over the imprisonment of Wei Jingsheng, declared that 'the Chinese judicial authorities had dealt with this issue according to the law and it was entirely an internal affair of China'. He added that 'China is a sovereign state' and that 'unwarranted remarks amounting to wilful interference in China's internal affairs by any foreign country or individuals [sic!] are totally unacceptable to us'.[75]

Human rights diplomacy has very different societies and governments as its addressees. The methods or forms of human rights diplomacy depend on agents, their interests and possibilities, as well as on the characteristics of the addressees. These methods vary from quiet diplomacy, open criticism, diplomatic protests and *démarches* to various sanctions.

Human rights diplomacy in a narrow sense is often reactive rather than pro-active. It deals with effects without addressing their causes. However, one should not underestimate the potential of such reactive diplomacy on human rights issues, especially if we take into account that sometimes by addressing the effects one may also reach the causes. At the same time, one should not forget that various characteristics of society, such as the level of its economic and political development, social cohesion, and its historical and religious traditions, put rather strict limits on what any human rights diplomacy can achieve at any given moment. Since these characteristics are not immutable it may be that what is not possible today may become feasible tomorrow. Often indirect methods, such as the activities of international financial bodies, international trade and other forms of economic cooperation, which open societies to the outside world, achieve more in changing the underlying conditions of human rights violations than direct human rights diplomacy. However, sometimes a threat to the most fundamental human rights, like the right to life for thousands of human beings, is, rephrasing the famous *Caroline* formula,[76] 'instant, overwhelming, leaving no choice of means and no moment for deliberation'. What should and could be the response of the world community to such situations will be discussed in the next chapter.

6 Human rights, peace and the use of force

As we have seen, improvements in human rights are, as a rule, only incremental; progress, if any, is usually slow; and 'shock therapy' is not a medicine which cures serious human rights situations. However, there can exist human rights emergencies which, using the medical analogy, do call for 'surgical interference'. In this chapter I will attempt to analyse the potential of, as well as the limits on, the use of force in order to protect human rights. In this context I will also discuss the new developments in UN field operations – operations whose aims may be primarily either political or military, with some human rights component; or primarily humanitarian with political or military aspects playing a supporting role.

ON HUMANITARIAN INTERVENTION

One of the most controversial problems of international law and politics has for many years been the issue of humanitarian intervention,[1] i.e., intervention when the professed reason for intervening is the violation of fundamental human rights, when the professed purpose of the intervention is redress of such violations and when the intervention is carried out in the name of the international community, or more generally, of humanity.[2]

Authorities on international law, such as Hugo Grotius and Emerich de Vattel, considered humanitarian intervention to be in conformity with natural law. Grotius wrote in 1625 in *De Jure Belli ac Pacis* that if a tyrant 'should inflict upon his subjects such treatment as no one is warranted in inflicting, the exercise of the right vested in human society is not precluded'.[3] Emmerich de Vattel, writing in 1758, believed that 'if a prince, by violating the fundamental laws, gives his subjects a lawful cause for resisting him; if, by his insupportable tyranny, he brings a national revolt against him, any foreign power may rightfully give assistance to oppressed people who ask for its aid'.[4]

One of the most authoritative and comprehensive studies of international law of the twentieth century, *Oppenheim's International Law*, has recognized through all its editions (to date there are nine of them), though cautiously and with many qualifications, the right to intervene on humanitarian grounds. In 1905, Oppenheim himself stated:

> Should a State venture to treat its own subjects or part of thereof with such cruelty as would stagger humanity, public opinion of the rest of the world would call upon the powers to exercise intervention for the purpose of compelling such a State to establish a legal order of things within its boundaries sufficient to guarantee to its citizens an existence more adequate to the ideas of modern civilization.[5]

Sir Hersch Lauterpacht, in his much-quoted fifth edition of *Oppenheim* which was published in 1955, was very close to his predecessor on the issue of humanitarian intervention:

> There is a substantial body of opinion and practice in support of the view that ... when a state renders itself guilty of cruelties against and persecution of its nationals in such a way as to deny their fundamental rights and to shock the conscience of mankind, intervention in the interest of humanity is legally permissible.[6]

In 1992, Sir Robert Jennings and Sir Arthur Watts, who edited the most recent edition of *Oppenheim*, are more cautious, but nevertheless conclude that:

> If humanitarian intervention is ever to be justified, it will only be in extreme and very particular circumstances. Crucial considerations are likely to include whether there is a compelling and urgent situation of extreme and large-scale humanitarian distress demanding immediate relief; whether the territorial state is itself incapable of meeting the needs of the situation or unwilling to do so (or is perhaps itself the cause of it); whether competent organs of the international community are unable to respond effectively or quickly enough to meet the demands of the situation; whether there is any practicable alternative to the action to be taken; whether there is likely to be any active resistance on the part of the territorial state; and whether the action taken is limited both in time and scope to the needs of the emergency.[7]

Richard Lillich,[8] Myres McDougal and Michael Reisman,[9] and

Fernando Teson[10] are probably most consistent supporters of humanitarian intervention. Teson, taking a rather extreme view on this issue, for example, writes:

> My main argument is that because the ultimate justification of the existence of states is the protection and enforcement of natural rights of the citizens, a government that engages in substantial violations of human rights betrays the very purpose for which it exists and so forfeits not only its domestic legitimacy, but its international legitimacy as well. Consequently, I shall argue, foreign armies are morally entitled to help victims of oppression in overthrowing dictators, provided that the intervention is proportionate to the evil which it is designed to suppress.[11]

However, there are probably more international lawyers who believe that international law does not recognize any right to intervene by force on humanitarian grounds.[12] Oscar Schachter, for example, argues that

> Two specific reasons [against humanitarian intervention] may be given. One is that any invasion or bombing of a State violates its territorial rights and its political independence.... The second ground for rejecting the permissive interpretation is that the maintenance of international peace is itself one of the purposes of the Charter – indeed, the very first. Hence, the use of force by a State in another country without that country's consent must be considered as inconsistent with a major Charter purpose.[13]

These are the views of some authorities in the doctrine of international law. What about international practice? Does it corroborate or refute these views?

State practice on humanitarian intervention is rather inconclusive. In the nineteenth century, as was mentioned in Chapter One, the European powers intervened more than once in the Ottoman Empire, and one of the declared motives was the protection of Christian subjects of the Sultan. However, as to pre-Charter interventions, especially those undertaken by Western powers in the Ottoman Empire, it is important to bear in mind that, as Judge Schwebel wrote in his dissenting opinion in *Nicaragua v. US*, 'in the pre-United Nations Charter era – or, at any rate, in the pre-Pact of Paris or pre-League of Nations era – states were free to employ force and go to war for any reason or no reason'.[14] It is therefore difficult to draw conclusions on the permissibility of humanitarian intervention from the practice of a time when there was no general prohibition on the use of force in international relations. However, even when intervention was not generally prohibited, it was not allowed for any cause or without a cause whatsoever; there should be a cause and it had to be lawful. Had it been lawful to use force for whatever purpose, it would not have been necessary, for example, for Grotius and Vattel to write about the permissibility of the use of force against tyrants who mistreat their subjects. Equally, it would not have been necessary for P. P. Shafirov, the Vice-Chancellor of the Russian Czar, Peter the Great, to write a book during the Northern War of 1700–21 (which was the first book on international law and diplomacy published in Russia in 1717) on the just causes which Peter the Great had in going to war against the Swedes.[15] According to Shafirov, Swedish policies and actions 'inevitably necessitated' Russia 'to begin this war against the crown of Sweden as an inveterate, perpetual and implacable enemy of the Russian crown ... '.[16]

Therefore the justifications and explanations which were given by states when they intervened by force in other states were not without legal significance; they constituted the *opinio juris* of states on the issue of intervention.

During the UN Charter period, either humanitarian concerns have been voiced in justification of some interventions or there have been consequences beneficial for human rights as a result of such interventions (for example, Belgian intervention in the Congo in 1960, Indian intervention in Eastern Pakistan in 1971, Vietnamese intervention in Kampuchea in 1978–79, Tanzanian intervention in Uganda in 1979, French intervention in Central Africa in 1979, US interventions in Grenada in 1983 and Panama in 1989). However, states have referred to humanitarian concerns as a moral rather than a legal basis for intervention (and certainly not the only or the main one), and humanitarian consequences have also not been the only, and often not even the main, result of such interventions.

Humanitarian aspects have indeed played some role in post-Second World War interventions. For example, in Eastern Pakistan, Kampuchea and Uganda, human rights violations were really massive and were committed against that most basic of human rights, the right to life. The International Commission of Jurists reported in the case of oppression in Eastern Pakistan that 'the principal features of this oppression were the indiscriminate killings of civilians ... the attempt to exterminate or drive out of the country a large part of the Hindu population ... the raping of women .... All this was done on a scale which is difficult to comprehend'.[17] As a result of these interventions, the human rights situation improved radically. There are authors who argue that these interventions and a corresponding reading of the UN

Charter and other relevant documents confirm the existence of the right of humanitarian intervention. So Myres McDougal and Michael Reisman believe that the advent of the United Nations 'neither terminated nor weakened the customary institution of humanitarian intervention'.[18] They even believe that the Charter strengthened and extended humanitarian intervention because it confirmed the 'homo-centric character of international law'.[19]

This last point, however, is definitely wrong, and corresponds more to the ideals of the authors (and of others, of course) than to the existing reality. Though the UN Charter contains several articles which, in rather general terms, speak of human rights, it is manifestly a state-centric document. Adam Roberts and Benedict Kingsbury correctly emphasize that the Charter 'was designed to accommodate the UN in the system of states rather than to pose a direct challenge to that system'.[20]

Louis Henkin writes that 'Article 2(4) [the principle of non-use of force in international relations] is the most important norm of international law, the distillation and embodiment of the primary value of the inter-state system, the defence of state independence and state autonomy'.[21] He believes that the UN Charter 'declares peace as supreme value, to secure not merely state autonomy, but fundamental order for all. It declares peace to be more compelling than inter-state justice, more compelling even than human rights or other human values'.[22]

I do not doubt that, in 1945, the founding fathers of the United Nations put international peace higher than any other value. However, as we saw in Chapter One, by then it was already clear that there were links between peace and justice, international security and human rights. Post-Second World War developments in international law and relations have further undermined the exclusivity of the inter-state nature of the international system. Therefore, when Professor Henkin writes that 'autonomy and impermeability [of the state] imply also immunity from having the state veil pierced by the system, or even permeated by international law that would have effect inside the state, inside its society' (it is interesting that he does not say 'inside society, inside its state', since it seems to me that the state should belong to society, to be an emanation from it, and not *vice versa*), he overstresses the state-centricity of international law and the international system.[23]

Taking into account that, notwithstanding a certain erosion of the state-centric nature of the contemporary international system and international law, states nevertheless remain major actors, it is not surprising that there is state practice and theoretical arguments which strongly militate against the right of humanitarian intervention, and there are probably more authors denying the existence of such a right than there are its advocates. A special study carried out in the United Kingdom concluded that:

> The overwhelming majority of contemporary legal opinion comes down against the existence of a right of humanitarian intervention for three main reasons: first, the UN Charter and the corpus of modern international law do not seem specifically to incorporate such a right; secondly, state practice in the past two centuries, and especially since 1945, at best provides only a handful of genuine cases of humanitarian intervention, and, on most assessments, none at all; and finally, on prudential grounds, the scope for abusing such a right argues strongly against its creation.[24]

International lawyers have naturally dealt with the issue of the legality of humanitarian intervention, asking questions such as: Is such an intervention in conformity with international law? Should such an intervention be authorized by the UN Security Council and linked with threats to international peace? Are there any moral or legal grounds for unilateral or regional intervention with humanitarian objectives? Specialists on international relations and philosophers have concentrated their attention on the moral aspects of outside intervention: Is outside intervention morally justified? Or, looked at another way, can an abstention from intervention be morally right if the only practicable way to protect the lives of thousands is by means of forceful outside intervention?

One of the moral as well legal arguments against humanitarian intervention is that it interferes with the internal affairs of states. For example, the Declaration on the Inadmissibility of Intervention, passed by the UN General Assembly on 21 December 1965, condemns armed intervention 'for any reason whatsoever' in the internal affairs of states and contains no exceptions.[25] There are many other documents which strongly emphasize the principle of non-intervention.

However, human rights and their violation are no longer simply the internal affairs of states. In 1923 the Permanent Court of International Justice, in its advisory opinion on *Nationality Decrees in Tunis and Morocco*, had emphasized that the question of whether a matter was solely within the jurisdiction of a state was essentially a relative question, depending on the development of international relations.[26] The development of international relations, especially after the Second World War, has led to the emergence of a substantial body of international human rights norms. Therefore the Vienna World

Conference on Human Rights of 1993 had good reason to declare that 'the promotion of human rights is a legitimate concern of the international community'.[27]

However, the conclusion that human rights is not an internal affair of a state, and that, therefore, competent international bodies and other states may have a legitimate interest in human rights in other countries, does not yet give an answer to the question of the legality of humanitarian intervention. It means that the norm which stipulates that states must not intervene in the internal affairs of other states 'for any reason whatsoever' does not apply in cases of violations of international human rights standards, since such violations are not an internal affair of a state. It does not say that an armed intervention for the sake of human rights is lawful.

The lawfulness, like the morality of outside interference in human rights situations, depends on the character of the violations and the modalities of responses to these violations. As it is in almost every domain of international law, the principle of proportionality is also important in choosing counter-measures to human rights violations. The more serious a violation, the more intrusive can be the counter-measures. Therefore any interference to protect human rights should be proportional to the character and scale of the human rights violations in the target state.

It is often asserted that humanitarian intervention, as does any intervention by force, violates the right of peoples to self-determination. Cultural relativists even view international human rights policy as a form of moral imperialism that shows inadequate respect for cultural and historical diversity.[28]

This can hardly be true. Obviously, any intervention which contravenes the principal of self-determination is not humanitarian. Intervention to humanitarian ends could be used, if used at all, only against regimes which lack popular support and, as the very aim of such an intervention is the protection of the population, it is absolutely necessary that the majority of the latter welcome the intervention. One should not even try to bring happiness to other peoples who have not asked for it. Michael Walzer believes that one can speak of humanitarian intervention only 'when the violation of human rights...is so terrible that it makes talk of community or self-determination...seem cynical and irrelevant'.[29] It is certainly true that humanitarian intervention can be justified, if justified at all, only in cases of human rights violations which, under international law, are defined as international crimes. Crimes against humanity, including genocide as a special kind of this category of international crime, have been condemned by a series of international instruments (for example, the Statute and Judgement of the Nuremberg Tribunal, the 1948 Convention on the Prevention and Punishment of the Crime of Genocide,[30] the Statutes of the International Criminal Tribunals for the former Yugoslavia[31] and Rwanda[32]) as international crimes for which not only states but also individuals bear responsibility directly under international law.

A much stronger argument against humanitarian intervention is the legal prohibition on the use of force in international relations. The UN Charter contains only two express exclusions to this prohibition: it provides for the use of force in self-defence against an armed attack, and for the use of force on the authorization of the UN Security Council in the case of a threat to international peace and security. In other circumstances the legality of the use of force is, at best, debatable. That is why Ian Brownlie has a strong point in concluding that it is 'extremely doubtful whether [a right of humanitarian intervention] has survived the express condemnations of intervention which have occurred in recent times or the general prohibition of resort to force to be found in the United Nations Charter'.[33]

However, there has been at least one category of cases of the unilateral use of force which has made this strict Charter interpretation somewhat divorced from reality. Limited operations to save one's nationals abroad (when their lives are really in danger, the government of the 'host' country being unable or unwilling to protect these people and there being no other realistic way to save their lives except using limited purposeful force) are recognized by many specialists as acts of the lawful use of force. Practice, though rather limited and controversial, seems to give, if not unequivocal support, then at least considerable ground for arguments in favour of the legality of intervention to save nationals abroad. For example, a British minister stated in the House of Commons in November 1964 that 'we take the view that under international law a State has the right to land troops in foreign territory to protect its nationals in an emergency if necessary'.[34] Some other states and many authors have taken the same view.[35] The ninth edition of *Oppenheim* states that 'although intervention for that reason may be open to abuse and lead to unjustifiably extensive intervention in another state's affairs, there has been little disposition on the part of states to deny that intervention properly restricted to the protection of nationals is, in emergencies, justified'.[36]

As was mentioned earlier, the UN Charter prohibits any use of force 'against the territorial integrity or political independence of any state, or in any other manner inconsistent with the Purposes of the United Nations' [Article 2(4)] and explicitly provides for its use only on two occasions: on the authorization of the Security Council 'to maintain or restore international peace and security' (Article 42) and in self-defence (Article 51).

However, humanitarian intervention is not *per se* inconsistent with the purposes of the Charter, since one of the purposes of the United Nations, which has developed considerably since 1945, is the promotion and protection of human rights. It is also arguable that humanitarian intervention does not violate either territorial integrity or the independence of a state. McDougal and Reisman even argue that,

> Since a humanitarian intervention seeks neither a territorial change nor a challenge to the political independence of the State involved and is not only not inconsistent with the purposes of the United Nations but is rather in conformity with the most fundamental peremptory norms of the Charter, it is a distortion to argue that it is precluded by Article 2(4).[37]

It would probably be too extreme too argue that there is no conflict whatsoever between an intervention for humanitarian purposes and the peremptory norms of the Charter such as the prohibition to use force in Article 2(4). Here we may have a collision between two peremptory norms: one which prohibits the use of force and the other which prohibits an infringement of human rights, and especially prohibits the violation of basic rights on a massive scale and the commitment of acts which are considered to be crimes under international law. There is no reason why in all cases of such a collision the prohibition of the use of force should inevitably prevail.

Moreover, though it is true that an intervention which is undertaken without the consent of a government which is itself guilty of gross human rights violations may constitute a threat to the very survival of such a government, it does not necessarily mean that it constitutes a threat to the independence of the target state. Government is only one of the three elements (government, population and territory) of statehood. When the government and the population are fighting each other, or the government is trying to exterminate a part of the population and the survival of the latter is at stake, an outside intervention on behalf of the population does not violate the independence of the target state. To think otherwise would be to equate the state and the government, leaving the other components out of the equation.

It is possible, of course, to argue, as has often been done, that such a right of humanitarian intervention cannot exist because it can be too easily abused. This argument is put forward even by those who cautiously support humanitarian intervention. Thomas Franck and Nigel Rodley write that one of the problems not resolved by those who argue for a right of states individually or collectively to use force to ameliorate the oppression of peoples by their own regimes is that they cannot devise a means 'that it is both conceptually and instrumentally credible to separate the few sheep of legitimate humanitarianism from the herds of goats which can too easily slip through'.[38]

But almost every right is open to abuse. For example, a right such as the right to self-defence, which is considered to be an inherent right of every state, has probably, been abused more often than any other right related to the use of force. However, as Rosalyn Higgins observes, that does not lead us to say that there should be no right of self-defence today, and she continues: 'We must face the reality that we live in a decentralised international legal order, where claims may be made either in good faith or abusively'.[39]

Moreover, those who criticize humanitarian intervention because it is, allegedly, susceptible to easy abuse, contradict themselves because their other argument against humanitarian intervention which is often put forward is that intervening states, even in cases when the intervention has resulted in improvement of the human rights situation (for example, in Eastern Pakistan in 1971–72, Uganda in 1979 or in Kampuchea in 1979), have not justified their acts by references to humanitarian grounds. However, we simply cannot speak of the abuse of a right to humanitarian intervention in cases when intervening states do not refer to humanitarian concerns as the basis for their intervention. Since India, Tanzania and Vietnam all put an emphasis on self-defence in the justifications of their respective interventions, it would be possible to speak of the abuse of the right to self-defence and not that of humanitarian intervention in the aforementioned cases.

Moreover, Michael Mandelbaum seems to be correct that, at least for the moment, 'the forces that have historically driven the governments of the powerful to intervene beyond their borders have all but vanished'.[40] War booty, or even territorial aggrandizement, are no longer among the factors which make states prosperous and strong. A certain level of economic development, education, and a skilled population matter more than the size of a state's territory or, as Professor Julian Simon has reminded us in his book *The Ultimate Resource*, the decisive element in achievement and progress is human intelligence.[41] The notable exception may currently be Russia, which is still trying to impose its 'Monroe doctrine' on what it terms the 'near-abroad' (see Chapter Two). However, I believe that generally there is much less incentive in the post-Cold War world to intervene militarily abroad for whatever purposes. Therefore, the risk of abuse of the doctrine of humanitarian intervention has greatly diminished, if not disappeared altogether. The instances of Russia, Serbia or Croatia may be rather exceptional cases, because they involve intervention in circumstances of territorial uncertainty which emerged as the result of the dissolution of multi-ethnic states. There is thus probably one exception to the general reluctance to intervene: attempts at intervention to protect ethnic kinsmen in other countries.

Intervention to save thousands, or even millions, of lives threatened by their own oppressive governments seems to be morally, if not legally, even more justifiable than intervention to rescue a few of one's own nationals abroad. However, there are still some substantial differences between these two categories of intervention which seem to speak more against humanitarian intervention than they do against operations to rescue one's nationals abroad. First, in contrast to rescue operations to save nationals, humanitarian intervention can hardly be a short-term 'surgical' interference. To be meaningful, it has to be considerably more intrusive. Second, in the case of humanitarian intervention, outside forces take care not of their own nationals, but of foreigners, and therefore the concept of self-defence, which is sometimes used to cover the rescue operations of nationals abroad, can hardly be stretched to embrace humanitarian intervention as well. Derek Bowett is right to say that 'it seems impossible, in the absence of the link of nationality, to regard [humanitarian intervention] as a species of self-defence...'.[42]

From the point of view the relationship between the morality and the legality of humanitarian intervention, it is interesting to note that those authors who are against humanitarian intervention on moral or political grounds, or because of the possibility of the abuse of any such right, also consider intervention on humanitarian grounds to be contrary to the spirit and letter of the UN Charter. Others, who find humanitarian intervention morally acceptable or even necessary, interpret the Charter in a way which is more favourable to intervention. This means that not a textual but a contextual answer is needed to the question of the legality of humanitarian intervention.

Thomas Franck and Nigel Rodley try to reconcile the legality and morality of intervention when these considerations seem to contradict each other:

Undeniably, there are circumstances in which the unilateral use of force to overthrow injustice begins to seem less wrong than to turn aside. Like civil disobedience, however, this sense of superior 'necessity' belongs in the realm not of law but of moral choice, which nations, like individuals, must sometimes make, weighing the costs and benefits to their cause, to the social fabric, and to themselves.[43]

But is not such a 'necessity' closer to the right of peoples to overthrow their rulers who have violated the social contract and have become tyrants than that simply to engage in acts of civil disobedience? And could there be a place in international relations for acts which, being morally justified or even necessary, can be nevertheless condemned as illegal? Does not such a dichotomy between morality and law do disservice to both? Should there be a place in the international system for somebody who is a moral hero but a legal villain?

David Scheffer puts it well: 'To argue today that norms of sovereignty, non-use of force, and sanctity of internal affairs are paramount to the collective human rights of people, whose lives and well-being are at risk, is to avoid the hard questions of international law and to ignore the march of history'.[44]

I believe that in certain rather limited and extreme circumstances humanitarian intervention can be justified not only from the point of view of morality but also that of law. As was mentioned above, the very existence of universal human rights is a proof of a certain, albeit rather weak, unity of humankind. That is why peoples, states, and the world community as a whole are concerned with human rights in other societies. Raymond Plant even finds that 'intervention to enforce human rights is in fact a logical or necessary feature of talking about rights at all and that doctrines about human rights do imply not only the possibility of intervention, but indeed the obligation to do so'.[45] And he correctly points out that the 'rights discourse must involve a radical modification of state sovereignty and non-intervention' and that 'this approach to rights undermines the "romance of the nation state"'.[46]

Indeed, from the point of view of morality, and also that of common sense, it seems to be not only possible but also necessary to argue that, if there are international standards of human rights, then reaction to the violation of these standards cannot be interference in either the internal or external affairs of the states where violations take place. The issue of the modalities of such a reaction should depend on the character of the violations. In cases where there is a threat to the survival of a people as a whole or of a substantial part of the people, which presumes that genocide or other similar crimes against humanity are being committed against the population of a country, and a forcible outside intervention is the only way to stop the extinction of the people, such an intervention can hardly be called immoral. Can, for example, Tanzanian intervention in Uganda, or that of India in Eastern Pakistan, be called immoral? I believe that, in terms of morality, non-intervention in such cases may deserve condemnation. Godfrey Binaisa, the successor to the deposed Ugandan dictator Idi Amin, in the UN General Assembly rebuked UN member-states for not coming to the aid of the Ugandans when they were oppressed by Amin: 'For eight years they cried out in the wilderness for help; unfortunately, their cries seem to have fallen on deaf ears'.[47] Therefore it seems to me that John Vincent has a point when he writes that 'this is the doctrine of humanitarian intervention which obliges a response from outsiders if a state by its conduct outrages the conscience of mankind'.[48] Or, to quote Michael Walzer again:

> All states have an interest in global stability and even in global humanity, and in the case of wealthy and powerful states like ours, this interest is seconded by obligation.... Grossly uncivilised behaviour... unchallenged, tends to spread, to be imitated and reiterated. Pay the moral price for silence and callousness, and you will soon have to pay the political price of turmoil and lawlessness nearer home.... Now obligation is seconded by interest.[49]

It seems that the issue of the legality of humanitarian intervention is one of those 'hard' cases, and may even be the 'hardest' case in international law related to the use of force, where a simple 'yes' or 'no' answer is hardly possible. Nguen Quoc Dinh, Patrick Dailler and Alan Pellet write that

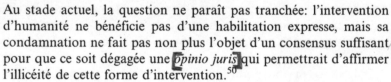

> Au stade actuel, la question ne paraît pas tranchée: l'intervention d'humanité ne bénéficie pas d'une habilitation expresse, mais sa condamnation ne fait pas non plus l'objet d'un consensus suffisant pour que ce soit dégagée une *opinio juris* qui permettrait d'affirmer l'illicéité de cette forme d'intervention.[50]

International law is based on and includes not only moral, but also practical political considerations and, although questions concerning the legality and morality of humanitarian intervention remain relevant, it seems that in our disorderly world the most important questions to be asked should be: can an outside intervention really protect human rights; and are other states and peoples ready to use sufficient resources and efforts in order not only to stop atrocities being committed by authorities against their own people, but also to guarantee that such atrocities do not recur immediately after the intervention has ended?

I believe that issues of political expediency put even more severe constraints on humanitarian intervention than the requirements of legality and morality. It is not easy for an outside intervenor to stop massive human rights violations (see, for example, the experience of Somalia or Liberia). It is even more difficult for outsiders, by way of military intervention, to change the underlying causes of such violations and to guarantee that violations do not recur immediately after the withdrawal of the intervening forces. Failed interventions only aggravate the suffering of those who have to be saved. The road to hell is paved not only with abuses; it is often paved, as we all well know, with good intentions. Therefore humanitarian intervention, in order to be morally and legally justifiable, has also to be successful. This means that to justify an intervention, one should be able to justify its aims and its means, as well as its results.

An intervention to save the lives of thousands or millions of people in a foreign country is usually such a difficult, costly and even dangerous mission that a humanitarian motivation alone may not be sufficient to trigger it. In the three cases mentioned previously of intervention during the Cold War era, where humanitarian considerations played a role and humanitarian consequences were unquestionable – the Indian intervention in Eastern Pakistan, Tanzanian in Uganda and Vietnamese in Democratic Kampuchea – other motives, especially security imperatives, were paramount.

Importantly, the intervening states did not even invoke humanitarian concerns as a main legal justification for their intervention, though as a result of these interventions genocide or genocide-like crimes came to an end. These states appealed to more traditional legal grounds – those of self-defence and threats to their security – though humanitarian aspects were referred to in order to justify the interventions from the moral and political points of view.[51] For example, in December 1971 the Indian Ambassador to the UN declared: 'We have on this particular occasion absolutely nothing but the purest of motives and the purest of intentions: to rescue the people of East Bengal from what they are suffering'.[52] Later, however, the Indian government referred only to the right of self-defence as a legal basis for its intervention. Tanzania, on the other hand, justified its intervention at first in terms of self-defence against the Ugandan aggression, but later referred also to humanitarian motives. The Tanzanian Foreign Ministry stated that the fall of Idi Amin had been 'a tremendous victory for the people of Uganda and a singular triumph for freedom, justice and human dignity'.[53] And Julius Nyerere stated that 'if Africa, as such, is unable to take up its responsibilities, it is incumbent upon each state to do so'.[54]

Such cautious references to humanitarian motives were due not only to the fact that the self-defence argument provided more solid ground for the use of force under traditional Charter law, but also because the intervening states did not dare to use a humanitarian justification lest it become a general rule which may eventually be used against them as well.

In favour of the legality of humanitarian intervention seems to speak the fact that, though there was some criticism of the acts of these states at the time (it is hardly possible to undertake any important action in international relations without criticism from at least some states), in two of these three cases – the Indian and Tanzanian interventions – the results of their interventions were nevertheless rather quickly recognized by the world community. For example, Bangladesh – a state which resulted from the Indian intervention – became a member of the United Nations in 1974, just a little over two years after it had gained independence with the help of the Indian army. Neither the United Nations nor the Organization of African Unity condemned the Tanzanian intervention, and many states quickly recognized the new government of Uganda.[55]

The reaction to the Vietnamese intervention in Kampuchea was different, basically because it threatened the regional balance of power and touched upon sensitive interests of the great powers in the Cold War context.

The tragic events in Liberia are well known, and they are considered in this book in a different context. But here it is interesting to note that one episode, which, in the days of the Cold War, might have caused at least angry verbal exchanges in the UN, remained without any official reaction whatsoever. In April 1996 the US sent its Marines to Liberia,[56] where law and order had completely broken down and the peacekeeping efforts of ECOMOG (the Cease-fire Monitoring Group of the Economic Community of Western African States) had failed to prevent the resumption of fighting between the warring factions. No state protested when four US warships with 1,500 Marines on board appeared offshore from Monrovia and helicopters dropped 200 Marines at the American Embassy as replacements for the paratroopers guarding the compound. Certainly this was a small-scale and low-key military operation, whose main purpose was to protect American diplomats and other foreigners in this small West African country without effective government. But the acquiescence of other states in this intervention indicates that the world community is ready to accept military operations in other countries which are in the throes of civil war or inter-ethnic conflict, or where law and order has otherwise broken down. The question is not so much about the legality of an intervention in such circumstances as it is about the willingness to intervene, and about what outside intervention can achieve.

There are authors who reject humanitarian intervention, *inter alia*, on the ground of non-purity of motives of the intervening states. Setting out the criteria for an intervention to qualify as humanitarian, they suggest that 'the intervening state's objective must be essentially limited to protecting human rights',[57] or that 'humanitarian considerations clearly provided the only major objectives and that no overriding or equally important political or economic considerations were involved'.[58]

Such a requirement seems to be rather voluntary. Why should not other motives be equally important or even overriding? As we will discuss further, even UN interventions, for example, in Haiti or northern Iraq were not and could not, by definition, be mainly or purely humanitarian, since the Security Council can authorize actions involving the use of force only if there is a threat to international peace and security. Richard Gardner is right to say that 'what the members of the Security Council will not do is authorise military intervention in a country on human rights grounds alone'.[59]

There have not been and there probably cannot be such a thing as a purely humanitarian intervention, i.e., an intervention exclusively with humanitarian aims. 'Interest, prudence, and political opportunism remain key factors in state behaviour, and have powerfully influenced decisions favouring humanitarian action in some situations, and opposing it in others'[60], writes Adam Roberts.

Even if we assume that states may intervene (especially collectively) on almost purely humanitarian grounds, the results of such an intervention would always be political as well. Michael Mandelbaum is right that 'the task of alleviating suffering inevitably involves political consequences when suffering has political causes'.[61] It would be a Sisyphean effort to intervene in the case of a humanitarian emergency and to withdraw without addressing the causes of such an emergency. One of the lessons of the UN and US intervention in Somalia, according to Walter Clarke and Jeffrey Herbst, is that 'the international community should discard the illusion that one can intervene in a country beset by widespread civil violence without affecting domestic politics and without including a nation-building component'.[62] Only operations which can be called humanitarian relief operations or operations of humanitarian assistance, i.e., operations which have the limited objectives of providing food, medicines and shelter for victims of humanitarian emergencies, may be carried out more or less independently from political processes, though, as the experience of Bosnia has vividly shown, even in these efforts politics and humanitarianism are closely entangled.[63]

Individual states, regional organizations and even the UN, when they intervene on humanitarian grounds, have, as a rule, mixed motives. Security imperatives or economic interests, rather than pure humanitarian concerns, can be the primary motives which trigger an intervention. Still I tend to agree with Fred Halliday, who writes about the intervention by the US, the UK and France to save the Kurds in northern Iraq: 'This was a practical and innovative implementation of the policy of humanitarian intervention, meaning by this not that the intervening powers had only humanitarian motives, a condition that would be impossible to meet, but that it had in part a humanitarian motivation and that its consequences were of clear and substantial benefit to the populations concerned'.[64]

If we look, in the light of this comment, at the interventions of India in Eastern Pakistan, Tanzania in Uganda and Vietnam in Kampuchea, we have to admit that they all had as one of their consequences a 'clear and substantial benefit to the population concerned'. Therefore I find it rather inconsistent for Arend and Beck to write that 'although the ouster of the Khmer Rouge regime put an end to Pol Pot's reign of terror, Vietnam's use of force against Kampuchea should not be considered a genuine "humanitarian intervention".'[65]

However, humanitarian intervention has to satisfy too many requirements for it to be considered a 'normal' instrument of human rights protection. These requirements concern the moral, political and legal aspects of intervention and they can basically be divided into two categories: those pertaining to humanitarian concerns, and those stemming from imperatives of *Realpolitik*. The first category of minimum requirements are:

(a) human rights violations have to be massive and concern funda-mental rights such as the right to life (this is the only condition which is fulfilled more than rarely);[66]
(b) intervention should be accepted or welcomed by at least the overwhelming majority of the population (this is not always the case, even in instances of most heinous crimes against human rights).

The minimum requirements of *Realpolitik* are:

(a) an outside intervention should be able to stop these violations and guarantee that they do not recur, at least immediately, after the withdrawal of the intervenors (a rather difficult condition to fulfil);
(b) the cost of an intervention in human, political and financial terms should be acceptable from the point of view of the governments of the intervening states (this also seems to be a condition which is rather difficult to fulfil);
(c) an intervention itself should not endanger international peace and security (as I will discuss further, there are interventions where humanitarian efforts are instrumental in peace-making or peace-building; however, there may be cases when an intervention undertaken, *inter alia*, on humanitarian grounds, like the Vietnamese intervention in Democratic Kampuchea, may have a destabilizing effect on international relations);
(d) for an intervention to be plausible, other interests in addition to humanitarian concerns, such as national, regional or international security, should also usually be at stake;
(e) public opinion in the intervening states should support intervention (there may be short-term support, but if longer-term efforts are needed, such support may vanish quickly).

As it would be rare for all or even most of these requirements to be fulfilled, I suggest that in the post-Cold War world, where one of the biggest threats to international stability stems from internal conflicts which are caused, among other factors, by, or result in, the massive violation of basic human rights, humanitarian intervention, i.e., an intervention by force to protect human rights in other countries, will remain a rare and exclusive instrument in the protection of human rights. The reason for such a conclusion is not so much that states ought not to intervene because of moral or legal restraints, but because in most cases (though probably not in all) it is next to impossible to protect human rights in other countries by using military means, and even when it may be possible, states are rarely ready for the necessary sacrifices. As Michael Mandelbaum writes, 'the United Nations lacks the means to carry out its resolutions [on intervention] and its member states lack the will to do so'.[67]

However, there are certain rare situations where outside interference, including a military component, usually, but not always, with the consent (though sometimes reluctant or semi-imposed) of the parties to a conflict caused, *inter alia*, by or resulting in, human rights violations, may change a human rights situation for the better and restore domestic and international stability. This is where the United Nations comes in.

CURRENT TENDENCIES: HUMAN RIGHTS IN UN FIELD OPERATIONS

The end of the Cold War has blurred many previously clear distinctions. It seems that nowadays the rather modest but nevertheless real achievement of the UN period – peace-keeping – is being cross-fertilized with the much bolder but, at the same time, much more controversial concept of humanitarian intervention dating back centuries. There is a tendency for issues of human rights and international peace to become more and more entwined in operations on the maintenance or restoration of peace and security.[68]

In many of the post-Cold War UN operations authorized by the Security Council, humanitarian or human rights issues have played a rather important role. This is clear evidence that humanitarian concerns and security imperatives are often interlinked.

Operations in Namibia, Angola, El Salvador, Cambodia and Mozambique have all had a substantial human rights component. Comprehensive settlements have included such issues as the verification of respect for human rights by all sides of a conflict, the design and supervision of constitutional, judicial and electoral reforms, the observation, supervision, organization and conduct of elections, and the creation of national institutions, including civilian police forces. As the UN Secretary General has reported in his 1995 Supplement to 'An Agenda for Peace', these elements have played an especially important role in the process of post-conflict peace-building measures, which he calls 'the institutionalization of peace'.[69] He has also emphasized the link between human rights and peace-keeping: 'La plupart des opérations de maintien de la paix prévoient, en effet, à la fois la restauration de la démocratie et la protection des droits de l'homme'.[70]

As peace and security are often threatened not by overt cross-border attacks but by domestic violence and instability, which may spill over and affect international relations as well as other countries, there is no way of dealing with such threats without addressing the underlying human rights issues. If the absence or violation of human rights may play a role in the genesis of internal conflicts with international repercussions, measures aimed at the improvement of human rights situations may become a necessary element of the resolution of such conflicts. While there are situations where, without stopping human rights violations, it is impossible to obtain a sustainable peace, there are also cases where the restoration of peace is a *conditio sine qua non* for putting an end to human rights abuses. Often these tasks (the restoration of peace and protection of human rights) have to be implemented at the same time, and they are not always complementary, particularly in the short term.

The Paris Agreement on a Comprehensive Political Settlement of the Cambodia Conflict of 23 October 1991 provided, *inter alia*, that 'UNTAC (UN Transitional Authority in Cambodia) shall be responsible during the transitional period for fostering an environment in which respect for human rights shall be ensured' and that 'after the end of the transitional period, the United Nations Commission on Human Rights should continue to monitor closely the human rights situation in Cambodia'.[71] The San José Agreement on Human Rights signed between the Government of El Salvador and the Frente Farabundo Martí (FMLN) on 26 July 1990 stipulated that the United Nations human rights verification mission would 'perform its functions with a view to promoting respect for human rights and their guarantee in El Salvador and helping to do away with those situations in which such respect and guarantees are not duly observed'.[72]

ONUSAL (the United Nations Observer Mission in El Salvador) had a Human Rights Division which monitored the compliance of the Government of El Salvador and the FMLN with the Agreement on Human Rights. Even Americas Watch, which criticized the timidity of ONUSAL's approach to human rights issues and called for bolder pressure on the Government, concluded nevertheless that ONUSAL's impact in El Salvador has been extremely positive.[73] A research by the Aspen Institute found that, in El Salvador 'between 1992, when the cease-fire took effect, and 1994, there was a dramatic decrease in the number of the most serious human rights violations, such as summary executions, torture, and improper treatment of detainees'.[74] Given the country's previous record on human rights, these developments are encouraging.

Creating conditions for, and the organization and monitoring of, free elections in the process of post-conflict peace-building (Namibia, Nicaragua, El Salvador, Cambodia, Mozambique) is an important human rights component of these processes. UNTAG (United Nations Transition Assistance Group) in Namibia was the first operation to combine peacekeeping with electoral supervision. UNTAG supervised the cease-fire and the brief cantonment of guerilla forces, assisted voter-registration and education, and monitored the elections that brought Namibia to independence.[75] It is one of the success stories of this new type of UN field operation.[76]

Not all of these operations have been successful. Probably the most prominent failure was the United Nations Angola Verification Mission (UNAVEM II), which did not succeed in putting an end to civil war in Angola. The lack of political will of the parties to the conflict (especially that of UNITA), the weakness of the UN mission, and defects in the peace accord signed by the Angolan government and UNITA, are all components which made the failure inevitable.[77]

In some cases the jury is still out. The most extensive and expensive UN operation ($2.6 billion) – UNTAC in Cambodia, where Co-Prime Minister Hun Sen is behaving more and more like a dictator (especially after the arrest and expulsion of Prince Norodom Sirivudh, the half-brother of the King Norodom Sihanouk[78]) – belongs in this category.

However, it is clear that in all conflicts where human rights are often abused by all sides it is impossible to achieve any sustainable peace without a radical improvement of the human rights situation. Gareth Evans, Australia's Minister for Foreign Affairs, writing of the lessons of the UNTAC experience, emphasizes that 'the observance of human rights is critical to the comprehensive settlement of a conflict – and this is arguably so in most operations'.[79]

Traditional, so-called first-generation or pure peacekeeping operations did not have any human rights component.[80] So-called second-generation missions have more intrusive mandates and ambitious goals: free elections, civic order and human rights, in addition to the monitoring of cease-fires or the decommissioning of weapons. While the earlier missions primarily sought to minimize external conflict by monitoring cease-fires, the latest efforts strive to advance more fundamental goals: civil order and domestic tranquillity; human rights, from those most basic to human dignity to those empowering a people to choose its government; and economic and social development.[81]

These human rights tasks are being carried out in circumstances which are not conducive to the observance of human rights. Obviously, an armed conflict, even if followed by a cease-fire, implies that human rights are constantly in jeopardy. Equally, the concurrent implementation of different tasks (political, military and humanitarian) is not easy because of conflicting priorities.

The experience of UN missions in El Salvador, Namibia or Cambodia shows that it is not easy to reconcile the impartiality needed for peace-building efforts with a human rights mandate which often calls, if not for taking sides in the conflict, then at least for taking steps against one of the sides. As the Lawyers' Committee for Human

Rights observes in the context of the UN operation in Haiti, 'the confusion between *objectivity* – as a monitor of human rights violations – and *neutrality* – as the instrument of political settlement leading to the return of the constitutionally elected government – dogged MICIVIH [the United Nations/Organization of American States International Mission in Haiti] at every step'.[82] Steven Ratner writes about ONUSAL, which has so far been one of the most successful missions in peace-building and human rights promotion: 'ONUSAL had a mandate as executor to promote human rights and report on violations. Yet this often proved hard to reconcile with its role as mediator to move the parties along in the implementation of all the accords (not merely the human rights agreement). ONUSAL needed the government's cooperation, yet also had a responsibility to challenge ongoing serious violations of human rights'.[83]

An 'either–or' approach to this dilemma would be wrong. It is equally impossible to recommend either that human rights tasks should always take precedence over political processes or that political solutions are so important that the humanitarian component of a mission should be sacrificed for the sake of finding a political solution. It is necessary to remember not only that there can be no human rights without peace but also that peace without justice is often fictitious. Therefore compromises and accommodation between the different tasks are usually needed.

Stephen Stedman writes that 'if getting the parties to reach a political settlement of their conflict is the goal, the other goals that may be good in and of themselves (such as the provision of humanitarian assistance, protection of civilians, or the investigation and prosecution of war crimes), must be subordinate to the larger goal of making peace'.[84]

I would agree that, for the sake of peace (and we should not forget that without peace there are no human rights but only humanitarian laws), it may be possible to sacrifice other goals. However, it seems that in internal conflicts it is impossible to achieve sustainable peace when massive human rights violations continue and when leaders who are guilty of such violations are not punished and, even worse, remain in their posts. If it is possible to separate warring sides in an international armed conflict by withdrawing armed forces behind internationally recognized borders so that peace may prevail, it is much more difficult to separate factions in an internal conflict. Here, peace without justice can hardly prevail. It would mean, among other things, that the victims would be forced to live together with, or even under, the offenders. In such cases any political settlement can hardly be lasting.

Therefore, the necessity of compromises between humanitarian tasks and the political settlement of a conflict cannot be stretched infinitely. If egregious human rights violations either continue on the part of a government (as happened in Haiti before the military junta was ousted by the Americans) or are committed by all sides of the conflict (as in Somalia), this usually means also that the situation in the country involved is not ripe for a political solution. In El Salvador or in Namibia, though humanitarian tasks were sometimes at odds with the search for a political solution, influential political forces had come to understand of the necessity of a political settlement, and therefore compromises in specific cases were possible and generally it was not necessary to sacrifice one task for the sake of the other.

At the same time, the sacrificing of the human rights task in Haiti for the sake of reaching a political settlement did not help in any way to make the political mission of the MICIVIH more successful. At the end of the day it was forced to evacuate.[85]

Sometimes concerns for human rights and international stability are so closely interrelated in operations authorized by the Security Council that it can be rather difficult to distinguish a peace-making operation from a humanitarian intervention. Was, for example, the UN-authorized US operation in Haiti an operation to eliminate a threat to international peace and security, or was it an intervention for the restoration of democracy and the establishment of law and order on the island, in other words a humanitarian intervention? It seems that, according to the United Nations mandate, it was primarily a peace-making operation, while in practice it turned out to be an operation on the re-initiation of the democratic process which had been interrupted by the military coup.

In June 1994 the Security Council in its resolution 929,[86] finding that the humanitarian crisis in Rwanda constituted a threat to peace and security in the region and acting under Chapter VII of the UN Charter, authorized UN member states cooperating with the Secretary General to establish a temporary operation to achieve humanitarian objectives set out in resolution 925,[87] contributing, *inter alia*, to the security and protection of displaced persons, refugees and civilians at risk in Rwanda. This was the legal basis for the French intervention. Here also it is difficult to separate security imperatives from humanitarian concerns.

The creation of safe areas for the Kurds in northern Iraq and the use of force to protect them were also in substance humanitarian operations, although references to international security were used to legitimize these actions undertaken for humanitarian reasons. Security

Council Resolution 688 of 5 April 1991 condemned 'the repression of the Iraqi civilian population in many parts of Iraq, including most recently in Kurdish populated areas, the consequences of which threaten international peace and security in the region'.[88] The resolution further demanded that Iraq immediately end this repression and insisted that Iraq allow immediate access by international humanitarian organizations to the devastated Kurdish areas. The resolution did not authorize the use of force to enforce its requirements. However, when the Iraqi repressions continued, the US, the UK and France launched operation 'Provide Comfort' in order to create safe areas for the Kurds in northern Iraq. President Clinton declared on 16 April 1991 that:

> Consistent with United Nations Security Council Resolution 688 and working closely with the United Nations and other international relief organizations and our European partners, I have directed the US military to begin immediately to establish several encampments in northern Iraq where relief supplies for these refugees will be made available in large quantities and distributed in an orderly way.[89]

Two days later, on 18 April, the Iraqi Foreign Minister signed a Memorandum of Understanding in which Iraq had reluctantly to agree to the UN presence in the country and with the delivery of humanitarian aid to the Kurds through its territory.[90]

Here we had a human rights emergency which constituted a threat to international peace and security in the region. We had the Security Council resolution requesting Iraq to put an end to human rights violations. We also had a military action undertaken by three UN member-states to enforce the requirements of the resolution although the resolution itself did not authorize the use of these measures.

The situation in and around Iraq was rather unique, but it seems that in the post-Cold War world we have more and more such unique situations which call for unique answers.

The UN Security Council has started to use rather widely the concept of a 'threat to international peace and security' when dealing with grave human rights violations. In the cases of Southern Rhodesia and South Africa, the Security Council had used the same concept before. In 1963, the Council found that the regime of apartheid in South Africa was 'seriously disturbing international peace and security'.[91] In 1966, it decided that the 'illegal' regime of Ian Smith in Southern Rhodesia constituted a 'threat to the peace'.[92] In 1970, it determined that the 'continued application of the policies of apartheid and the constant build-up of the South African military and police forces... constitutes a potential threat to international peace and security'.[93] Again, in 1977, the acquisition of arms and related materials by South Africa was found by the Security Council to constitute a 'threat to the maintenance of international peace and security'.[94] The Council imposed economic sanctions and arms embargos against these regimes.

In the 1990s, the operations in Somalia, the former Yugoslavia, Haiti, northern Iraq and Rwanda were all authorized by the Security Council because it had found that the situation in these countries, or in parts of them, constituted a threat to international peace and security. Some of these humanitarian emergencies may really have had serious security implications (e.g., the situation in the former Yugoslavia), while others have hardly had any (for example, the situation in Haiti) or may have had security implications in a non-traditional, i.e., a non-military, sense (for example, refugee flows of Iraqi Kurds to Turkey). But as the Security Council under the Charter can use or authorize the use of force only in the case of a threat to international peace or security, the Council has employed this concept when dealing with human rights emergencies under Chapter VII.

How may we evaluate such a tendency in the interpretation of the UN Charter? Rosalyn Higgins has written that 'there is simply no getting away from the fact that the Charter could have allowed for sanctions for gross human rights violations, but deliberately did not do so. The only way in which economic or military sanctions for human rights purposes could lawfully be mounted under the Charter is by the legal fiction that human rights violations are causing a threat to international peace'.[95] This means that only a creative interpretation of Chapter VII allows the Security Council to authorize in cases of humanitarian emergencies the measures provided for in Articles 41 and 42 of the Charter.

I believe that this rather wide interpretation generally corresponds to changes which are taking place in the post-Cold War international system. International bodies, as well as individual states, should be able to respond adequately to challenges such as terrorist acts, drug-trafficking or inter-ethnic conflicts which, during the Cold War, were suppressed or at least overshadowed by the East–West conflict and its most important component – the threat of a thermo-nuclear war. The use of old articles in these changed circumstances may sometimes require some stretching of the traditional reading of these articles.

Moreover, even if we cannot say that developments in Haiti or Rwanda threatened international peace in the traditional – military –

sense, they had significant destabilizing effects on international relations. John Vincent observed some time ago that the concept of security in foreign policy studies was at once too narrow and too broad.[96] It was too narrow 'in being concentrated on safety against military threats', and too broad 'in having safety against military threats trumping all other considerations in the external relations of the state'.[97]

A re-definition of threats to international security is even more urgent in the post-Cold War world. I agree with Michael Clarke that 'for the future, international security should not be so exclusively regarded as – by definition – the study of relationships between states. It must, instead, be defined as the study of those forces which affect the outbreak of violent conflict between any significant groups of people in the world'.[98]

The 1995 report of the Commission on Global Governance puts an emphasis on the security of people and finds that this security may be challenged by threats to the Earth's life support systems, by extreme economic deprivation, by the proliferation of conventional arms, by terrorism, and by gross violations of human rights.[99] The report concludes that, quite often, 'threats to the security of people that justify international action may not constitute threats to international peace and security',[100] and it proposes to amend the UN Charter, permitting intervention by the international community in cases that 'constitute a violation of the security of people so gross and extreme that it requires an international response on humanitarian grounds'.[101]

Amendments to the Charter are certainly necessary. Proposals made in the report of the Commission on Global Governance contain many interesting and rational ideas whose realization would transfer the UN into a more effective and representative body. However, it will take time. Some of the proposals would meet strong resistance from various states. The inclusion into the Charter of a clause dealing with intervention on humanitarian grounds undoubtedly belongs to this category. Therefore creative interpretation of the Charter on a case-by-case basis may be a way out of the legal impasse the world community may find itself in when urgent humanitarian action is needed.

Finally, I should like to echo a point made by Tom Farer: 'Why the Council's creative interpretation of its constitutional obligation to maintain international peace and security should occasion alarm among people other than members of brutal parasitic governments in relatively weak states is unclear'.[102]

A new and interesting link between human rights and international security, apart from their intermingling in second-generation peacekeeping operations, is to be seen in the creation and functioning of two international criminal tribunals – one for the former Yugoslavia,[103] the other for Rwanda[104] – which exist to try those persons accused of violations of international humanitarian law, genocide and crimes against humanity.

If the immediate purpose of these two international *ad hoc* judicial bodies is to try individuals for crimes against human rights, i.e., to do justice, their longer-term declared aim is to contribute to the restoration and maintenance of international peace and security. The Security Council could create, under its mandate, these bodies only because it had established this link between justice and peace. So the Council, in the Resolution which contained the Statute of the Tribunal for Rwanda, determining that the situation in Rwanda continued to constitute a threat to international peace and security, was convinced that 'in the particular circumstances of Rwanda, the prosecution of persons responsible for serious violations of international humanitarian law would...contribute to the process of national reconciliation and maintenance of peace'.[105]

It seems to me that, at least in the short term, the creation and functioning of these tribunals could hardly have contributed in any way to the *restoration* of peace and stability in the former Yugoslavia or Rwanda. However, I do not share the views of those who believe that the accusations against and trials of politicians or military leaders who may have been negotiating partners in the peace efforts in the former Yugoslavia could have hindered these efforts or could have even created conditions for an all-out war in the region. I believe, simply, that such tribunals cannot have any short-term impact whatsoever upon on-going conflicts. They may have a positive impact only in the long run. If these tribunals will be able to claim some success (for example, if a significant number of perpetrators of crimes against humanity or war crimes are tried, or if some of the leaders, even if they are not tried but only indicted, become *persona non grata* in all civilized countries), this may contribute to the gradual change of attitude towards massive human rights violations (this attitude may become less cynical and more intolerant towards such violations). It may also be true that, although the tribunals may not contribute to the restoration of peace in these regions, they may be necessary for making peace, achieved through other means, more sustainable. It seems to me that any peace would hardly be *sustainable* without at least some justice done.

A similar role is served by various 'truth commissions' in some Latin American countries, and in South Africa where human rights violations have been so massive that they continue to have an impact on domestic tranquillity. These efforts show that there is an understanding that without justice, without punishing those who are guilty of egregious human rights violations or at least revealing the truth about their crimes, it is difficult to create conditions for sustainable peace, be it domestic or international. Or as Alexander Solzhenitsyn wrote in *The Gulag Archipelago*, 'when we neither punish nor reproach evildoers, we are not simply protecting the trivial old age, we are thereby ripping the foundations of justice from beneath new generations'.[106]

However, there have been different approaches to this issue as well. Amnesty laws which pardoned those guilty of gross human rights violations were passed in Argentina, Brazil, Chile, Uruguay, Guatemala, El Salvador, Nicaragua, Namibia, and Surinam.[107] In Angola and Cambodia, where the atrocities committed by all sides in the conflict were far greater than in the Balkans, neither UNITA nor the Khmer Rouge were prosecuted.

In some cases such prosecutions may be impossible; in other cases they may be fraught with the danger of breaking a fragile peace. One could hardly recommend doing something which is too dangerous or simply impossible. However, where possible, past atrocities and crimes should not be left without any response.

The Peace Agreement for Bosnia and Herzegovina,[108] initialled in Dayton, Ohio, and signed in Paris on 14 December 1995 by Presidents Izetbegovic, Milosevic and Tudjman, deals not only with issues concerning territorial and constitutional arrangements, the role of NATO and many other problems, but in Annex 6 it contains the Agreement on Human Rights. The Agreement stipulates in Article I that:

> The Parties shall secure to all persons within their jurisdiction the highest level of internationally recognized human rights and fundamental freedoms, including the rights and freedoms provided in the European Convention for the Protection of Human Rights and Fundamental Freedoms and its Protocols and the other international agreements listed in the Appendix to this Annex.

The Annex provides for the establishment of a Commission of Human Rights which consists of the office of the Ombudsman and the Human Rights Chamber. These bodies should pay particular attention to an alleged or apparent discrimination on any ground such as sex, race, colour, language, religion, political or other opinion, national or social origin, association with a national minority, property, birth or other status (Article II of Annex 6).

The Parties also agreed to invite the United Nations Commission on Human Rights, the OSCE, the United Nations High Commissioner for Human Rights, and other inter-governmental bodies, to monitor closely the human rights situation in Bosnia and Herzegovina, and promised to allow full and effective access to non-governmental organizations for the purposes of investigating and monitoring human rights conditions in the country (Article XIII of Annex 6).

It is difficult to tell at this stage whether these efforts will succeed. The biggest unknown is the fate of Bosnia-Herzegovina as a state. It seems that the Dayton agreement may be a step towards the division of the country. Zoran Pajic observes that 'the document's fundamental contradictions – declaring a unified state while recognising two antagonised entities and ethnically based parties, re-affirming individual rights while legitimising ethnic majoritarianism – raise serious concerns about which vision for Bosnia will prevail'.[109] It should be also noted that the Dayton Agreement, containing human rights provisions such as the direct applicability of the European Convention on Human Rights and all of its eleven Protocols, as well as references to all major UN human rights instruments (it is safe to say that the US – the main driving force behind the Agreement – could never have agreed to such human rights obligations), is quite detached from the reality reigning in the Balkans. However, in any case, the improvement of the current human rights situation is a necessary precondition for peace in the area.

FUTURE PERSPECTIVES

Tom Farer made an interesting comment on the 'Santiago Commitment to Democracy and the Renewal of the International System', adopted by the Organization of American States General Assembly in June 1991, which provides for measures to be taken by the OAS member-states when representative democracy, which is 'an indispensable condition for the stability, peace and development of the region', is suddenly or irregularly interrupted. He wrote that such a change of attitude among countries which have always emphasized non-interference in internal affairs more than any other group of states, has surely something to do with the end of the Cold War: 'For the passing of that conflict sharply reduced the risk that resolutions endorsing Hemispheric action on behalf of democracy would be treated as licences for the pursuit of political ends related loosely if at all to the consolidation and preservation of representative government'.[110]

The most amazing example of changing attitudes after the end of the Cold War occurred in 1989, when Washington and Paris allegedly let Moscow know that they would not mind if the Soviet Union interfered in Romania to put an end to the atrocities committed by the Ceaucescu regime. This, of course, happened during the 'honeymoon' period between the West and the then Soviet Union, and did not in itself create any new tendencies. Nevertheless, it may still be considered as a blow to certain existing stereotypes.

In Liberia, where grave human rights violations resulted in a civil war, which in its turn led to further humanitarian tragedies, ECOWAS (the Economic Community of West African States) intervened unilaterally.[111] This intervention, which had both humanitarian and security implications, was later legitimized by the Security Council. Salim A. Salim, the Secretary General of the OAU, argued on ECOWAS's operation in Liberia:

> To tell the truth, the Charter [of the OAU] was created to preserve the humanity, dignity, and the rights of the African. You cannot use a clause of the Charter to oppress the African and say that you are implementing the OAU Charter. What has happened is that people have interpreted the Charter as if to mean that what happens in the next house is not one's concern. This does not accord with the reality of the world'.[112]

David Wippman, analysing the intervention by ECOWAS in Liberia, writes that:

> the willingness of the international community to acquiesce in but not overtly approve forcible intervention in Liberia suggests that, as in the past, states and groups of states willing to undertake interventions perceived as genuinely humanitarian will not incur condemnation or international sanction, especially when the decision to intervene stems from a multilateral decision-making process.[113]

This approach also differs radically from the traditional doctrine of non-interference adopted by African leaders.

However, almost every tendency has its counter-tendency. There are states which try to avoid legalizing even rather modest UN-authorized interventions on humanitarian grounds. Thus the Indian representative explained that he had abstained in voting for the Security Council resolution 688 (1991) on safe havens for the Kurds in northern Iraq because his delegation wanted to draw attention to the threat, be it actual or latent, to peace and stability in the region rather than to the facts which were at the origin of that situation.[114] Zimbabwe, voting against the resolution, stated that 'while we realise that the humanitarian dimensions affect neighbouring states, we do not believe that this in any way makes the internal conflict in Iraq an issue that the Council should be seized of'.[115]

This is a strange position. Such an approach would effectively mean that, at the international level, it would often be possible to deal only with the effects, rather than the causes, of real problems. However, the root causes of threats to international stability often lie in matters which are still believed by some states to be domestic affairs, while only the effects are considered to be issues of international concern. In practice, such a policy would mean that international action is possible only when it is too late to act effectively. Rwanda and the former Yugoslavia are examples of the situation where earlier and more decisive interference by the world community might have prevented calamities which also constituted a threat to international stability. The report of the Commission on Global Governance concludes that 'in many of today's crises, it is clear that an early intervention could have prevented later negative developments, and might have saved many lives'.[116]

There were reliable reports before the April 1994 massacre in Rwanda which warned that the human rights situation in that country was rapidly deteriorating, to such an extent that mass ethnic killings would be an imminent reality. Bacre Waly N'Diaye, a Senegalese lawyer and the UN representative on human rights, warned as early as August 1993 of such a threat.[117] However, the report of Mr N'Diaye was not given due attention by either the UN Human Rights Commission or any other competent body, and the report and accurate prediction of the development of the human rights situation could not perform the role of providing an early warning which could have been acted upon.

The Security Council, in passing resolutions authorizing intervention on mixed humanitarian–security grounds (Somalia, Iraq, Liberia, Rwanda), has always considered all these cases as exceptional and unique. For example, in July 1994 it recognized 'the unique character of the present situation in Haiti and its deteriorating, complex and extraordinary nature, requiring an exceptional response'.[118] The Security Council's earlier resolution, No. 794 on Somalia, authorizing the UN intervention on humanitarian grounds, also stressed 'the unique character of the present situation in Somalia'.[119]

Therefore it seems that even a UN-authorized intervention on humanitarian grounds will remain a rather exceptional remedy. However, developments in different parts of the world show that these unique cases still occur, and therefore the world community should be ready to respond to these cases with exceptional measures.

Taking into account all these difficulties with *ex post facto* interventions in those human rights situations which may constitute a threat to international peace and security, the efforts of the world community should be aimed at preventing situations which are marked by humanitarian emergencies. Not intervention, but prevention, should be the main strategy for the future, though it may be the case that prevention can sometimes call for early and more decisive interference.

Conclusion

With the end of the Cold War, human rights diplomacy is at a crossroads. During the Cold War, human rights issues in international relations were often used for political purposes which were far from a genuine concern for human rights. On the other hand, human rights were too often forgotten for the sake of *raison d'état*.

There is no doubt that, Cold War or not, human rights issues in diplomacy cannot be separated from politics, since inter-state relations are by definition and will always remain political relations. They are also political because radical changes in the human rights situation in many countries will require deep political, economic and social reforms.

At the same time, human rights diplomacy should not be (and usually it is not, though it is sometimes described as such by not-so-human-rights-friendly regimes) power-politics in disguise. It is politics which is cross-fertilized with morality, and which should be exercised in a legal framework. And even if there is still quite a lot of hypocrisy and double standards in human rights diplomacy, this does not mean that it is necessary to curtail human rights diplomacy. One should try instead to get rid of the hypocrisy and double standards.

The end of the Cold War has increased the importance of human rights diplomacy. On the one hand, human rights seem to affect post-Cold War international relations more than before because there is no longer an overwhelming security threat; instead there are multifarious threats to international stability, many of which have their origin in the human rights situation of a particular country. In the present international system – which is much looser than the rather rigid, disciplined, bipolar Cold War international system – in a world which is becoming more and more interdependent, the domestic characteristics of states and internal developments in those states affect international relations much more directly. Hence the increase in the importance of human rights issues in foreign policy. On the other hand, there is less reason for the misuse or abuse of human rights issues in foreign policy, and there is more room for relatively effective diplomatic efforts with a view to promoting and protecting human rights.

Human rights diplomacy can be and should be exercised at different levels and through various methods and forms. Multifarious human rights bodies, such as the UN Commission on Human Rights, the Human Rights Committee and other treaty-bodies, regional mechanisms and procedures represent the first, and basically the legal level. In urgent cases the UN Security Council, regional bodies or individual states, preferably in cooperation with the Security Council, may be used to deal with humanitarian emergencies. This is mainly the political level of human rights diplomacy. The activities of human rights NGOs, the mass media and public opinion form the third level of human rights diplomacy. Their role is emotional and mobilizational as well as practical. Without this support, official human rights diplomacy would not only be ineffective, it would probably wither completely away. Finally, economic growth, the integration of states with human rights problems into the world economy, progress in education, health care and other areas which form the basis for societal development, are factors which work slowly, but without progress on these issues the promotion of human rights cannot be steady and sustainable.

After the Teheran 1968 World Conference on Human Rights, Richard Bilder in summary of the first twenty-five years of UN human rights experience wrote:

> Perhaps the principal lesson to be learned is patience. For the ultimate test of the usefulness of current international human rights efforts may lie less in their immediate accomplishments than in their long-run, evolutionary impact. Even if declarations and conventions are now less than fully effective, even if government professions of support for human rights aims are often insincere, such activities are nevertheless sowing seeds which are gradually sifting down and taking root in popular attitudes. One generation's hypocrisy may be the next generation's fighting creed. Perceptions of people about themselves, what they want and what they are entitled to, are slowly changing. History suggests that such widespread ideas and hopes are not easily stifled. To have planted the human rights idea in fertile soil throughout the world may

ultimately prove a sufficient achievement of present international activity.[1]

These words seem to remain true more than a quarter of a century later, now that the UN has celebrated its fiftieth anniversary and the second World Conference on Human Rights has been held in Vienna in 1993. The last twenty-five years have shown not only frustration at the abuses of human rights and the atrocities committed in Africa, America, Asia and Europe. They have also shown significant progress on human rights in many countries of all of these continents. In October 1995, the heads of states and governments addressing the jubilee session of the United Nations did not praise its achievements but instead were rather critical of the UN, and sometimes even of themselves (though unfortunately not so often as perhaps they should have been). It was rather different from many other international events, where stilted language, unrealistic hopes and promises and self-praise have often been a kind of norm. I found this change of tonality cautiously encouraging. Taken together with some other developments, it may mean that the UN and other international bodies, having reached a point when it is necessary either 'to put up or to shut up', are going to stop sacrificing precision for the sake of politeness and deeds for the sake of words.

It is difficult to be optimistic regarding the progress in the domain of human rights worldwide if in order to be an optimist it is necessary to believe that, in the foreseeable future, there will be no inhumanitarian hells in any part of the world or that there will be a paradise for human rights somewhere on the Earth. But it is possible to be slightly more optimistic regarding the possibility of gradual progress in a number of countries and regions of the world, and I believe that at least some of the human rights hells may be healed more or less successfully. Something, certainly, can be and, therefore, should be done. Active and skilful human rights diplomacy is needed, not only for the sake of international stability, but for the sake of humankind as a whole and for every human being, since that is what human rights are for.

Notes

INTRODUCTION

1 On human rights in foreign policy and international relations see, for example, D. Newsom (ed.), *The Diplomacy of Human Rights* (New York: University Press of America, 1986); R. J. Vincent, *Human Rights and International Relations* (Cambridge: Cambridge University Press, 1986); J. Egeland, *Impotent Superpower – Potent Small State* (Oslo: Norwegian University Press, 1988); J. Donnelly, *International Human Rights. Dilemmas in World Politics* (Boulder: Westview Press, 1993); D. Forsythe, *Human Rights and Peace. International and National Dimensions* (Lincoln: University of Nebraska Press, 1993); P. Baher, *The Role of Human Rights in Foreign Policy* (London: Macmillan, 1994); J. Tang (ed.), *Human Rights and International Relations in the Asian Pacific* (London: Pinter, 1995).

2 For example, as of 1 July 1996: 133 states were parties to the International Covenant on Civil and Political Rights; 134 states participated in the Covenant on Economic, Social and Cultural Rights; 147 states had become parties to the Convention on Elimination of All Forms of Racial Discrimination; 147 were bound by the Convention on Elimination of All Forms of Discrimination against Women; and 187 states had ratified the Convention on the Rights of the Child (I thank Mr Alexander Tikhonov from the UN Centre on Human Rights in Geneva for these updated numbers).

3 The literature on human rights is too impressive to be enumerated. Human rights issues are the domain of moral philosophers, lawyers and specialists on international relations. Among the works which deal with human rights issues rather comprehensively, and which have inspired my work, I would single out the following books: T. Meron (ed.), *Human Rights in International Law: Legal and Policy Issues* (Oxford: Clarendon Press, 1984); J. Donnelly, *Universal Human Rights in Theory and Practice* (Ithaca: Cornell University Press, 1989); Z. Arat, *Democracy and Human Rights in Developing Countries* (London: Lagneia Rainier Publishers, 1991); A. An-Na'im (ed.) *Human Rights in Cross-Cultural Perspectives. A Quest for Consensus* (Philadelphia: University of Pennsylvania Press, 1992); P. Alston (ed.), *The United Nations and Human Rights. A Critical Appraisal* (Oxford: Clarendon Press, 1992); B. Johnson (ed.), *Freedom and Interpretation. The Oxford Amnesty Lectures 1992* (New York: Basic Books, 1993); S. Shute

and S. Hurley (eds), *On Human Rights. The Oxford Amnesty Lectures on Human Rights 1993* (New York: Basic Books, 1993); O. Hufton (ed.), *Historical Change and Human Rights. The Oxford Amnesty Lectures 1994* (New York: Basic Books, 1995).

4   See, e.g., *Restatement of the Law. The Foreign Relations Law of the United States*, Third edition, vol. 2, pp. 161–7 (St Paul: American Law Institute Publishers, 1987); L. Henkin, *International Law: Politics and Values* (Dordrecht: Nijhoff, 1995).

5   Commission on Human Rights. Report of the Fiftieth Session (31 January–11 March 1994), pp. 391–3 (New York: United Nations, 1994).

6   The International Institute for Strategic Studies, *Strategic Survey: 1994/95*, p. 16 (Oxford: Oxford University Press, 1995).

7   *Oxford English Dictionary*, Second edition, vol. XVI, p. 430 (Oxford: Oxford University Press, 1980).

8   J. Baker, with T. M. DeFrank, *The Politics of Diplomacy*, p. 672 (New York: G. P. Putnam's Sons, 1995).

9   B. Buzan, C. Jones and R. Little, *The Logic of Anarchy*, p. 166 (New York: Columbia University Press, 1993).

10   Here I am omitting a detailed discussion as to the meaning of the concept of 'gross and systematic violations of human rights'. This concept has evolved basically in the framework of the UN, though sometimes different terminology is used. Thus the ECOSOC Resolution 1503 of 27 May 1970 speaks of a special procedure for the consideration of individual communications, if such communications 'appear to reveal a consistent pattern of gross and reliably attested violations of human rights and fundamental freedoms' (UN Doc. E/4832-/Add.1). The Maastricht Seminar on the Right to Restitution, Compensation and Rehabilitation for Victims of Gross Violations of Human Rights and Fundamental Freedoms of 15 March 1992 provides that 'the notion of gross violations of human rights and fundamental freedoms includes at least the following practices: genocide, slavery and slavery-like practices, summary and arbitrary executions, torture, disappearances, arbitrary and prolonged detention, and systematic discrimination', and it concludes that 'violations of other human rights, including violation of economic social and cultural rights, may also be gross and systematic in scope and nature' (Seminar on the Right to Restitution, Compensation and Rehabilitation for Victims of Gross Violations of Human Rights and Fundamental Freedoms, Maastricht, 11–15 March 1992, SIM Special No. 12, p. 17). Section 502B of the US Foreign Assistance Act prohibits security aid, except in extraordinary circumstances, to any country 'which engages in a constant pattern of gross violations of internationally recognized human rights, including torture or cruel, inhuman or degrading treatment or punishment; prolonged detention without charges; or other flagrant denials of the right to life, liberty, and security of the person' (D. Weissbrodt, 'Human Rights Legislation and United States Foreign Policy', Georgia Journal of International and Comparative Law, 7, 242 (1977)). One of the most comprehensive definitions of the term is given by Cecilia Medina Quiroga, who writes that 'gross, systematic violations of human rights are those violations, instrumental to the achievement of governmental policies, perpetrated in such a quantity and in such a manner as to create

a situation in which the right to life, to personal integrity or to personal liberty of the population as a whole or of one or more sectors of the population of a country are continuously infringed or threatened' (C. M. Quiroga, *The Battle of Human Rights*, p. 16 (Dordrecht: Nijhoff, 1988)).

11 See R. Falk's 'Foreword' to B. S. Chimni, *International Law and World Order*, p. 9 (London, Sage, 1993).
12 *The Economist*, 28 October 1995, p. 86.
13 35 ILM 357 (1996).
14 Ibid., p. 373.
15 Ibid., p. 398.
16 A. Renteln, *International Human Rights: Universalism Versus Relativism* (Newbury Park, Sage, 1990).

1 THE *RAISON D'ÊTRE* OF HUMAN RIGHTS DIPLOMACY

1 L. Henkin, *International Law: Politics and Values*, p. 106 (Dordrecht: Nijhoff Publishers, 1995).
2 The laws of war, which aim at the protection of individuals in international armed conflicts, emerged, of course, much earlier than international norms on the rights of religious or ethnic minorities. In contrast to human rights norms, which protect the individual *vis-à-vis* his or her own state, the rules and customs of war (or international humanitarian law) emerged to protect only enemy or alien nationals. Expected reciprocity was the very reason for such a concern for the rights of enemy nationals. Therefore the laws of war are international by definition.
3 I. Brownlie, *International Law and the Use of Force by States*, p. 340 (Oxford: Clarendon Press, 1963).
4 See A. de Balogh, *La protection internationale des minorités*, p. 23 (Paris: Les editions internationales, 1930).
5 See F. L. Israel, *Major Peace Treaties of Modern History, 1648–1967*, vol. 1, pp. 7–49 (New York: Chelsea House in association with McGraw-Hill, 1967).
6 See P. Thornberry, *International Law and the Rights of Minorities*, p. 27 (Oxford: Clarendon Press, 1991).
7 See E. C. Stowell, *Intervention in International Law*, pp. 126, 489 (Washington, DC: Henry Holt & Company, 1921).
8 See Stowell 1921.
9 F. Capotorti, *Study on the Rights of Persons Belonging to Ethnic, Religious and Linguistic Minorities*, p. 17 (New York: United Nations, 1991).
10 Ibid., pp. 17–18.
11 D. Welch, *Justice and the Genesis of War*, p. 48 (Cambridge: Cambridge University Press, 1993).
12 Quoted by W. Laqueur in 'The Issue of Human Rights', *Commentary*, 64:5, 33 (1977).
13 B. Russet, *Grasping the Democratic Peace*, p. 135 (Princeton: Princeton University Press, 1993).

14 See, e.g., C. Thomas, 'Third World Security', in R. Carey and T. C. Salmon (eds), *International Security in the Modern World*, p. 106 (London: St Martin's Press, 1992).

15 F. Halliday, *Islam and the Myth of Confrontation: Religion and Politics in the Middle East*, p. 70 (London, Tauris, 1996).

16 *The Economist*, 14 May 1994, p. 88.

17 M. Doyle, 'Kant, Liberal Legacies, and Foreign Affairs', *Philosophy and Public Affairs*, 12:3 (1983).

18 Russet 1993.

19 C. Layne, 'Kant or Cant: The Myth of the Democratic Peace', *International Security*, 19:2 (1994); D. Spiro, 'The Insignificance of the Liberal Peace', *International Security*, 19:2 (1994).

20 Welch 1993, p. 73.

21 See Russet 1993, pp. 11–35.

22 *The Economist*, 1 April 1995, p. 21.

23 A. Moravcsik, 'Letter to the Economist', *The Economist*, 29 April 1995, p. 8.

24 *Sunday Times*, 9 July 1995, p. 15.

25 UNHCR, *The State of the World's Refugees. The Challenge of Protection*, p. 1 (New York: Penguin Books, 1993).

26 Ibid., p. 3.

27 The 1994 Human Development Report prepared by the UNDP counts only three inter-state wars in the period between 1989 and 1992, while there had been seventy-nine cases of intra-state conflicts within the same period (*UNDP, Human Development Report 1994*, p. 47 (New York: Oxford University Press, 1994)).

28 See *Country Reports on Human Rights Practices for 1994*, US State Department, February 1995.

29 The Parliamentary Assembly of the Council of Europe, in its Resolution of 2 February 1995, declared that although the political conflict between Chechnya and the central authorities of the Russian Federation belonged to the internal affairs of Russia, the methods used by these authorities violate Russia's international obligations (*Human Rights in Russia – International Dimension* (in Russian), Moscow: *Prava Cheloveka* (Human Rights) 1995, p. 179). In January 1996, though the Parliamentary Assembly voted for the admission of Russia to the Council of Europe, its government was severely criticized by many members of the Assembly for its human rights record generally and especially for its handling of the hostage crisis in Dagestan. The main reasoning behind the vote in favour of Russia seems to be that positive changes in the country would become a reality through its inclusion into European structures rather than its exclusion from them.

30 T. Hobbes, *Leviathan*, Part 2, Chapter 17.

31 T. Hobbes, *Behemoth or the Long Parliament* (ed. F. Tonnies), Second edition (London: Frank Cass & Co., 1969).

32 R. Dahrendorf, *Law and Order*, p. 158 (London: Stevens & Sons, 1985).

33 *The Economist*, 28 August 1993, p. 15.

34 See M. Singer and A. Wildavski, *The Real World Order: Zones of Peace/Zones of Turmoil* (Chatham: Chatham House Publishers, 1993).

35 F. Halliday, *Rethinking International Relations*, p. 149 (London: Macmillan, 1994).
36 R. Keohane, 'Hobbes's Dilemma and Institutional Change in World Politics: Sovereignty in International Society', in H. H. Holm and G. Sorensen (eds), *Whose World Order*, p. 180 (Boulder: Westview Press, 1995).
37 S. Hoffman, 'In Defence of Mother Teresa: Morality in Foreign Policy', *International Affairs*, 75:2 (March–April 1996), 175.
38 *The Times*, 27 November 1995, p. 9.
39 *The Times*, 29 November 1995, p. 21.
40 J. B. Goodno, *The Philippines: Land of Broken Promises*, p. 67 (London, Zed Books, 1991).
41 *The Economist*, 27 August 1994, p. 17.
42 Ibid., p. 19.
43 E. Hobsbawm, *Age of Extremes*, p. 370 (London: Michael Joseph, 1994).
44 *Time*, 22 May 1995, p. 57.
45 O. Sunkel, 'Uneven Globalization, Economic Reform, and Democracy: A View from Latin America', in H. H. Holm and G. Sorensen (eds), *Whose World Order*, p. 57 (Boulder: Westview Press, 1995).
46 *The Economist*, 22 April 1995, p. 77.
47 Keohane 1995, p. 224.
48 Ibid.
49 R. Rorty, 'Human Rights, Rationality, and Sentimentality', in S. Shute and S. Hurley (eds.) *On Human Rights. The Oxford Amnesty Lectures 1993*, p. 134 (New York: Basic Books, 1993).
50 Ibid.
51 Henkin 1995, p. 183.
52 *The Economist*, 25 February 1995, p. 22.
53 L. Ferry, *L'homme-Dieu ou le Sens de la vie*, p. 225 Paris: Grasset, 1996).

2 HUMAN RIGHTS AND INTERNATIONAL STABILITY

1 T. Franck and N. Rodley, 'After Bangladesh: The Law of Humanitarian Intervention by Military Force', *American Journal of International Law*, 67, 300, (1973).
2 R. Manning, 'Clinton and China: Beyond Human Rights', *Orbis* 38:2, 202, (1995).
3 However, votes given for the communists (more than 20 per cent) in the Parliamentary elections in Russia in December 1995 show that hardships stemming, *inter alia*, from instability created by the reforms are too much for quite a large part of the population of Russia. They would prefer the previous stability and certainty, without rights and freedoms, to the risks and hardships which often come together with reforms.
4 H. Bull, *The Anarchical Society: A Study of Order in World Politics*, p. 83 (London: Macmillan, 1977).
5 *The Times*, 16 December 1995, p. 12.
6 A. Mazrui, *Towards a Pax Africana*, p. 144 (Chicago: University of Chicago Press, 1967).
7 *The Times*, 22 October 1994, p. 17.

8   A. Mazrui, 'The Bondage of Boundaries', *The Economist*, 28 August 1993, p. 34.
9   Ibid.
10 D. C. Bach, 'Reappraising Postcolonial Geopolitics: Europe, Africa and the End of the Cold War', in T. Ranger and O. Vaughan (eds), *Legitimacy and the State in Twentieth-Century Africa*, p. 247 (Oxford: Macmillan, 1993).
11 M. Singer and A. Wildavski, *The Real World Order: Zones of Peace/Zones of Turmoil*, p. 140 (Chatham: Chatham House Publishers, 1993).
12 H. Kissinger, *Diplomacy*, p. 623 (London: Simon & Schuster, 1994).
13 Singer & Wildavski 1993, p. 80.
14 See, e.g., K. Roosevelt, *Countercoup: The Struggle for the Control of Iran* (New York: McGraw-Hill, 1979).
15 D. Forsythe, *Human Rights and Peace: International and National Dimensions*, p. 38 (Lincoln: University of Nebraska Press, 1993).
16 J. Donnelly, 'International Human Rights after the Cold War', in M. T. Clare and D. C. Thomas (eds), *World Security: Challenges for a New Century*, p. 236 (London: St Martin's Press, 1994).
17 Sattareh Farman Farmaian with Dona Munker, *Daughter of Persia*, p. 385 (London: Corgi Books, 1995).
18 Ibid., p. 365.
19 J. Donnelly, *Universal Human Rights in Theory and Practice*, p. 247 (Ithaca: Cornell University Press, 1989).
20 Z. F. Arat, *Democracy and Human Rights in Developing Countries*, p. 81 (London: Lagneia Rainier Publishers, 1991).
21 F. Halliday, *Islam and the Myth of Confrontation: Religion and Politics in the Middle East*, p. 47 (London: Tauris, 1996).
22 Ibid., p. 51.
23 Ibid., p. 65.
24 Ibid., p. 9.
25 Ibid., p. 56.
26 Forsythe 1993, p. 68; Arat 1991.
27 H. Shue, *Basic Rights: Subsistence, Affluence and US Foreign Policy*, pp. 24–5 (Princeton: Princeton University Press, 1980).
28 D. Türk, 'Development and Human Rights', in L. Henkin and J. Hargrove (eds), *Human Rights: An Agenda for the Next Century*, p. 176 (Washington DC: The American Society of International Law, 1995).
29 UN Doc. E/1993/22, para. 10.
30 See J. Tang (ed.), *Human Rights and International Relations in the Asian Pacific*, pp. 214–15 (London: Pinter, 1995).
31 S. Hewlett, *The Cruel Dilemmas of Development: Twentieth Century Brazil*, p. 4 (New York: Basic Books, 1980).
32 Donnelly 1989, p. 187.
33 Ibid., p. 188.
34 Ibid.
35 Banco Central de Chile, Departamente de Estudios, 1995.
36 *The Economist*, 1 July 1995, p. 21.
37 D. Welsh, 'Domestic Politics and Ethnic Conflict', in M. Brown (ed.) *Ethnic Conflict and International Security*, p. 56 (Princeton: Princeton University Press, 1993).

38 See J. Snyder, 'Nationalism and the Crisis of the Post-Soviet State', in M. Brown (ed.), *Ethnic Conflict and International Security*, p. 80 (Princeton: Princeton University Press, 1993).
39 UN Doc. A/50/36.
40 C. Black, 'Canada's Continuing Identity Crisis', *Foreign Affairs*, 74:2 110 (1995).
41 H. Hannum, *Autonomy, Sovereignty, and Self-Determination. The Accommodation of Conflicting Rights*, p. 276 (University of Pennsylvania Press, 1990).
42 P. Brogan, *World Conflicts*, p. 574 (London: Bloomsbury, 1992).
43 Ibid., p. 572.
44 *The Times*, 2 September 1995, p. 12.
45 Brogan 1992, p. 412.
46 See, e.g., UN Doc. CCPR/C/42/Add.12, p. 2.
47 T. Franck, *Fairness in the International Legal and Institutional System,- Fairness in the International Legal and Institutional System*, General Course on Public International Law, pp. 125–50 (Academy of International Law, 1993–III).
48 See more on this in T. Franck, *The Power of Legitimacy Among Nations* (Oxford: Oxford University Press, 1990); R. Müllerson, *International Law, Rights and Politics* (London: Routledge, 1994).
49 UN Doc. CCPR/C/94/Add.1, p. 9.
50 UN Doc. CCPR/C/64/Add.12, pp. 4–5.
51 J. Chipman, 'Managing the Politics of Parochialism', in M. E. Brown (ed.), *Ethnic Conflict and International Security*, p. 245 (Princeton: Princeton University Press, 1993).
52 Hannum 1990, p. 455.
53 Helsinki Document (1992), paras 2–3.
54 Documents/Statements on or of the CSCE High Commissioner on National Minorities (1993), Reference No. 206/93/L/Rev.
55 Ibid.
56 *Guardian*, 7 July 1993, p. 8; EPC Press Release, P.66/93, Brussels, 9 July 1993.
57 Documents/Statements on or of the CSCE High Commissioner on National Minorities (1993), Reference No. 251/93/L.
58 Ibid., Reference No. 2556/94/L.
59 Ibid.
60 M. Jeziorski, *Former Yugoslav Republic of Macedonia – Background Paper for the Expert Consultation on Minority Education*, p. 4, The Hague, 18 November 1995.
61 The Framework Convention on the Protection of National Minorities, Council of Europe Doc. H(1995)10.
62 Constitution of the Republic of Hungary (as amended by Act No. XXXI of 1989), in G. Kilenyi and V. Lamm (eds), *Democratic Changes in Hungary (Basic Legislations on a Peaceful Transition from Bolshevism to Democracy)*, p. 35 (Budapest, 1990).
63 Constitution of the Republic of Macedonia (Skopje, 1991), p. 17.
64 Y. Shaposhnikov, 'On the Concept of the National Security of Russia', *Miezhdunarodnaya Zhizn [International Affairs]* (1993), no. 9, pp. 9–10.

65 C. Pleshakov, 'Human Rights in Russia: the Dragon is not Defeated', in Tang 1995, p. 132.
66 Ibid., p. 133.
67 *Rossiiskaya Gazeta*, 24 August 1994.
68 'Main Provisions of the Military Doctrine of the Russian Federation (Digest)', *Military News Bulletin*, 11 November 1993.
69 Ibid., p. 2.
70 G. I. Morozov, 'The UN at the Turn of the Century', *Moscow Journal of International Law*, 1, 39, (1995).
71 See more on this in Müllerson 1994, pp. 78–9.
72 Frontier Dispute (*Burkina Faso* v. *Republic of Mali*) 1986 *ICJ Reports* 565.
73 Opinion No. 3 of the Arbitration Commission of the International Conference on Yugoslavia, *European Journal of International Law*, 3:1, 184 (1992).
74 See more on the recognition of Croatia and Bosnia-Herzegovina in Müllerson 1994, chapter 4.
75 D. Owen, *Balkan Odyssey*, pp. 342–3 (London: Victor Gollancz, 1995).
76 H. Ekwe-Ekwe, *Africa 2001: The State, Human Rights and the People*, p. 95 (Reading: International Institute for Black Research, 1993).
77 W. Kymlicka, *Multicultural Citizenship. A Liberal Theory of Minority Rights*, p. 185 (Oxford: Clarendon Press, 1995).
78 Ibid.
79 See *The Times*, 30 September, 1995, p. 14.
80 The Framework Convention on the Protection of National Minorities, Council of Europe Doc. H(1995)10.
81 See M. Marty and R. Scott Appleby (eds), *Fundamentalisms Observed* (Chicago: The University of Chicago Press, 1991).
82 Ibid., p. ix.
83 D. Swearer, 'Fundamentalist Movements in Theravada Buddhism', in Marty and Scott Appleby 1991, p. 648.
84 *Sunday Times Magazine*, 9 May 1993, p. 51.
85 P. Kennedy, *Preparing for the Twenty-First Century*, p. 208 (London: HarperCollins, 1993).
86 F. Fukuyama, *The End of History and the Last Man*, p. 46 (London: Hamish Hamilton, 1992).
87 A. A. Sachedina, 'Activist Shi'ism in Iran, Iraq, and Lebanon', in Marty and Scott Appleby 1991, p. 450.
88 *The Economist*, 9 December 1995, p. 64.
89 F. Halliday, 'Review Article: The Politics of "Islam" – A Second Look', *British Journal of Political Science*, 25, 404 (1995).
90 See, e.g., ibid.; A. E. Mayer, *Islam and Human Rights: Tradition and Politics*, Second edition (Boulder: Westview Press, 1995).
91 A. A. An-Na'im, *Toward an Islamic Reformation: Civil Liberties, Human Rights and International Law* (Syracuse University Press, 1990); A. A. An-Na'im (ed.), *Human Rights in Cross-Cultural Perspectives. A Quest for Consensus* (Philadelphia: University of Pennsylvania Press, 1992); B. Tibi, 'Islamic Law/Shari'a, Human Rights, Universal Morality and International Relations', *Human Rights Quarterly*, 16 (1994).
92 See, e.g., UN Doc. CCPR/C/SR./1253, 30 July 1993.
93 UN Doc. E/CN.4/1993/41.

94 An-Na'im 1990, p. 163.
95 Bangkok NGO Declaration on Human Rights, 27 March 1993, pp. 10–11.
96 UN Doc. CCPR/C/SR.1263, p. 7.
97 Ibid.
98 H. Shahidian, 'National and International Aspects of Feminist Movement: The Example of Iranian Revolution of 1978–79', Critique, *Journal of Critical Studies of Iran and the Middle East*, Spring, 1, 46 (1993).
99 An-Na'im 1990, p. 184.
100 Ibid., p. 187.
101 Mayer 1995, p. xii.
102 Ibid., p. 27.
103 Ibid., p. 28.
104 Halliday 1995, p. 417.
105 Halliday 1995, pp. 149–50.
106 *Guardian*, 13 May 1995, p. 11.
107 Jason Abrams, 'Burundi: Anatomy of an Ethnic Conflict', *Survival*, 37:1, 150 (1995).
108 E. D. Mansfield and J. Snyder, 'Democratization and War', *Foreign Affairs*, 74:3, 79–80 (1995).
109 Ibid., p. 80.
110 Ibid., p. 81.
111 Ibid., p. 89.
112 B. Roberts, 'Human Rights, International Security and the Crisis of Communism', in V. Mastny and J. Zielonka (eds), *Human Rights and Security. Europe on the Eve of a New Era*, p. 52 (Oxford: Westview Press, 1991).

3 THE ROLE OF CULTURAL FACTORS, SOCIETAL DEVELOPMENT AND POWER INTERESTS IN THE HUMAN RIGHTS DISCOURSE

1 I. Brownlie (ed.), *Basic Documents on Human Rights*, Third edition, p. 22 (Oxford: Clarendon Press, 1992).
2 World Conference on Human Rights. The Vienna Declaration and Programme of Action, p. 28 (New York: United Nations, 1993).
3 *American Anthropologist*, 49 (1947), pp. 539–43.
4 Ibid., p. 543.
5 B. Kausikan, 'Asia's Different Standard', *Foreign Policy* Fall, 35 (1993).
6 M. Walzer, *Thick and Thin: Moral Argument at Home and Abroad*, p. 8 (Notre Dame, Ind.: University of Notre Dame Press, 1994).
7 A. H. Robertson and J. G. Merrills, *Human Rights in the World*, Third edition, p. 8 (Manchester University Press, 1993).
8 F. Fukuyama, *Trust*, p. 41 (London: Hamish Hamilton, 1995).
9 E. Hobsbawm, *Age of Extremes*, p. 9 (London: Michael Joseph, 1994).
10 D. Selbourne, *The Principle of Duty* p. 57 (London: Sinclair-Stevenson, 1994),.
11 A. Schlesinger Jr, 'The Opening of the American Mind', *New York Times Book Review*, 23 July 1989, p. 26.

12 A. Pollis, 'Eastern Orthodoxy and Human Rights', *Human Rights Quarterly*, 15, 344, 353 (1993).
13 F. Halliday, *Islam and the Myth of Confrontation: Religion and Politics in the Middle East*, p. 140 (London: Tauris, 1996).
14 W. Durant, *Age of Faith*, vol. 4 of *The Story of Civilization*, p. 544 (London: Simon & Schuster, 1950).
15 J. Donnelly, 'Cultural Relativism and Universal Human Rights', *Human Rights Quarterly*, 6:4, 414–15 (1984).
16 *Independent*, 8 June 1995, p. 15.
17 *The Times*, 10 January 1996, p. 10.
18 The new offence of 'dowry death' was included in the Indian Penal Code; and there is the Commission of Sati (Prevention) Act of 1987 (Second Periodic Report of India to the UN Human Rights Committee, 12 July 1989, UN Doc. CCPR/C/137/Add.13, paras. 117, 119).
19 'The Real World of Human Rights', statement by Foreign Minister Wong Kan Seng of Singapore at the World Conference on Human Rights, Vienna, 16 June 1993, p. 2.
20 Ibid., p. 4.
21 27 L.N.T.S. 2113.
22 46 U.N.T.S. 169.
23 Brownlie 1993, pp. 132–3.
24 Ibid., p. 127.
25 Bangkok Inter-Governmental Declaration on Human Rights in J. Tang (ed.), *Human Rights and International Relations in the Asian Pacific*, p. 205 (London: Pinter, 1995).
26 World Conference on Human Rights. The Vienna Declaration and Programme of Action, p. 30 (New York: United Nations, 1993).
27 J. Donnelly, *Universal Human Rights in Theory and Practice*, p. 119 (Ithaca: Cornell University Press, 1989).
28 Bangkok NGO Declaration on Human Rights, 27 March 1993, p. 1.
29 Aung San Suu Kyi, 'Listen: the Culture of Human Rights and Democracy is Universal', *International Herald Tribune*, 7 December 1994, p. 4.
30 P. Windsor, 'Cultural Dialogue in Human Rights', in M. Desai and P. Redfern (eds), *Global Governance: Ethics and Economics of the World Order*, p. 185 (London: Pinter, 1995).
31 A. E. Mayer, *Islam and Human Rights: Tradition and Politics*, Second edition, p. 176 (Boulder: Westview Press, 1995).
32 R. Scruton, *Modern Philosophy*, p. 32 (London: Sinclair-Stevenson, 1994).
33 Howard, 'Evaluating Human Rights in Africa: Some Problems of Implicit Comparisons', *Human Rights Quarterly*, 6:2, 175 (1984).
34 Donnelly 1989, p. 119.
35 M. Djilas, *The New Class. An Analysis of the Communist System* (New York: Praeger, 1965).
36 Yash Ghai, 'Asian Perspectives of Human Rights', in Tang 1995, p. 61.
37 A. Etzioni, *The Spirit of Community*, p. 3 (London: Simon & Schuster, 1993).
38 *The Times*, 3 June 1995.
39 Selbourne 1994, p. 83.
40 'Citizens' Responsibilities', Discussion Seminar with Experts, Research and Planning Unit, 16 December 1994, p. 2.

41 *The Times*, 8 November 1995, p. 16.
42 *Our Global Neighbourhood. The Report of the Commission on Global Governance*, p. 56 (Oxford: Oxford University Press, 1995).
43 Etzioni 1993, p. 25.
44 H. McRae, *The World in 2020. Power, Culture and Prosperity: A Vision of the Future*, p. 204 (London: HarperCollins, 1994).
45 S. M. Lipset, *American Exceptionalism: A Double-Edged Sword*, p. 98 (New York: Norton, 1996).
46 Fukuyama 1995, p. 157.
47 M. Ch. Bassiouni (ed.), *International Criminal Law*, vol. 1, p. 363 (New York: Transnational, 1986).
48 *Longman's Illustrated Encyclopedia of World History*, p. 463 (London: Ivy Leaf, 1991).
49 Ibid., p. 410.
50 A. Ross, *Statsret [State Law]*, Third edition, p. 707 (Copenhagen, 1980). (I am thankful to my LLM student Kristina Miskowiak who drew my attention to this interesting fact.)
51 L. Swidler, *After the Absolute: The Dialogical Future of Religious Reflection*, p. 63 (Minneapolis: Fortress Press, 1990).
52 One may, of course, argue that the death penalty is still used in some highly developed societies, such as, for example, the United States. However, the US, while being a highly developed, democratic society, is at the same time a society which has developed very unevenly, especially in comparison with the Western European democracies. Extreme richness and extreme poverty, the highest academic excellence and widespread illiteracy, are to be found in the United States. The very high crime rate and the use of the death penalty as a response seem to reflect this controversial character of the country.
53 Donnelly 1989, p. 70.
54 Howard 1984, pp. 169–70.
55 Hobsbawm 1994, p. 15.
56 See, e.g., G. D. Ganby, 'Power of the People via Personal Electronic Media', *Washington Quarterly*, Spring, 5–22 (1991); S. Shane, *Dismantling Utopia: How Information Ended the Soviet Union* (Chicago: Ivan Dee, 1994).
57 'News Review', *Sunday Times*, 3 September 1995, p. 3.
58 The fact that certain ideas, practices or discoveries which originate in some societies, are taken over by others, does not mean that the former are inherently superior to the latter. Societies and civilizations develop unevenly. The West did not only borrow gunpowder from China, and a lot of mathematics from the Arab world, but the very *homo sapiens* himself, to all appearances, originated in Africa. It seems quite plausible that, in the foreseeable future, the West will have to borrow rather heavily from the East.
59 In 1993 Samuel Huntington wrote: 'The great divisions among humankind and the dominating source of conflict will be cultural. Nation states will remain the most powerful actors in world affairs, but principal conflicts of global politics will occur between nations and groups of different civilizations' (S. Huntington, 'The Clash of Civilizations', *Foreign Affairs* , 72:3, 22 (1993)).

60   R. Rorty, 'Human Rights, Rationality, and Sentimentality', in S. Shute and S. Hurley (eds), *On Human Rights. Oxford Amnesty Lectures 1993* , p. 119 (New York: Basic Books, 1993).
61   Windsor 1995, pp. 177–8.
62   Rorty 1993, p. 128.
63   Ibid.
64   P. Abramson and R. Inglehart, *Value Change in Global Perspective* (Ann Arbor: University of Michigan Press, 1995).
65   *The Economist*, 1 July 1995, p. 54.
66   M. Freeman, 'Human Rights: Asia and the West', in Tang 1995, pp. 16–17.
67   K. Waltz, *Theory of International Politics*, p. 97 (London: Addison-Wesley, 1979).
68   F. Halliday, 'International Society as Homogeneity: Burke, Marx, Fukuyama', *Millennium*, 21:3, 435 (1992).
69   Maly Gaballero-Anthony writes that 'Thailand's economic growth resulted in a growing middle class which eventually played a crucial role in breaking the monopoly of military power.... Buoyed by its political development, Thailand is now working towards a more stable and sustainable democratic system' (M. Gaballero-Anthony, 'Human Rights, Economic Change and Political Development', in Tang 1995, p. 44).
70   Fukuyama 1995, p. 356.
71   W. Brands, 'Human Rights and US Policy Towards Asia', in Tang 1995, p. 81.
72   Yash Ghai, in Tang 1995, p. 65.
73   R. L. Bartley, 'The Case for Optimism. The West Should Believe in Itself', *Foreign Affairs*, 72:4, 17 (1993).
74   UN Doc. E/1995/23; E/CN.4/1995/176, p. 391.
75   Ibid., p. 417.
76   In this context, it is interesting to note that half a year later, after the military regime had executed nine activists for the independence of Ogoniland, including writer Ken Saro-Wiwa, the Commonwealth suspended Nigeria's membership. These developments show that certain events related to human rights which, thanks to mass media attention, are able to 'shock the conscience of mankind' may trigger even some sanctions, while more important developments remain without any response. The execution of Ken Saro-Wiwa was only one episode in a whole chain of massive human rights violations in Nigeria. Obviously the most important among them, causing many other violations, occurred when the military regime in 1993 annulled the result of the elections which gave victory to Chief Abiola.
77   UN Doc. E/1995/23; E/CN.4/1995/176, p. 351.
78   Even democratic governments are guilty of misleading parliaments and the public, and committing human rights violations in order to stay in power. Different Watergates, Irangates, Iraqgates and similar scandals show that even democratically elected governments tap telephones, contrary not only to international human rights standards, but to their own laws as well, try to suppress the freedom of the press, and commit other human rights violations.
79   See Mayer 1995, pp. 29–31

80 F. Halliday, 'Review Article: The Politics of "Islam" – A Second Look', *British Journal of Political Science*, 25, 405 (1995).
81 Liu Binyan, 'Civilization Grafting', *Foreign Affairs*, 72:4, 20 (1993).
82 Mayer 1995, p. xv.
83 B. Anderson, *Imagined Communities* (London: Verso, 1991).

4 SOME LESSONS OF COLD WAR HUMAN RIGHTS DIPLOMACY

1 See, e.g., H. H. Wilson, 'Some Principal Aspects of British Efforts to Crush the African Slave Trade', *AJIL*, 44:2 (1950).
2 See, e.g., P. Collinson, 'Religion and Human Rights: The Case of and for Protestantism', in *Historical Change and Human Rights. The Oxford Amnesty Lectures 1994*, pp. 51–52 (New York: Basic Books, 1995).
3 G. Scelle, *Précis de droit des gens*, p. 53 (Paris: Libraire du Recueil Sirey, 1934).
4 See C.W. Jenks, *Social Justice in the Law of Nations: The ILO Impact after Fifty Years* (Oxford: Oxford University Press, 1970).
5 L. Henkin, *International Law: Politics and Values*, p. 171 (Dordrecht: Nijhoff, 1995).
6 J. Donnelly, 'Security, Human Rights, and East–West Relations: Theoretical Bases of the Linkage', in V. Mastny and J. Zielonka (eds), *Human Rights and Security. Europe on the Eve of A New Era*, p. 29 (Oxford: Westview Press, 1991).
7 R. Bilder, 'Rethinking International Human Rights: Some Basic Questions', *Human Rights Law Journal*, II, 573–4 (1969).
8 S. Davidson, *Human Rights*, p. 120 (Buckingham: Open University Press, 1993). See also D. Harris, M. O'Boyle and C. Warbrick, *The Law of the European Convention on Human Rights* (London: Butterworth, 1995).
9 Ibid., p. 29.
10 See, e.g., Ch. Horner, 'Human Rights and the Jackson Amendment', in D. Fosdick (ed.), *Staying the Course* (Washington DC: Washington University Press, 1987).
11 C. J. Nolan, *Principled Diplomacy. Security and Rights in U.S. Foreign Policy*, p. 133 (London: Greenwood Press, 1993).
12 Ibid., p. 134.
13 The literature on the Helsinki process and its human dimension is vast. See, e.g., V.-Y. Ghebali, *La diplomatie de la détente: la C.S.C.E., 1973–1989* (Brussels: Bruylant, 1989); A. Bloed and P. van Dijk (eds), *The Human Dimension of the Helsinki Process: The Vienna Follow-up Meeting and the Aftermath* (Dordrecht: Nijhoff, 1991); A. Heraclides, *Security and Cooperation in Europe: The Human Dimension, 1972–1992* (London: Frank Cass, 1993).
14 For the text of The Helsinki Final Act, see I. Brownlie (ed.), *Basic Documents on Human Rights*, Third edition, pp. 391–449 (Oxford: Clarendon Press, 1993).
15 A. Cassese, *Human Rights in a Changing World*, p. 57 (Cambridge: Polity, 1994).
16 Ibid., p. 58.

17 J. Kirkpatrick, 'Dictatorship and Double Standards', *Commentary*, November, 34–45 (1979).
18 J. Egeland, *Impotent Superpower – Potent Small State*, pp. 135–6 (Oslo: Norwegian University Press, 1988).
19 P. Baehr, *The Role of Human Rights in Foreign Policy*, p. 83 (London: Macmillan, 1994).
20 See D. Newsom (ed.), *The Diplomacy of Human Rights*, p. 10 (New York: University Press of America, 1986).
21 See ibid., pp. 67–139.
22 D. C. McGaffey, 'Policy and Practice: Human Rights in the Shah's Iran', in Newsom 1986, p. 75.
23 D. Newsom, 'Release in Indonesia', in Newsom 1986, pp. 106–7.
24 Egeland 1988, p. 44.
25 See I. Brecher (ed.), *Human Rights, Development and Foreign Policy: Canadian Perspectives*, p. 126 (Ottawa: The Institute for Research on Public Policy, 1989).
26 J. J. C. Voorhoeven, *Peace, Profits and Principles*, p. 222 (Dordrecht: Nijhoff, 1979).
27 Ibid., p. 223.
28 T. Carothers, 'Democracy Promotion under Clinton', *The Washington Quarterly*, 18:4, 15 (1995).
29 R. J. Vincent, 'The Response of Europe and the Third World to United States Human Rights Diplomacy', in Newsom 1986, p. 37.
30 Ibid.
31 J. Dugard, *International Law. A South African Perspective*, p. 202 (Kenwin: Juta & Co., 1994).
32 Ibid., p. 305.
33 Ibid., pp. 202–3.
34 Ibid., p. 307.
35 *Restatement of the Law. The Foreign Relations Law of the United States*, vol.1, p. 382 (St Paul: American Law Institute Publishers, 1987).
36 L. de Villiers, *In Sight of Surrender: The US Sanctions Campaign against South Africa* (Westport: Praeger, 1995).
37 B. Russell, P. Van Ness and Beng Hewn Chua, 'Australia's Human Rights Diplomacy', *Australian Foreign Policy Papers*, 36–7 (1992).
38 C. J. Nolan, *Principled Diplomacy: Security and Rights in U.S. Foreign Policy*, p. 142 (London: Greenwood Press, 1993).
39 D. Forsythe, *Human Rights and Peace: International and National Dimensions*, p. 7 (Lincoln: University of Nebraska Press, 1993).
40 The State Department Legal Advisor, Davis Robinson, gave three reasons which, in his view, legally justified the US invasion in Grenada. These were: protection of nationals abroad; collective action under Article 52 of the UN Charter; and response to a request by lawful authority ('Letter of Davis Robinson to Edward Gordon', in J. N. Moore (ed.), *Law and the Grenada Mission*, pp. 125–9 (1984)). Most international lawyers criticized the invasion (see, e.g., W. C. Gilmore, *The Grenada Invasion: Analysis and Documents* (London: Mansell, 1984)) and the General Assembly voted 108 to 9 to condemn the US use of force as a violation of international law (ibid., p. 153). The landing in Panama in 1989 was justified by the US government as an act of self-defence, and on the grounds of: the need to

restore democracy in Panama in the face of the arbitrary refusal by Noriega to honour election results; the need to defend the Panama canal; the consent of the constitutional authority (Guillermo Endara); and the need to protect US military and other personnel (R. Jennings and A. Watts (eds.), *Oppenheim's International Law*, Ninth edition, vol. I, Introduction, and Part 1, p. 436 (London: Longman, 1993).

41 Kishore Mahbubani, 'The Pacific Impulse', *Survival*, 37:1, 116 (1995).
42 Ibid.
43 See, e.g., J. Harriss (ed.), *The Politics of Humanitarian Intervention* (London: Pinter, 1995); D. Owen, *Balkan Odyssey* (London: Victor Gollancz, 1995).
44 R. Falk, *On Humane Governance: Toward a New Global Politics*, p. 207 (Cambridge: Polity Press, 1995).

5 A NEW ERA: WHAT SHOULD, AND WHAT CAN, BE DONE?

1   S. M. Lipset, *Political Man*, p. 77 (New York: Doubleday, 1960).
2   See D. Forsythe, *Human Rights and Peace: International and National Dimensions*, pp. 61–76 (Lincoln: University of Nebraska Press, 1993).
3   M. Weber, 'Legitimacy, Politics and the State', in W. Connelly (ed.), *Legitimacy and the State*, p. 34 (Oxford: Basil Blackwell, 1984).
4   Forsythe 1993, p. 63.
5   *Country Reports on Human Rights Practices for 1994*, p. 1165 (US State Department, February 1995).
6   See *The Times*, 1 July 1994, p. 11; *The Times*, 10 July 1994, p. 15.
7   See *Human Rights Watch World Report 1994*, p. 325 (New York: Human Rights Watch, 1993).
8   See ibid.
9   *The Economist* writes that, although 'outwardly Saudi Arabia appears as affluent as ever... whereas a year ago Saudis would have spent without thought, now they must sometimes think first' (*The Economist*, 17 September 1994, p. 66).
10 *The Times*, 2 August 1995, p. 7.
11 Ibid., p. 13.
12 T. Carothers, 'Democracy Promotion under Clinton', *TheWashington Quarterly*, 18:4, 23 (1995).
13 C. W. Maynes, 'Relearning Intervention', *Foreign Policy*, 98, 113 (1995).
14 T. Franck, 'The Emerging Right to Democratic Governance', *American Journal of International Law*, 86 (1992).
15 Virginia Page Fortna, 'Success and Failure in Southern Africa: Peacekeeping in Namibia and Angola', in D. Daniel and B. Hayes (eds), *Beyond Traditional Peacekeeping*, p. 293 (London: Macmillan, 1995).
16 *Our Global Neighbourhood. The Report of the Commission on Global Governance*, pp. 59–60 (Oxford: Oxford University Press, 1995).
17 See M. Weller (ed.), *Regional Peace-Keeping and International Enforcement: the Liberian Crisis*, pp. 24–32 (Cambridge: Cambridge University Press, 1994).
18 *The Economist*, 23 December 1995, p. 81.
19 UN Doc. CCPR/C/79/Add. 59, 9 November 1995, paras. 16, 18, 19, 20.

20 Ibid., paras. 12, 22, 23.
21 During the Cold War, the causes of many negative phenomena, such as international tension, under-development, terrorism and human rights violations, were seen or presented by the major political and ideological adversaries not only differently but also in a distorted and simplified manner. If for the Kremlin it was Western – and especially American – imperialism, Zionism or capitalist exploitation which was to be blamed, Washington saw the arm of Moscow where frequently poverty, corruption and injustice were the main causes of various troubles. Therefore one could hardly speak of causes of, for example, international terrorism or human rights violations when discussing these issues at international fora. Though different visions of these and other problems will always remain inevitable, the Cold War lens which distorted and simplified many issues seems to have gone for good.
22 UN Doc. A/47/277, S/24111, 17 June 1992.
23 UN Doc. E/CN.4/1995/176, p. 260.
24 *Country Reports on Human Rights Practices for 1994*, p. xiv (US State Department, February 1995).
25 Carothers 1995, p. 20.
26 As quiet diplomacy is usually also confidential, we know little of it, and it is difficult to find any references. However, as an example, it is possible, I believe, to refer to the activities of the OSCE High Commissioner on National Minorities Max van der Stoel. He rarely condemns or accuses, but often recommends governments to adopt different measures, offers good offices, and praises governments even for minor progress made in the domain of minority issues. And governments have changed their laws and policies because of, *inter alia*, his recommendations and insistence.
27 L. F. Damrosch, 'The Civilian Impact of Economic Sanctions', in L. F. Damrosch (ed.), *Enforcing Restraint*, p. 275 (New York: Council of Foreign Relations Press, 1993).
28 Ibid., p. 278.
29 D. Keen, 'Short-Term Interventions and Long-Term Problems: The Case of the Kurds in Iraq', in J. Harriss (ed.), *The Politics of Humanitarian Intervention*, pp. 182–3 (London: Pinter, 1995).
30 WFP, *News Update*, 26 September 1995, Rome.
31 *The Economist*, 21 October 1995, p. 81.
32 *The Economist*, 29 July 1995, p. 13.
33 J. Lilley, 'Freedom through Trade', *Foreign Policy*, 94, 40 (1994).
34 *The Economist*, 23 March 1996, p. 16.
35 L. Henkin, *International Law: Politics and Values*, p. 45 (Dordrecht: Nijhoff, 1995).
36 It seems that economic sanctions against Yugoslavia (Serbia and Montenegro) played a role in bringing Milosevic to the negotiating table and changing his policy towards Bosnia-Herzegovina and the Serb-held territories in Croatia.
37 See *The Times*, 29 July 1995, p. 14.
38 *The Economist*, 19 July 1995, p. 37.
39 *The Financial Times*, 14 December 1995, p. 2.
40 The suppression of Nigeria's membership of the Commonwealth, and the EU's arms embargo against Nigeria (*The Times*, 21 November 1995, p. 10)

because of its outrageous human rights record, are measures which will not negatively affect Nigeria's population. Equally, freezing the assets of the military regime will not hurt ordinary Nigerians.

41 For detailed information, see a comprehensive and excellent study of the activities of the UN in the field of human rights during a period of almost fifty years in P. Alston (ed.), *The United Nations and Human Rights. A Critical Appraisal* (Oxford: Clarendon Press, 1992).
42 Ibid., p. 154.
43 UN Doc. A/50/36.
44 Ibid., para. 38.
45 Ibid., para. 46.
46 Ibid., para. 38.
47 UN Doc. A/50/36, para. 22.
48 Ibid., para. 23.
49 The presentation of Mr Mavrommatis at the Conference on Administrative and Expert Monitoring of International Legal Norms (New York, New York University, February 1996).
50 Professor Philip Alston's study on possible long-term approaches to enhancing the effective operation of existing and prospective bodies established under United Nations human rights instruments (UN Doc. A/44/668, para. 180).
51 *European Treaty Series*, 148 (1992).
52 *The Framework Convention on the Protection of National Minorities* (Council of Europe Doc. H (1995) 10).
53 *The Economist*, 2 December, 1995, p. 45.
54 *European Journal of International Law* 72 (1993).
55 I. Brownlie, *Basic Documents on Human Rights*, pp. 495–530 (Oxford: Clarendon Press, 1993).
56 Ibid., pp. 551–66.
57 A. H. Robertson and J. G. Merrills, *Human Rights in the World*, p. 221 (Manchester: Manchester University Press, 1993).
58 European Bank for Reconstruction and Development, Annual Report 1994, p. 7.
59 A. Newburg, 'The European Bank for Reconstruction and Development: Democracy, Human Rights and Market Economics', *Law in Transition* (A Newsletter on Legal Cooperation and Training from the EBRD), pp. 2–3 (Autumn 1993).
60 I. F. I. Shihata, *The World Bank in a Changing World*, Selected Essays and Lectures, vol. II, p. 133 (Dordrecht: Nijhoff, 1995).
61 Ibid., p. 137.
62 Ibid., p. 175.
63 Ibid., p. 176.
64 Ibid., p. 177.
65 Ibid., p. 561.
66 UN Doc. E/1995/ 23-E/CN.4/1995/176.
67 D. Weissbrodt, 'The Contribution of International Non-Governmental Organizations to the Protection of Human Rights', in T. Meron (ed.), *Human Rights in International Law: Legal and Policy Issues*, vol. II, p. 411 (Oxford: Clarendon Press, 1984).

68 P. J. Spiro, 'New Global Communities: Nongovernmental Organizations in International Decision-Making Institutions', *The Washington Quarterly*, 18:1, 53 (1994).

69 UN Doc. E/C.12/1989/4 (1988), p. 27.

70 M. Craven, *The International Covenant on Economic, Social and Cultural Rights: A Perspective for Development*, p. 81 (Oxford: Clarendon Press, 1995).

71 For example, during the consideration of the UK's third periodic report on the implementation of the Covenant on Civil and Political Rights by the Human Rights Committee in New York in 1989, some NGOs put great pressure on the Committee members, trying to focus the main attention of the Committee upon human rights in Hong Kong, in view of the Chinese takeover in 1997. Had the Committee gone along with this lobbying, many other important aspects of the human rights situation in the UK would not have been addressed at all.

72 P. Taylor, 'Options for the Reform of the International System for Humanitarian Assistance', in Harriss 1995, p. 124.

73 P. Spiro 1994, p. 46.

74 UN Doc. A/50/36, para. 12.

75 I thank the Legal Department of the FCO for the text of the statement of China's Foreign Ministry spokesman.

76 In connection with the *Caroline* incident in 1837, Daniel Webster, the American Secretary of State, laid out the conditions for the exercise of the right to self-defence. The formula is still widely used when the admissibility of so-called anticipatory self-defence is discussed.

6 HUMAN RIGHTS, PEACE AND THE USE OF FORCE

1 For different views on humanitarian intervention, see, e.g., R. Lillich (ed.), *Humanitarian Intervention and the United Nations* (Charlottesville: University Press of Virginia, 1973); M. Verwey, 'Humanitarian Intervention', in A. Cassese (ed.), *The Current Legal Regulation of the Use of Force* (Dordrecht: Nijhoff, 1986); F. Teson, *Humanitarian Intervention* (New York: Transnational, 1988); D. Scheffer, R. Gardner and G. Helman, *Post-Gulf War Challenges to the UN Collective Security System: Three Views on the Issue of Humanitarian Intervention* (Washington, DC: Carnegie Endowment for International Peace, 1992); A. Clark Arend and R. J. Beck, *International Law and the Use of Force* (London: Routledge, 1993); A. Roberts, 'Humanitarian War: Military Intervention and Human Rights', *International Affairs* 63:3 (1993).

2 See N. Lewer and O. Ramsbotham, *Something Must Be Done: Towards an Ethical Framework for Humanitarian Intervention in International Social Conflict*, pp. 2–3 (Bradford: University of Bradford, 1993).

3 Hugo Grotius, *De Jure Belli ac Pacis*, trans. Francis W. Kelsey, ch. VII, para. 2, p. 584 (Oxford: Clarendon Press, 1925).

4 Emmerich de Vattel, *The Law of Nations or the Principles of Natural Law Applied to the Conduct and to the Affairs of Nations and Sovereigns*, trans. Charles G. Fenwick, p. 325 (Washington, DC: Carnegie Institute, 1916).

5 L. Oppenheim, *International Law*, p. 347 (London: Longman, 1905).
6 H. Lauterpacht (ed.), *Oppenheim's International Law*, p. 312 (London: Longman, 1955).
7 Sir Robert Jennings and Sir Arthur Watts (eds) *Oppenheim's International Law*, Ninth edition, p. 443 (London: Longman, 1992).
8 R. Lillich, 'Humanitarian Intervention: A Reply to Ian Brownlie and a Plea for Constructive Alternatives', in J. Moore (ed.), *Law and Civil War in the Modern World* (Baltimore: The Johns Hopkins University Press, 1974).
9 M. McDougal and M. Reisman, 'Humanitarian Intervention to Protect Ibos', in Lillich 1973.
10 Teson 1988.
11 Ibid., p. 15.
12 See, e.g., I. Brownlie, *International Law and the Use of Force by States* (Oxford: Clarendon Press, 1963); M. Akehurst, 'Humanitarian Intervention', in H. Bull (ed.) *Intervention in World Politics* (Oxford: Clarendon Press, 1984).
13 O. Schachter, *International Law in Theory and Practice*, p. 118 (Dordrecht: Nijhoff, 1991).
14 S. Schwebel, 'Military and Paramilitary Activities (*Nicaragua* v. *US*) Merits: Dissenting Opinion of Judge Stephen Schwebel' (para. 200), *ICJ Reports*, p. 352 (1986).
15 P. P. Shafirov, *A Discourse Concerning the Just Causes of the War Between Russia and Sweden*, trans. W. E. Butler (Yorkshire, The Scolar Press, 1973).
16 Ibid., p. 239.
17 *International Commission of Jurists Report: The Events in East Pakistan 1971*, pp. 26–7 (Geneva, 1972).
18 McDougal and Reisman 1973, p 171
19 Ibid.
20 A. Roberts and B. Kingsbury, 'Roles of the United Nations after the Cold War', *Oxford International Review*, VI:2, Spring, 5 (1995).
21 L. Henkin, *International Law: Politics and Values*, p. 113 (Dordrecht: Nijhoff, 1995).
22 Ibid.
23 However, Professor Henkin later admits that 'international human rights law reflects a major derogation by the international system from its commitment to basic state values – state autonomy and impermeability' (ibid., p. 203).
24 *British Yearbook of International Law*, 57, 614 (1986).
25 G. A. Res. 2131 (XX), 21 December 1965.
26 1923 *PCIJ, Series B*, No. 4, pp. 23–4.
27 World Conference on Human Rights. The Vienna Declaration and Programme of Action (New York: United Nations, 1993), para. 4.
28 See more on this in J. Donnelly, *Universal Human Rights in Theory and Practice*, pp. 229–37 (Ithaca: Cornell University Press, 1989).
29 M. Walzer, *Just and Unjust Wars*, Second edition, p. 90 (New York: Basic Books, 1992).
30 Brownlie 1963, pp. 31–4.
31 UN Doc. S/RES/827 (1993), 25 May 1993.

32 UN Doc. S/RES/955 (1994), 8 November 1994.
33 Brownlie 1963, p. 342.
34 *Parliamentary Debates (Commons)*, vol. 702, col. 911.
35 See, e.g., D. Bowett, 'The Use of Force for the Protection of Nationals Abroad', in A. Cassese (ed.), *The Current Legal Regulation of the Use of Force* (Dordrecht: Nijhoff, 1986).
36 *Oppenheim's International Law*, Ninth edition, p. 440 (Jennings and Watts 1992).
37 McDougall and Reisman 1973, p. 177.
38 T. Franck and N. Rodley, 'After Bangladesh: The Law of Humanitarian Intervention by Military Force', *American Journal of International Law*, 67, 284 (1973).
39 R. Higgins, *Problems and Process: International Law and How We Use It*, p. 247 (Oxford: Clarendon Press, 1994).
40 M. Mandelbaum, 'The Reluctance to Intervene', *Foreign Policy*, 95, 16 (1994).
41 J. Simon, *The Ultimate Resource*, p. 346 (Oxford: Martin Robertson & Company, 1981).
42 D. W. Bowett, 'The Interrelation of Theories of Intervention and Self-Defence', in J. Moore (ed.), *Law and Civil War in the Modern World*, p. 44 (Baltimore: The Johns Hopkins University Press, 1974).
43 Franck & Rodley 1973, p. 304.
44 D. Scheffer, 'Toward a Modern Doctrine of Humanitarian Intervention', *University of Toledo Law Review*, 23, Winter, 259 (1992).
45 R. Plant, 'Rights, Rules and World Order', in M. Desai and P. Redfern (eds), *Global Governance. Ethics and Economics of the World Order*, pp. 203–4 (London: Pinter, 1995).
46 Ibid., p. 204.
47 UN Doc. A/34/PV.14 (1979).
48 R. J. Vincent, *Human Rights and International Relations*, p. 125 (Cambridge: Cambridge University Press, 1986).
49 M. Walzer, 'The Politics of Rescue', *Social Research*, 62:1, Spring, 60 (1995).
50 Nguen Quoc Dinh, P. Dailler and A. Pellet, *Droit international public*, Fifth edition, p. 892 (Paris, L.G.D.J., 1994).
51 See, e.g., Clark Arend and Beck 1993, pp. 121–5.
52 UN Doc. S/PV.1606, 4 December 1971, p. 86.
53 Clark Arend and Beck 1993, p. 124.
54 Ibid.
55 See Teson 1988, pp. 165–6.
56 See *The Times*, 22 April 1966, p. 10.
57 Clark Arend and Beck 1993, p. 119.
58 Verwey 1986, p. 66.
59 R. Gardner, 'International Law and the Use of Force: Paper II', *Adelphi Paper No. 266*, p. 72 (Winter 1991/1992).
60 A. Roberts, 'Humanitarian War: Military Intervention and Human Rights', *International Affairs* 69:3, 446 (1993).
61 Mandelbaum 1994, p. 4.
62 W. Clarke and J. Herbst, 'Somalia and the Future of Humanitarian Intervention', *Foreign Affairs'* 75:2, (March–April), 78 (1996).

63 It seems that there is a tendency towards legalizing humanitarian assistance or aid even without the territorial state's consent. Article 18(2) of the 1977 Protocol II (concerning armed conflicts of non-international character) to the Geneva conventions on international humanitarian law stipulates that:

> If the civilian population is suffering undue hardships owing to the lack of supplies essential for its survival... relief actions for the civilian population which are of an exclusively humanitarian and impartial nature and which are conducted without any adverse distinction shall be undertaken *subject to the consent of the High Contracting Party concerned.*
>
> (Emphasis added.)

In 1989 the *Institut de Droit International* passed a resolution providing that

> an offer by a state, a group of states, an international organization or an impartial humanitarian body such as the International Committee of the Red Cross, of food or medical supplies to another state in whose territory the life or health of the population is seriously threatened, cannot be considered an unlawful intervention in the internal affairs of that state. However, such offers of assistance shall not... take a form suggestive of a threat of armed intervention or any other measure of intimidation.... *States in whose territories these emergency situations exist should not arbitrarily reject such offers of humanitarian assistance.*
>
> (Article 5 of the Resolution 'The Protection of Human Rights and the Principle of Non-Intervention in Internal Affairs of States', in *Annuaire de l'Institut de Droit International*, p. 345 (Paris: Editions A. Pedone, 1989). (Emphasis added.)

In 1986, the ICJ in the *Nicaragua* case stipulated that 'there can be no doubt that the provision of strictly humanitarian aid to persons or forces in another country, whatever their political affiliations or objectives, cannot be regarded as unlawful intervention, or as in any other way contrary to international law' (1986 ICJ 124).

64 F. Halliday, *Rethinking International Relations*, p. 238 (London: Macmillan, 1994).

65 Clark Arend and Beck 1993, p. 122.

66 The UNDP Human Development Report for 1994 argues that there are four situations which would appear to warrant international intervention: mass slaughter of the population by the state; decimation through starvation or the withholding of health or other services; forced exodus; and occupation and the denial of the right to self-determination (UNDP, *Human Development Report 1994*, p. 57 (New York: Oxford University Press, 1994)).

67 Mandelbaum, 1994, p. 17.

68 See more on peacekeeping and human rights in: M. Berdal, *Whither UN Peacekeeping*, Adelphi paper (London: Brassey/IISS, 1993); D. Daniel and B. Hayes (eds), *Beyond Traditional Peacekeeping* (London: Macmillan, 1995); A. Henkin (ed.), *Honouring Human Rights and Keeping the Peace. Lessons from El Salvador, Cambodia, and Haiti* (New York: The Aspen

Institute, 1995); S. Ratner, *The New Peacekeeping* (London: Macmillan, 1995); C. Thornberry, *The Development of International Peacekeeping*, LSE Centenary Lectures (London: LSE Books, 1995).

69   UN Doc. A/50/60, S/1995/1, 3 January 1995.
70   Boutros Ghali, B. 'Démocratie et droit de l'homme', *Le Monde Diplomatique*, October 1992, p. 32.
71   See Ratner 1995, p. 253.
72   UN Doc. A/44/971. S/21541.
73   Americas Watch. El Salvador: Successes and Shortcomings of the United Nations Observer Mission in El Salvador, 2 September 1992, p. 2.
74   A Henkin 1995, p. 47.
75   S. J. Stedman, 'UN Intervention in Civil Wars: Imperatives of Choice and Strategy', in Daniel and Hayes 1995, p. 41.
76   See more about UNTAG in Thornberry 1995.
77   See Virginia Page Fortna, 'Success and Failure in Southern Africa: Peacekeeping in Namibia and Angola', in Daniel and Hayes 1995, pp. 282–300.
78   See *The Economist*, 25 November 1995, pp. 88–9.
79   *NATO Review* (August 1994), 4, p. 26.
80   The 1960–64 UN operation in the Congo (now Zaire) had a mandate which included: assistance to the central government in maintaining law and order; the prevention of tribal conflict and civil war; maintenance of the territorial integrity of the country; the prevention of external intervention; and the protection of individual rights (see I. J. Rikhue, 'United Nations Operation in Congo: Peacekeeping, Peacemaking and Peacebuilding', in Daniel and Hayes 1995, p. 220). This means that the Congo operation (ONUC) had certain characteristics by which it differed from other peacekeeping missions of that period and which relate it to so-called second-generation operations.
81   See Ratner 1995, p. 1.
82   *Haiti. Learning the Hard Way: The UN/OAS Human Rights Monitoring Operation in Haiti 1993–1994*, p. 54 (New York: Lawyers' Committee for Human Rights, 1995).
83   Ratner 1995, p. 130.
84   Stedman 1995, p. 54.
85   See *Haiti. Learning the Hard Way*.
86   UN Doc. S/RES/929, 22 June 1994.
87   UN Doc. S/RES/925, 8 June 1994.
88   SC Res. 688 (1991) of 5 April 1991, para. 1.
89   M. Weller, *Iraq and Kuwait: The Hostilities and Their Aftermath*, p. 717 (Cambridge: Cambridge University Press, 1993).
90   *International Legal Materials* 860–2 (1991).
91   UN Doc. S/RES/181 (1963).
92   UN Doc. S/RES/221 (1966).
93   UN Doc. S/RES/282 (1970).
94   UN Doc. S/RES/418 (1977).
95   R. Higgins, *Problems and Process: International Law and How We Use It*, p. 255 (Oxford: Clarendon Press, 1994).
96   R. J. Vincent, *Human Rights and International Relations*, p. 140 (Cambridge: Cambridge University Press, 1986).

97 Ibid., pp. 140–1.
 98 M. Clarke, 'Politics as Government and Politics as Security', in M. Clarke (ed.), *New Perspectives on Security*, p. 57 (London: Brassey's, 1993).
 99 *Our Global Neighbourhood*, p. 79.
100 Ibid., p. 89.
101 Ibid., p. 90.
102 T. Farer, 'A Paradigm of Legitimate Intervention', in L. Damrosch (ed.), *Enforcing Restraint*, p. 330 (New York: Council on Foreign Relations Press, 1993).
103 UN Doc. S/25704, 3 May 1993.
104 UN Doc. S/RES/955, 8 November 1994.
105 Ibid. The Tribunal for the former Yugoslavia is often criticised of dealing only with small fry: while Tadić is before the Tribunal, Karadžić and Mladić, though indicted, are at the time of writing still free. However, though it is very important to try to punish those who give orders and plan genocidal acts, I disagree that Tadić, as a willing executioner, is small fry. Luc Ferry writes on atrocities committed in places like former Yugoslavia and Rwanda: 'Or tout se passe comme si la guerre fournissait l'occasion de glisser insensiblement, en toute impunité, du mauvais au méchant, comme si mal n'était plus un moyen mais une fin, non plus une réalité tragique mais une passetemps, pour ne pas dire un exaltant projet...' [L. Ferry, *L'homme-Dieu ou le Sens de la vie* (Paris: Grasset, 1996, p. 92)]. As historical figures all of them may be rather unimportant and mean. But as criminals, they are all great; as agents of evil, they are equal. None of those who torture, rape and kill in the context of crimes against humanity should be seen as small fry in the fires of Hell.
106 A. Solzhenitsyn, *The Gulag Archipelago*, trans. T. Whitney, p. 178 (London: Fontana 1974).
107 D. F. Orentalicher, 'Settling Accounts: The Duty to Prosecute Human Rights Violations of a Prior Regime', *The Yale Law Journal* 100:8, 2537–615 (1991).
108 *The Peace Agreement for Bosnia and Herzegovina* (Paris, 14 December 1995).
109 Z. Pajic, 'Constitution of Bosnia and Herzegovina: A Critical Appraisal of its Human Rights Provisions', (a paper presented at the Conference on Constitutional Reforms on Eastern and Central Europe and Russia and International Law, King's College, London, 30 March 1996) p. 11.
110 T. Farer, 'Collectively Defending Democracy in a World of Sovereign States: the Western Hemisphere Prospect', in *Essays on Human Rights and Democratic Development*, p. 20 (International Centre for Human Rights and Democratic Development, 1994).
111 Under the UN Charter interventions by regional organizations without the authorization of the Security Council are on the same footing as interventions by individual states.
112 See Damrosch 1993, p. 181.
113 D. Wippman, 'Enforcing the Peace: ECOWAS and the Liberian Civil War', in Damrosch 1993, p. 193.
114 Conseil de Securité. Proces-verbal 1982e séance. S/PV 2982, 5–4-1991.
115 Weller 1993, p. 127.

116 *Our Global Neighbourhood*, p. 110.
117 See 'Rwanda: Death, Despair and Defiance', *African Rights*, 666 (1994).
118 UN Doc. S/RES/940, 31 July 1994.
119 UN Doc. S/RES/794, 3 December 1992.

CONCLUSION

1 R. B. Bilder, 'Rethinking International Human Rights: Some Basic Questions', *Human Rights Law Journal*, II, 607 (1969).

Bibliography

Abrams, Jason, 'Burundi: Anatomy of an Ethnic Conflict', *Survival*, 37:1 (1995).

Abramson, P. and R. Inglehart, *Value Change in Global Perspective* (Ann Arbor: University of Michigan Press, 1995).

Akehurst, M., 'Humanitarian Intervention', in H. Bull (ed.) *Intervention in World Politics* (Oxford: Clarendon Press, 1984).

Alston, P. (ed.), *The United Nations and Human Rights. A Critical Appraisal* (Oxford, Clarendon Press, 1992).

Americas Watch, *El Salvador: Successes and Shortcomings of the United Nations Observer Mission in El Salvador*, 2 September 1992.

Anderson, B., *Imagined Communities* (London: Verso, 1991).

An-Na'im, A. A., *Toward an Islamic Reformation: Civil Liberties, Human Rights and International Law* (Syracuse University Press, 1990).

—— (ed.), *Human Rights in Cross-Cultural Perspectives. A Quest for Consensus* (Philadelphia: University of Pennsylvania Press, 1992).

Arat, Z. F., *Democracy and Human Rights in Developing Countries* (London: Lagneia Rainier Publishers, 1991).

Aung San Suu Kyi, 'Listen: the Culture of Human Rights and Democracy is Universal', *International Herald Tribune*, 7 December 1994.

Bach, D. C., 'Reappraising Postcolonial Geopolitics: Europe, Africa and the End of the Cold War', in T. Ranger and O. Vaughan (eds), *Legitimacy and the State in Twentieth-Century Africa* (Oxford: Macmillan, 1993).

Baehr, P., *The Role of Human Rights in Foreign Policy* (London: Macmillan, 1994).

Baker, J. with T. M. DeFrank, *The Politics of Diplomacy* (New York: G. P. Putnam's Sons, 1995).

Bangkok NGO Declaration on Human Rights, 27 March 1993.

Bartley, R. L., 'The Case for Optimism. The West Should Believe in Itself', *Foreign Affairs*, 72:4 (1993).

Bassiouni, M. Ch. (ed.), *International Criminal Law*, vol. 1 (New York: Transnational, 1986).

Berdal, M., *Whither UN Peacekeeping*, Adelphi paper (London: Brassey/IISS, 1993).

Bilder, R., 'Rethinking International Human Rights: Some Basic Questions', *Human Rights Law Journal*, II (1969).

Binyan, Liu, 'Civilization Grafting', *Foreign Affairs*, 72:4 (1993).

Black, C., 'Canada's Continuing Identity Crisis', *Foreign Affairs*, 74:2 (1995).

Bloed, A. and P. van Dijk (eds), *The Human Dimension of the Helsinki Process: The Vienna Follow-up Meeting and the Aftermath* (Dordrecht: Nijhoff, 1991).

Boutros Ghali, B., 'Démocratie et droit de l'homme', *Le Monde Diplomatique*, October 1992.

Bowett, D. W., 'The Interrelation of Theories of Intervention and Self-Defence', in J. N. Moore (ed.), *Law and Civil War in the Modern World* (Baltimore: The Johns Hopkins University Press, 1974).

—— 'The Use of Force for the Protection of Nationals Abroad', in A. Cassese (ed.), *The Current Legal Regulation of the Use of Force* (Dordrecht: Nijhoff, 1986).

Brands, W., 'Human Rights and US Policy Towards Asia', in J. Tang (ed.), *Human Rights and International Relations in the Asian Pacific* (London: Pinter, 1995).

Brecher, I. (ed.), *Human Rights, Development and Foreign Policy: Canadian Perspectives* (Ottawa: The Institute for Research on Public Policy, 1989).

Brogan, P., *World Conflicts* (London: Bloomsbury, 1992)

British Yearbook of International Law, 57 (1986).

Brown, M. E. (ed.), *Ethnic Conflict and International Security* (Princeton University Press, 1993).

Brownlie, I., *International Law and the Use of Force by States* (Oxford: Clarendon Press, 1963).

—— (ed.), *Basic Documents on Human Rights*, Third edition (Oxford: Clarendon Press, 1993).

Bull, H., *The Anarchical Society: A Study of Order in World Politics* (London: Macmillan, 1977)

—— (ed.) *Intervention in World Politics* (Oxford: Clarendon Press, 1984).

Buzan, B., C. Jones and R. Little, *The Logic of Anarchy* (New York: Columbia University Press, 1993).

Capotorti, F., *Study on the Rights of Persons Belonging to Ethnic, Religious and Linguistic Minorities* (New York: United Nations, 1991).

Carothers, T., 'Democracy Promotion under Clinton', *The Washington Quarterly*, 18:4 (1995).

Cassese, A., *Human Rights in a Changing World* (Cambridge: Polity, 1994).

Chipman, J., 'Managing the Politics of Parochialism', in M. E. Brown (ed.), *Ethnic Conflict and International Security* (Princeton University Press, 1993).

Clark Arend, A., and R. J. Beck, *International Law and the Use of Force* (London: Routledge, 1993).

Clarke, M., 'Politics as Government and Politics as Security', in M. Clarke (ed.), *New Perspectives on Security* (London: Brassey, 1993).

Clarke, W. and J. Herbst, 'Somalia and the Future of Humanitarian Intervention', *Foreign Affairs*, 75:2 (March–April 1996).

Collinson, P., 'Religion and Human Rights: The Case of and for Protestantism', in *Historical Change and Human Rights. The Oxford Amnesty Lectures 1994* (New York: Basic Books, 1995).

Commission on Human Rights. Report of the Fiftieth Session (31 January–11 March 1994), pp. 391–3 (New York: United Nations, 1994).

Country Reports on Human Rights Practices for 1994 (US State Department, February 1995).

Craven, M., *The International Covenant on Economic, Social and Cultural Rights: A Perspective for Development* (Oxford: Clarendon Press, 1995).

Dahrendorf, R., *Law and Order* (London: Stevens & Sons, 1985).

Damrosch, L. F., 'The Civilian Impact of Economic Sanctions', in L. F. Damrosch (ed.), *Enforcing Restraint* (New York: Council of Foreign Relations Press, 1993).

Daniel, D. and B. Hayes (eds), *Beyond Traditional Peacekeeping* (London: Macmillan, 1995).

Davidson, S., *Human Rights* (Buckingham: Open University Press, 1993).

De Balogh, A., *La protection internationale des minorités* (Paris: Les editions internationales, 1930).

De Vattel, Emmerich, *The Law of Nations or the Principles of Natural Law Applied to the Conduct and to the Affairs of Nations and Sovereigns*, trans. Charles G. Fenwick (Washington, DC: Carnegie Institute of Washington, 1916).

De Villiers, L., *In Sight of Surrender: The US Sanctions Campaign against South Africa* (Westport: Praeger, 1995).

Dinh, Nguen Quoc, P. Dailler and A. Pellet, *Droit international public*, Fifth edition, (Paris: L.G.D.J., 1994).

Djilas, M., *The New Class. An Analysis of the Communist System* (New York: Praeger, 1965).

Donnelly, J., 'Cultural Relativism and Universal Human Rights', *Human Rights Quarterly*, 6:4 (1984).

—— *Universal Human Rights in Theory and Practice* (Ithaca: Cornell University Press, 1989).

—— 'Security, Human Rights, and East–West Relations: Theoretical Bases of the Linkage', in V. Mastny and J. Zielonka (eds), *Human Rights and Security. Europe on the Eve of A New Era* (Oxford: Westview Press, 1991).

—— *International Human Rights. Dilemmas in World Politics* (Boulder: Westview Press, 1993).

—— 'International Human Rights after the Cold War', in M. T. Clare and D. C. Thomas (eds), *World Security: Challenges for a New Century* (London: St Martin's Press, 1994).

Doyle, M., 'Kant, Liberal Legacies, and Foreign Affairs', *Philosophy and Public Affairs*, 12:3 (1983).

Dugard, J., *International Law. A South African Perspective* (Kenwin: Juta & Co., 1994).

Durant, W., *Age of Faith*, vol. 4, *The Story of Civilization* (London: Simon & Schuster, 1950).

Egeland, J., *Impotent Superpower – Potent Small State* (Oslo: Norwegian University Press, 1988).

Ekwe-Ekwe, H., *Africa 2001: The State, Human Rights and the People* (Reading: International Institute for Black Research, 1993).

Etzioni, E., *The Spirit of Community* (London: Simon & Schuster, 1993).

European Bank for Reconstruction and Development, Annual Report 1994.

Falk, R., 'Foreword' to B. S. Chimni, *International Law and World Order* (London: Sage, 1993).

—— *On Humane Governance: Toward a New Global Politics* (Cambridge: Polity Press, 1995).

Farer, T., 'A Paradigm of Legitimate Intervention', in L. F. Damrosch (ed.), *Enforcing Restraint and some more* (New York: Council of Foreign Relations Press, 1993).

—— 'Collectively Defending Democracy in a World of Sovereign States: the Western Hemisphere Prospect', in *Essays on Human Rights and Democratic Development* (International Centre for Human Rights and Democratic Development, 1994).

Farmaian, Sattareh Farman with Dona Munker, *Daughter of Persia* (London: Corgi, 1995).

Ferry, L. *L'homme-Dieu ou le Sens de la vie* (Paris: Grasset, 1996).

Forsythe, D., *Human Rights and Peace: International and National Dimensions* (Lincoln: University of Nebraska Press, 1993).

Fortna, Virginia Page, 'Success and Failure in Southern Africa: Peacekeeping in Namibia and Angola', in D. Daniel and B. Hayes (eds), *Beyond Traditional Peacekeeping* (London: Macmillan, 1995).

Franck, T., *The Power of Legitimacy Among Nations* (Oxford: Oxford University Press, 1990).

——'The Emerging Right to Democratic Governance', *American Journal of International Law*, 86 (1992).

—— *Fairness in the International Legal and Institutional System*, General Course on Public International Law (Academy of International Law, 1993–III).

Franck, T. and N. Rodley, 'After Bangladesh: The Law of Humanitarian Intervention by Military Force', *American Journal of International Law*, 67 (1973).

Freeman, M., 'Human Rights: Asia and the West', in J. Tang (ed.), *Human Rights and International Relations in the Asian Pacific* (London: Pinter, 1995).

Fukuyama, F., *The End of History and the Last Man*, (London: Hamish Hamilton, 1992).

—— *Trust* (London: Hamish Hamilton, 1995).

Gaballero-Anthony, M., 'Human Rights, Economic Change and Political Development', in J. Tang (ed.), *Human Rights and International Relations in the Asian Pacific* (London: Pinter, 1995).

Ganby, G. D., 'Power of the People via Personal Electronic Media', *Washington Quarterly*, Spring 1991.

Gardner, R., 'International Law and the Use of Force: Paper II', *Adelphi Paper No. 266* (Winter 1991/1992).

Ghai, Yash, 'Asian Perspectives of Human Rights', in J. Tang (ed.) *Human Rights and International Relations in the Asian Pacific* (London: Pinter, 1995).

Ghebali, V.-Y., *La diplomatie de la détente: la C.S.C.E., 1973–1989* (Brussels: Bruylant, 1989).

Gilmore, W. C., *The Grenada Invasion: Analysis and Documents* (London: Mansell, 1984).

Goodno, J. B., *The Philippines: Land of Broken Promises* (London: Zed Books, 1991).

Grotius, Hugo, *De Jure Belli ac Pacis*, trans. Francis W. Kelsey (Oxford: Clarendon Press, 1925).

Haiti. Learning the Hard Way: The UN/OAS Human Rights Monitoring Operation in Haiti 1993–1994 (New York: Lawyers' Committee for Human Rights, 1995).

Halliday, F., 'International Society as Homogeneity: Burke, Marx, Fukuyama', *Millennium*, 21:3 (1992).

—— *Rethinking International Relations* (London: Macmillan, 1994).

—— 'Review Article: The Politics of "Islam" – A Second Look', *British Journal of Political Science*, 25 (1995).

—— *Islam and the Myth of Confrontation: Religion and Politics in the Middle East* (London: Tauris, 1996).

Hannum, H., *Autonomy, Sovereignty, and Self-Determination. The Accommodation of Conflicting Rights* (University of Pennsylvania Press, 1990).

Harris, D., M. O'Boyle and C. Warbrick, *The Law of the European Convention on Human Rights* (London: Butterworth, 1995).

Harriss, J. (ed.), *The Politics of Humanitarian Intervention* (London: Pinter, 1995).

Henkin, Alice (ed.), *Honouring Human Rights and Keeping the Peace. Lessons from El Salvador, Cambodia, and Haiti* (New York: The Aspen Institute, 1995).

Henkin, L., *International Law: Politics and Values* (Dordrecht: Nijhoff, 1995).

Heraclides, A., *Security and Cooperation in Europe: The Human Dimension, 1972–1992* (London: Frank Cass, 1993).

Hewlett, S., *The Cruel Dilemmas of Development: Twentieth Century Brazil* (New York: Basic Books, 1980).

Higgins, R., *Problems and Process: International Law and How We Use It* (Oxford: Clarendon Press, 1994),

Hobbes, T., *Leviathan*, (Harmondsworth: Penguin, 1981)

——*Behemoth or the Long Parliament* (ed. F. Tonnies), Second edition (London: Frank Cass, 1969).

Hobsbawm, E., *Age of Extremes* (London: Michael Joseph, 1994).

Hoffmann, S., 'In Defence of Mother Teresa: Morality in Foreign Policy', *International Affairs*, 75:2 (March–April 1996).

Horner, Ch., 'Human Rights and the Jackson Amendment', in D. Fosdick (ed.), *Staying the Course* (Washington, DC: Washington University Press, 1987).

Howard, 'Evaluating Human Rights in Africa: Some Problems of Implicit Comparisons', *Human Rights Quarterly*, 6:2 (1984).

Hufton, O. (ed.), *Historical Change and Human Rights. The Oxford Amnesty Lectures 1994* (New York: Basic Books, 1995).

Human Development Report 1994 (New York: Oxford University Press, 1994).

Human Rights in Russia – International Dimension (in Russian) (Moscow: Prava Cheloveka (Human Rights), 1995).

Human Rights Watch World Report 1994 (New York: Human Rights Watch, 1993).

Huntington, S., 'The Clash of Civilizations', *Foreign Affairs* , 72:3 (1993).

International Commission of Jurists Report: The Events in East Pakistan 1971 (Geneva, 1972).

Israel, F. L., *Major Peace Treaties of Modern History, 1648–1967*, vol. 1 (New York: Chelsea House in association with McGraw-Hill, 1967).

Jenks, C. W., *Social Justice in the Law of Nations: The ILO Impact after Fifty Years* (Oxford: Oxford University Press, 1970).

Jennings, Sir Robert and Sir Arthur Watts (eds) *Oppenheim's International Law*, Ninth edition (London: Longman, 1992).

Jeziorski, M., *Former Yugoslav Republic of Macedonia – Background Paper for the Expert Consultation on Minority Education*, The Hague, 18 November 1995.

Johnson, B. (ed.), *Freedom and Interpretation. The Oxford Amnesty Lectures 1992* (New York: Basic Books, 1993).

Kausikan, B., 'Asia's Different Standard', *Foreign Policy*, Fall 1993.

Keen, D., 'Short-Term Interventions and Long-Term Problems: The Case of the Kurds in Iraq', in J. Harriss (ed.), *The Politics of Humanitarian Intervention* (London: Pinter, 1995).

Kennedy, P., *Preparing for the Twenty-First Century* (London: HarperCollins, 1993).

Keohane, R., 'Hobbes's Dilemma and Institutional Change in World Politics: Sovereignty in International Society', in H. H. Holm and G. Sorensen (eds.), *Whose World Order* (Boulder: Westview Press, 1995).

Kilenyi, G. and V. Lamm (eds), *Democratic Changes in Hungary (Basic Legislations on a Peaceful Transition from Bolshevism to Democracy)* (Budapest, 1990).

Kirkpatrick, J., 'Dictatorship and Double Standards', *Commentary*, November 1979.

Kissinger, H., *Diplomacy* (London: Simon & Schuster, 1994).

Kymlicka, W., *Multicultural Citizenship. A Liberal Theory of Minority Rights* (Oxford: Clarendon Press, 1995).

Laqueur, W., 'The Issue of Human Rights', *Commentary*, 64:5 (1977).

Lauterpacht, H. (ed.), *Oppenheim's International Law* (London: Longman, 1955).

Layne, C., 'Kant or Cant: The Myth of the Democratic Peace', *International Security*, 19:2 (1994).

Lewer, N. and O. Ramsbotham, *Something Must Be Done: Towards an Ethical Framework for Humanitarian Intervention in International Social Conflict* (Bradford: University of Bradford, 1993).

Lilley, J., 'Freedom through Trade', *Foreign Policy*, 94 (1994).

Lillich, R. (ed.), *Humanitarian Intervention and the United Nations* (Charlottesville: University Press of Virginia, 1973).

—— 'Humanitarian Intervention: A Reply to Ian Brownlie and a Plea for Constructive Alternatives', in J. Moore (ed.), *Law and Civil War in the Modern World* (Baltimore: The Johns Hopkins University Press, 1974).

Lipset, S. M., *Political Man* (New York: Doubleday, 1960).

—— *American Exceptionalism: A Double-Edged Sword* (New York: W. W. Northon, 1996).

Longman's Illustrated Encyclopedia of World History (London: Ivy Leaf, 1991).

McDougal, M. and M. Reisman, 'Humanitarian Intervention to Protect Ibos', in R. Lillich (ed.), *Humanitarian Intervention and the United Nations* (Charlottesville: University Press of Virginia, 1973).

McGaffey, D. C., 'Policy and Practice: Human Rights in the Shah's Iran', in D.

Newsom (ed.), *The Diplomacy of Human Rights* (New York: University Press of America, 1986).

McRae, H., *The World in 2020. Power, Culture and Prosperity: A Vision of the Future* (London: HarperCollins, 1994).

Meron, T. (ed.), *Human Rights in International Law: Legal and Policy Issues* (Oxford: Clarendon Press, 1984).

Mahbubani, Kishore, 'The Pacific Impulse', *Survival*, 37:1 (1995).

'Main Provisions of the Military Doctrine of the Russian Federation (Digest)', *Military News Bulletin*, 11 November 1993.

Mandelbaum, M., 'The Reluctance to Intervene', *Foreign Policy* (1994).

Manning, R., 'Clinton and China: Beyond Human Rights', *Orbis*, 38:2 (1995).

Mansfield, E. and J. Snyder, 'Democratization and War', *Foreign Affairs*, 74:3 (1995).

Marty, M. and R. Scott Appleby (eds), *Fundamentalisms Observed* (Chicago: The University of Chicago Press, 1991).

Mayer, A. E., *Islam and Human Rights: Tradition and Politics*, Second edition (Boulder: Westview Press, 1995).

Maynes, C., 'Relearning Intervention', *Foreign Policy*, 98 (1995).

Mazrui, A., 'The Bondage of Boundaries', *The Economist*, 28 August 1993.

—— *Towards a Pax Africana* (Chicago: University of Chicago Press, 1967).

Moravcsik, A., 'Letter to the Economist', *The Economist*, 29 April 1995.

Morozov, G. I., 'The UN at the Turn of the Century', *Moscow Journal of International Law*, 1 (1995).

Müllerson, R., *International Law, Rights and Politics* (London: Routledge, 1994).

Newburg, A., 'The European Bank for Reconstruction and Development: Democracy, Human Rights and Market Economics', in *Law in Transition* (A Newsletter on Legal Cooperation and Training from the EBRD, Autumn 1993).

Newsom, D. (ed.), *The Diplomacy of Human Rights* (New York: University Press of America, 1986).

Nolan, C. J., *Principled Diplomacy. Security and Rights in U.S. Foreign Policy* (London: Greenwood Press, 1993).

'Opinion No. 3 of the Arbitration Commission of the International Conference on Yugoslavia', *European Journal of International Law*, 3:1 (1992).

Oppenheim, L., *International Law* (London: Longman, 1905).

Orentalicher, D. F., 'Settling Accounts: The Duty to Prosecute Human Rights Violations of a Prior Regime', *The Yale Law Journal*, 100:8 (1991).

Our Global Neighbourhood. The Report of the Commission on Global Governance (Oxford: Oxford University Press, 1995).

Owen, D., *Balkan Odyssey* (London: Victor Gollancz, 1995).

Pajic, Z., 'Constitution of Bosnia and Herzegovina: A Critical Appraisal of its Human Rights Provisions' (a paper presented at the Conference on Constitutional Reforms on Eastern and Central Europe and Russia and International Law, King's College, London, 30 March 1996).

Plant, R., 'Rights, Rules and World Order', in M. Desai and P. Redfern (eds), *Global Governance. Ethics and Economics of the World Order* (London: Pinter, 1995).

Pleshakov, C., 'Human Rights in Russia: the Dragon is not Defeated', in J.

Tang (ed.), *Human Rights and International Relations in the Asian Pacific* (London: Pinter, 1995).

Pollis, A., 'Eastern Orthodoxy and Human Rights', *Human Rights Quarterly*, 15 (1993).

Quiroga, C. M., *The Battle of Human Rights* (Dordrecht: Nijhoff, 1988).

Ratner, S., *The New Peacekeeping* (London: Macmillan, 1995).

Renteln, A., *International Human Rights: Universalism Versus Relativism* (Newbury Park: Sage, 1990).

Restatement of the Law. The Foreign Relations Law of the United States, Third edition (St Paul: American Law Institute Publishers, 1987).

Rikhue, I. J., 'United Nations Operation in Congo: Peacekeeping, Peacemaking and Peacebuilding', in D. Daniel and B. Hayes (eds), *Beyond Traditional Peacekeeping* (London: Macmillan, 1995).

Roberts, A., 'Humanitarian War: Military Intervention and Human Rights', *International Affairs*, 69:3 (1993).

Roberts, A. and B. Kingsbury, 'Roles of the United Nations after the Cold War', *Oxford International Review*, VI:2 (Spring 1995).

Roberts, B., 'Human Rights, International Security and the Crisis of Communism', in V. Mastny and J. Zielonka (eds), *Human Rights and Security. Europe on the Eve of a New Era* (Oxford: Westview Press, 1991).

Robertson, A. H. and J. G. Merrills, *Human Rights in the World*, Third edition (Manchester: Manchester University Press, 1993).

Roosevelt, K., *Countercoup: The Struggle for the Control of Iran* (New York: McGraw-Hill, 1979).

Rorty, R., 'Human Rights, Rationality, and Sentimentality', in S. Shute and S. Hurley (eds), *On Human Rights. The Oxford Amnesty Lectures 1993* (New York: Basic Books, 1993).

Ross, A., *Statsret [State Law]*, Third edition (Copenhagen: 1980).

Russell, B., P. Van Ness and Beng Hewn Chua, 'Australia's Human Rights Diplomacy', *Australian Foreign Policy Papers* (1992).

Russet, B., *Grasping the Democratic Peace* (Princeton: Princeton University Press, 1993).

Sachedina, A. A., 'Activist Shi'ism in Iran, Iraq, and Lebanon', in M. Marty and R. Scott Appleby (eds), *Fundamentalisms Observed* (Chicago: The University of Chicago Press, 1991).

Scelle, G., *Précis de droit des gens* (Paris: Libraire du Recueil Sirey, 1934).

Schachter, O., *International Law in Theory and Practice* (Dordrecht: Nijhoff, 1991).

Scheffer, D., 'Toward a Modern Doctrine of Humanitarian Intervention', *University of Toledo Law Review*, 23 (Winter 1992).

Scheffer, D., R. Gardner and G. Helman, *Post-Gulf War Challenges to the UN Collective Security System: Three Views on the Issue of Humanitarian Intervention* (Washington, DC: Carnegie Endowment for International Peace, 1992).

Schlesinger A. Jr, 'The Opening of the American Mind', *New York Times Book Review*, 23 July 1989.

Schwebel, S., 'Military and Paramilitary Activities (*Nicaragua* v. *US*) Merits: Dissenting Opinion of Judge Stephen Schwebel' (para. 200), *ICJ Reports* (1986).

Scruton, R., *Modern Philosophy* (London: Sinclair-Stevenson, 1994).

Selbourne, D., *The Principle of Duty* (London: Sinclair-Stevenson, 1994).

'Seminar on the Right to Restitution, Compensation and Rehabilitation for Victims of Gross Violations of Human Rights and Fundamental Freedoms', Maastricht, 11–15 March 1992, SIM Special No. 12.

Shafirov, P. P., *A Discourse Concerning the Just Causes of the War Between Russia and Sweden*, trans. W. E. Butler (Yorkshire: The Scolar Press, 1973).

Shahidian, H., 'National and International Aspects of Feminist Movement: The Example of the Iranian Revolution of 1978–79', critique, *Journal of Critical Studies of Iran and the Middle East* (Spring 1993).

Shane, S., *Dismantling Utopia: How Information Ended the Soviet Union* (Chicago: Ivan Dee, 1994).

Shaposhnikov, Y., 'On the Concept of the National Security of Russia', *Miezhdunarodnaya Zhizn [International Affairs]*, 9 (1993).

Shihata, I. F. I., *The World Bank in a Changing World*, Selected Essays and Lectures, vol. II (Dordrecht: Nijhoff, 1995).

Shue, H., *Basic Rights: Subsistence, Affluence and US Foreign Policy* (Princeton: Princeton University Press, 1980).

Shute, S. and S. Hurley (eds), *On Human Rights. The Oxford Amnesty Lectures on Human Rights 1993* (New York: Basic Books, 1993).

Simon, J., *The Ultimate Resource* (Oxford: Martin Robertson & Company, 1981).

Singer, M. and A. Wildavski, *The Real World Order: Zones of Peace/Zones of Turmoil* (Chatham: Chatham House Publishers, 1993).

Snyder, J., 'Nationalism and the Crisis of the Post-Soviet State', in M. E. Brown (ed.), *Ethnic Conflict and International Security* (Princeton: Princeton University Press, 1993).

Solzhenitsyn, A., *The Gulag Archipelago*, trans. T. Whitney (London: Fontana, 1974).

Spiro, D., 'The Insignificance of the Liberal Peace', *International Security*, 19:2 (1994).

Spiro, P. J., 'New Global Communities: Nongovernmental Organizations in International Decision-Making Institutions', *The Washington Quarterly*, 18:1 (1994).

Stedman, S. J., 'UN Intervention in Civil Wars: Imperatives of Choice and Strategy', in D. Daniel and B. Hayes (eds), *Beyond Traditional Peacekeeping* (London: Macmillan, 1995).

Stowell, E. C., *Intervention in International Law* (Washington DC: Henry Holt & Company, 1921).

Strategic Survey: 1994/95, The International Institute for Strategic Studies (Oxford: Oxford University Press, 1995).

Sunkel, O., 'Uneven Globalization, Economic Reform, and Democracy: A View from Latin America', in H. H. Holm and G. Sorensen (eds), *Whose World Order* (Boulder: Westview Press, 1995).

Swearer, D., 'Fundamentalist Movements in Theravada Buddhism', in M. Marty and R. Scott Appleby (eds), *Fundamentalisms Observed* (Chicago: The University of Chicago Press, 1991).

Swidler, L., *After the Absolute: The Dialogical Future of Religious Reflection* (Minneapolis: Fortress Press, 1990).

Tang, J. (ed.), *Human Rights and International Relations in the Asian Pacific* (London: Pinter, 1995).

Taylor, P., 'Options for the Reform of the International System for Humanitarian Assistance', in J. Harriss (ed.), *The Politics of Humanitarian Intervention* (London: Pinter, 1995).

Teson, F., *Humanitarian Intervention* (New York: Transnational, 1988).

The Peace Agreement for Bosnia and Herzegovina (Paris, 14 December 1995).

Thomas, C., 'Third World Security', in R. Carey and T. C. Salmon (eds), *International Security in the Modern World* (London: St Martin's Press, 1992).

Thornberry, C., *The Development of International Peacekeeping*, LSE Centenary Lectures (London: LSE Books, 1995).

Thornberry, P., *International Law and the Rights of Minorities* (Oxford: Clarendon Press, 1991).

Tibi, B., 'Islamic Law/Shari'a, Human Rights, Universal Morality and International Relations', *Human Rights Quarterly*, 16 (1994).

Türk, D., 'Development and Human Rights', in L. Henkin and J. Hargrove (eds), *Human Rights: An Agenda for the Next Century* (Washington DC: The American Society of International Law, 1995).

UNHCR, *The State of the World's Refugees. The Challenge of Protection* (New York: Penguin Books, 1993).

Verwey, M., 'Humanitarian Intervention', in A. Cassese (ed.), *The Current Legal Regulation of the Use of Force* (Dordrecht: Nijhoff, 1986).

Vincent, R. J., *Human Rights and International Relations* (Cambridge: Cambridge University Press, 1986).

—— 'The Response of Europe and the Third World to United States Human Rights Diplomacy', in D. Newsom (ed.), *The Diplomacy of Human Rights* (New York: University Press of America, 1986).

Voorhoeven, J. J. C., *Peace, Profits and Principles* (Dordrecht: Nijhoff, 1979).

Waltz, K., *Theory of International Politics* (London: Addison-Wesley, 1979).

Walzer, M., *Just and Unjust Wars*, Second edition (New York: Basic Books, 1992).

—— *Thick and Thin: Moral Argument at Home and Abroad* (Notre Dame, Ind.: University of Notre Dame Press, 1994).

—— 'The Politics of Rescue', *Social Research*, 62:1 (Spring 1995).

Weber, M., 'Legitimacy, Politics and the State', in W. Connelly (ed.), *Legitimacy and the State* (Oxford: Basil Blackwell, 1984).

Weissbrodt, D., 'Human Rights Legislation and United States Foreign Policy', *Georgia Journal of International and Comparative Law*, 7 (1977).

—— 'The Contribution of International Non-Governmental Organizations to the Protection of Human Rights', in T. Meron (ed.), *Human Rights in International Law: Legal and Policy Issues*, vol. II (Oxford: Clarendon Press, 1984).

Welch, D., *Justice and the Genesis of War* (Cambridge: Cambridge University Press, 1993).

Weller, M., *Iraq and Kuwait: The Hostilities and Their Aftermath* (Cambridge: Cambridge University Press, 1993).

—— (ed.), *Regional Peace-Keeping and International Enforcement: the Liberian Crisis* (Cambridge: Cambridge University Press, 1994).

Welsh, D., 'Domestic Politics and Ethnic Conflict', in M. Brown (ed.), *Ethnic Conflict and International Security* (Princeton: Princeton University Press, 1993).

Wilson, H. H., 'Some Principal Aspects of British Efforts to Crush the African Slave Trade', *AJIL*, 44:2 (1950).

Windsor, P., 'Cultural Dialogue in Human Rights', in M. Desai and P. Redfern (eds), *Global Governance: Ethics and Economics of the World Order* (London: Pinter, 1995).

Wippman, D., 'Enforcing the Peace: ECOWAS and the Liberian Civil War', in L. F. Damrosch (ed.), *Enforcing Restraint: Collective Intervention in Internal Conflicts* (New York: Council of Foreign Relations Press, 1993).

World Conference on Human Rights, The Vienna Declaration and Programme of Action (New York: United Nations, 1993).

Index